Reprints of Economic Classics

STUDIES
IN THE THEORY OF
MONEY AND CAPITAL

STUDIES

IN THE THEORY OF

MONEY AND CAPITAL

BY

ERIK LINDAHL

[1939]

REPRINTS OF ECONOMIC CLASSICS

AUGUSTUS M. KELLEY · PUBLISHERS

NEW YORK 1970

First Edition 1939

(London: George Allen & Unwin Ltd., 1939)

Reprinted 1970 By

AUGUSTUS M. KELLEY · PUBLISHERS

New York New York 10001

By Arrangement With George Allen & Unwin Ltd.

I S B N 0 678 00655 5
L C N 70 117915

Printed in the United States of America
by Sentry Press, New York, N. Y. 10019

STUDIES IN THE THEORY OF MONEY AND CAPITAL

by

ERIK LINDAHL
Professor at The University of Lund, Sweden

LONDON
GEORGE ALLEN & UNWIN LTD
MUSEUM STREET

PREFACE

THIS BOOK is the outcome of a desire expressed by some of my friends in England to have an English translation of some of my earlier works. While this idea was being carried out, the plan was slightly modified, since I wished to add a contribution from my later studies in the central field of economic theory. For this reason I have limited the selections from my earlier writings to two papers concerned with the same theme. The present volume therefore consists of three relatively independent parts, written at different times. Each part may be read by itself, but, since the three parts deal with related problems of economic theory seen from different angles, they may be considered as forming a connected whole.

An inverse chronological order has been followed in the book.* Part One has not previously appeared in print. Part Two contains the more important sections of the work *Penningpolitikens Medel* (Methods of Monetary Policy), printed for private circulation in 1929 and published in Swedish in 1930. Part Three is a translation of a study entitled "Prisbildningsproblemets uppläggning från kapitalteoretisk synpunkt" (The Pricing Problem from the Point of View of Capital Theory) which appeared in the *Ekonomisk Tidskrift* in 1929. A compressed version of another paper printed in the *Ekonomisk Tidskrift* in 1935, dealing with a much-discussed problem of public finance, has been added as an Appendix.

In the translations accuracy has been the principal aim. The main differences from the Swedish versions are the insertion of additional subheadings, and certain regroupings, compressions, and deletions, the purpose of which is

* Except in the case of the Appendix.

9

to make the argument easier to read. A few additions have also been made at some points in order to bring out the intended meaning more exactly. In the "Algebraic Discussions" of Part Three, the more elegant notation used by Professor Bowley and others has been substituted for the Walrasian notation used in the Swedish original. Passages which do not agree with the author's present views have been retained, with the addition either of new explanatory paragraphs, or of new notes. These are indicated by square brackets.

Differences of method between the two later parts and the first are the inevitable consequence of the development of the author's thought over the last ten years. It should nevertheless be possible for the reader to tackle the parts in their present sequence, starting with the more general problems and proceeding to more special ones.

Taking the sections, for the moment, chronologically, Part Three may be described as an attempt to approach gradually a realistic economic theory, beginning with a simplified static analysis and introducing successively more complicated assumptions. In the two first chapters an endeavour is made to fuse together the pricing theories of Walras and Cassel on the one hand and the capital theories of Böhm-Bawerk and Wicksell on the other. Subsequent chapters introduce dynamic problems within the static framework, this being possible under certain simplifying assumptions. If perfect foresight is assumed, the dynamic problem can evidently be handled in a manner quite parallel to the Walrasian scheme. I believe that this approach is not entirely unrealistic, since people actually do anticipate correctly much of what takes place. The analysis then continues by introducing unforeseen events, which may also be pressed into the static scheme if they are assumed to cause discontinuous shifts from one temporary equilibrium position to another.

The treatment of monetary problems in Part Two is mainly based on the same simplified method of analysing a dynamic process as a series of temporary equilibria, between which there occur unforeseen events with consequent gains and losses. For the rest these problems are dealt with on Wicksellian lines. The price level of consumers' goods is principally determined by the relation between consumption and saving on the one hand and the relation between the volume of consumers' goods and that of capital goods produced, on the other. These relations are in their turn determined by the level of interest rates and by expectations concerning the future. This line of thought is illustrated by an analysis of cumulative processes on various assumptions, taking into account among other things the important distinction between short and long term rates of interest. Finally, the Wicksellian concept of a "normal loan rate of interest" is shown to be wanting in precision when more dynamic assumptions are made.

The first of the studies of Part One summarizes my present views. The traditional approach to realistic dynamic theory (used in Part Three) is not regarded as necessary or even suitable in all cases. Instead, economic theory should if possible be so framed as to be applicable to real conditions from the beginning. This means that we should proceed from general terms to more differentiated and complex terms. The main outlines of the reorganization of the systematic structure of economic theory that follows from the adoption of this view are briefly indicated. The "Algebraic Discussion" which concludes this part is an endeavour to give a general formulation of some basic economic concepts, in such a way as to make them directly applicable to real situations; and to give a systematic account of the relations between these concepts. Although the task may seem elementary, it is of fundamental importance, and my exposition shows that it presents certain difficulties. It is my hope that I have been able, by utilizing the distinction, now well established in the Swedish school, between *ex ante* and *ex post* estimates, to find a simple solution of the much-debated question of the relation between saving and investment. It has not however been possible to include in the present volume that full analysis of the working of the economic process which is needed in order to complete the discussion.

Mrs. U. K. Hicks has with never-failing interest and patience followed the work from beginning to end, and if the result is a book worth publishing, this is due to her tireless efforts, extending down to the smallest details, and to her valuable advice concerning the planning and execution of the work. Professor J. R. Hicks has also followed the development of the book with interest from the start, and has in addition read the page proofs and given me much helpful advice. I wish to express my deep-felt thanks to them both. I am also indebted to Dr. P. N. Rosenstein-Rodan, who has aided me by word and deed throughout. Among my Swedish colleagues I desire to record my gratitude to Dr. Dag Hammarskjöld of the Finance Department for various improvements made as a result of my discussions with him concerning the contents of Part One, and for his kindness in reading the page proofs, and to Fil. lic. Tor Fernholm, who has not only translated the greater part of the book but has also, by his sound judgment, valuable suggestions, and keen criticisms, materially improved its contents.

ERIK LINDAHL

LUND, SWEDEN
June 1939

CONTENTS

PART ONE

THE DYNAMIC APPROACH TO ECONOMIC THEORY

INTRODUCTION TO THE STUDY OF DYNAMIC THEORY

ALGEBRAIC DISCUSSION OF THE RELATIONS BETWEEN SOME FUNDAMENTAL CONCEPTS

PART TWO

THE RATE OF INTEREST AND THE PRICE LEVEL (1930)

PART THREE

THE PLACE OF CAPITAL IN THE THEORY OF PRICE (1929)

I. THE TRADITIONAL SETTING OF THE PRICING PROBLEM

17

THE DYNAMIC APPROACH
TO ECONOMIC THEORY

INTRODUCTION TO THE STUDY OF
DYNAMIC THEORY

1. THE AIM OF ECONOMIC THEORY

The final aim of Economic Science is either to explain the economic phenomena of the past or to forecast the economic events that will, under given conditions, probably occur in the future. In the first case we are concerned with problems of Economic History, in the second with problems of our actual life, especially those referring to the domain of Economic Policy.

In both cases scientific treatment of the questions involves, not only the collecting of empirical material and its appropriate arrangement, but also the demonstration of causal connections between the phenomena studied. The first step in this analysis is *to explain a certain development as a result of certain given conditions* prevailing at the beginning of the period studied. These given conditions must be stated in such a way that they contain *in nuce* the whole subsequent development. Thus they should embrace not only the external facts and the plans in existence at the initial point of time, but also, as latent propensities of the economic subjects taking part in the system, their subsequent reactions to what happens during the period. If all this is known, it will be possible to give a theoretical construction of the development in question.

But the analysis should not stop there. We do not fully understand the importance of the initial conditions for the resulting development, unless we have undertaken a *comparison with hypothetical developments* that might be the result of an assumed variation of these conditions. We may elucidate this further by the aid of the following scheme:

Given conditions at an arbitrary point of time	Resulting developments during a following period of arbitrary length
a'	A'
a''	A''
. . .	. . .
b'	B'
b''	B''
. . .	. . .

The treatment of a historical problem includes first the description of the development in question (A'), then the ascertainment of which initial conditions (a') can be assumed to be the *joint* causes of the said development. In order to obtain an idea of the importance of each separate condition, we must make a further investigation as to the possible connections between initial conditions and subsequent developments, on the lines indicated in the scheme above. Thus if we can prove that a development of the actual type, A, can be occasioned either by our original set of conditions, a', or by some other combinations of conditions, a'', etc., and that a development of another type, B, can only be the result of certain other combinations, b', b'', etc., we can draw the following conclusion: the fact that our original set of conditions is of the type a instead of the type b, is the *cause* of the fact that the actual development has been of the A-type instead of the B-type.

Similar reasoning can be applied to the treatment of practical and political problems. In some cases a future development of a certain type (A) is given as a desirable *end* for our activities, and we have to find out the best *means* for attaining this end. The solution of this question involves firstly the statement that initial conditions of the a-type must be established, and, secondly, an investiga-

22

of the consequences of the alternative lines of action (a', a'', etc.) between which we then have to choose. In other cases the task of the economist may only be to make clear what developments will be the probable result of certain lines of action. He has then also to rely on a scheme showing the connections between initial conditions and resulting developments.

The purpose of this introduction is to make clear the aim of Economic Theory: *to provide theoretical structures showing how certain given initial conditions give rise to certain developments.* The structures are to be used as *instruments* with which to analyse historical and practical problems. Economic theory has thus no end in itself; it is only a servant of those parts of economic science which are devoted to the treatment of concrete economic problems.* But it is an indispensable servant. Even the arrangement of empirical material must be based on a system of concepts, elaborated by economic theory. And if we wish to go deeper and make judgments regarding the causal connections between the phenomena studied, it is, as we have seen, necessary to work with hypothetical cases in the form of theoretical structures.

The conclusions contained in these structures are of a

* This point of view is supported also by the authority of Professor Pigou: "None the less, the thought-tools of the economist are, I think, in themselves and for their own sake of little interest and importance. The pure mathematician would protest—and rightly—if anyone should regard his structures as merely tools for physics and other applied sciences. But then these structures—if one who knows them by repute may venture to speak—constitute immense and imposing triumphs of the human intellect. They are much more than tools: they are themselves works of art. No claim of that kind can be made for the structure of pure economics. These are tools only. Those of them that cannot be made to work in elucidating the problems of the real world must be scrapped: there is no place for them in the gallery of art. But, though they are only tools, as tools they are vital." Pigou and Robertson, *Economic Essays and Addresses*, p. 8.

purely formal nature, stating what series of events must be the consequences of the assumptions made about the situation at the start.* It is questionable whether propositions of this type should be honoured by the term of "economic laws," since their relevance to the real world cannot be determined from the content of these structures themselves. It is of course essential that the assumptions which are the data of the theoretical system should be related as much as possible to empirical phenomena. Only in this way can the theoretical structures acquire relevance for the solution of actual problems.†

If a historical case is analysed, the structures used should be based on assumptions that are in accordance with the real situation at the time. And if we have to deal with a problem of practical life, to explain the probable effects of possible alternative actions of a person, a firm or a public body in a certain situation, the data of our structures should correspond to this situation. Ideally the system of economic theory should include all the structures—showing the connections between different sets of data and the resulting developments—that could be of any relevance to the treatment of those historical and practical problems, the solution of which would be of interest, now or in the future.

In view of the infinite variety of economic phenomena

* Cf. L. Robbins, *An Essay on the Nature and Significance of Economic Science*, 2nd ed., pp. 78–9: "The propositions of economic theory, like all scientific theory, are obviously deductions from a series of postulates. . . . The truth of the deductions . . . depends, as always, on their logical consistency. Their applicability to the interpretation of any particular situation depends upon the existence in that situation of the elements postulated." Cf. also G. Mackenroth, *Theoretische Grundlagen der Preisbildungsforschung und der Preispolitik*, Berlin, 1933, where a good exposition of this and other methodological questions is given.

† Cf. the discussion of this problem in Cairnes, *The Character and Logical Method of Political Economy*, London, 1888, pp. 33 ff. and 110–11.

in the real world, it is of course impossible to reach this aim. As economic theory can contain only a limited number of structures, the working out of the special theories, needed for the analysis of actual problems, must to a large extent be left to the investigators of these problems. The claim that can be made on economic theory in its proper sense can therefore be formulated in the following way: *it should give as much assistance as possible in the elaboration of the special theories.* This means that the body of pure theory should be based on data which are of general relevance to the actual cases considered, so that it can be easily adapted for application to these cases.

2. General Concepts and General Theoretical Structures

From this point of view we may draw some conclusions on two methodological questions that are of fundamental importance for the elaboration of economic theory. The first concerns the *degree of generality* of systematic theory, the second the use of typical *simplified structures* as a means of dealing with the complex problems of reality. The primary distinction is between general theories on the one hand and special and concrete structures on the other. As a cross-classification* we can also distinguish between simplified theories, which may be more or less concrete, and complex or differentiated structures. The mark of a simplified theory, such as that of a "stationary state," "free competition," etc., is a certain uniformity in the data and the conceived developments. In the next section we return to the use of such simplifying assumptions but we will now take up the question of general versus special or particular structures.

If we use comparatively abstract terms which will

* Cf. the diagram below, p. 32.

25

cover many cases, the theory expounded becomes more generally important than if it is based on more concrete terms having reference to particular cases. On the other hand, a theory that may be used in a concrete case and which will thus be based on relatively determinate assumptions as to the content of the concepts used, can of course be carried much further than a theory referring only to an abstract and more indeterminate case.

Take for example the theory of capital itself. If we start from a very general definition of capital in its real sense, as including all external goods of economic relevance, and make no further assumptions about the attributes of these goods, our theory can be applied to all real cases but its content will be relatively poor. If we make more particular assumptions with regard to the form of the capital goods—and let them consist, e.g. of casks of wine of certain defined qualities, if we are studying circulating capital (Wicksell), or if we are especially interested in durable capital, a certain type of machine (Gustaf Åkerman)—we can of course obtain more definite results, but then the question remains how far these results are applicable when we are dealing with the more complicated cases of the real world.

Which of these methods is to be preferred, if we are to build up a system of economic theory?

In answering this question we may first consider the case of theories framed with reference to concrete examples of a comparatively simple character. If such theories are relatively easy to construct, they may be all the more difficult to apply to the complicated problems found in the real world. We may, for instance, have a theory of price developments in a closed system; in that case no safe conclusions can be drawn from this theory concerning the actual course of events in a country with foreign trade. We must instead first elaborate a more general theory

26

valid both for open and closed systems, and then proceed to apply this generalized theoretical structure to our case. In other words, *two* logical processes are necessary, first the production of a broader theory, and then, with its aid, the interpretation of reality.

If we neglect to restate the simplified theory in a more general form, and proceed directly to utilize it in a real and more complicated case, we run the risk of drawing false conclusions. There is plenty of evidence to show the dangers of such superficial application of simplified economic theories to real conditions. Economists who are investigating concrete problems in the domain of economic history or economic policy have often not sufficient time or patience to undertake the necessary restatement of the basic doctrines. This exacting task should therefore be left to those who are dealing with pure theory.

Our conclusion is therefore, that the body of pure theory should if possible be developed in terms general enough for it to be at least approximately applicable to the actual cases which are to be analysed with its help. If the terms are generalized to this extent, we get a theoretical groundwork that can serve as an established basis for the further development of the particular theories necessary for the analysis of concrete problems.*

This does not imply, however, that it should be the endeavour of the economist to carry the process of

---

* Cf. Myrdal, *Prisbildningsproblemet och föränderligheten* (*The Pricing Problem and Change*), Uppsala, 1927, p. 1, note 1: "The difference between the two types of theory becomes apparent when they are applied to concrete problems. If we start from a general theory, the particular data (referring to the special case) will fit into the scheme; the general theory is correct at the same time as the concrete conception. Any stage of intermediate theory may be imagined, each of which will fit into one another; only the equations have more terms. If on the other hand the theory is built on approximating assumptions of the said character, the inductive data that are introduced into the analysis will modify the scheme."

generalization as far as is logically possible. The urgent need is only for structures general enough for application to our present problems, not for constructions of a still more general character that might apply to other possible but at the moment irrelevant cases. If we carry the abstraction too far, the content of the theory will be too much diluted. It is therefore quite natural that the character given to economic theory in every epoch and in every country will be that which is suited to the economic institutions of the particular community.

Even with this restriction, it is not always feasible to generalize so widely that all actual cases are covered. Instead, we may frame alternative theories for different sets of conditions. Our theoretical system will then contain a set of alternatives, which between them embrace the entire subject-matter.

It can hardly be asserted that economic theory in its present stage fully satisfies the claims thus implicitly made on it by the investigators of historical and practical problems. The theoretical economists have hitherto, in the construction of their systems, shown a predilection for the method of treating concrete and simple cases; this is quite natural, especially when we realize that economics is a relatively young science. But we have now come to the point when it is necessary to *supplement* this procedure with the method of generalization. It can be regarded as an important task for the present generation of economists to restate and develop existing theory in this direction.

3. The Use of Simplifying Assumptions

We may now turn from the consideration of generalized structures to the role of simplifying assumptions in economic reasoning. Such assumptions are, as every economist instinctively feels, in many cases indispensable and in other cases very useful. In passing under review the various arguments brought forward in support of them it is convenient to distinguish between general and special theories.

(*a*) It must be noted that it is not always possible to develop the *general* doctrines that should represent the groundwork of economic theory, without a certain amount of simplification of the basic assumptions, as will appear later in this essay. The value of the resulting theory will depend on its degree of *approximation* to reality, i.e. on the ease with which the transition to real problems can be made without essential readjustments of the theoretical structure.

In other cases the simplification of our theories, even if not absolutely necessary from a logical point of view, will make the exposition very much easier without correspondingly diminishing its range of application. Thus the treatment of simple typical cases can be of great pedagogic value in the exposition of the central part of a theory. It is especially when we have to explain economic problems to readers who are not themselves economic experts, that it becomes necessary to simplify them to a certain extent, in order to evade clumsiness of exposition.

In this connection the following question presents itself: When we have to develop a general theory, would it not be an appropriate procedure to begin with comparatively simple structures and then progress successively to higher and higher degrees of abstraction?—In answering this question, we must distinguish between the working out and the exposition of a theory. Broadly it may perhaps be asserted that the method of beginning with simple cases is more justified in constructing a theory than in stating it. In other words, even if the construction of a theory has been the result of a laborious process, it is not always suitable to expound the results in the same heuristic manner. In any case, the common opinion that it is a logical necessity to begin with the simpler and concrete cases, must be confuted. The main defence of this very usual method of exposition should be based on its possible advantages from a pedagogic point of view as mentioned above. In a more systematic exposition it is preferable to begin with the general case and then to proceed to the more specialized ones. However, the question is not of first importance from a strictly scientific point of view.

(b) The great number and variety of *special* theories necessitates a choice among them. It is then wise to begin with simple and typical instances. In this way we also obtain useful *approximations*. For example the simplified exposition in static theory of the higher level of wages due to an increase in the quantity of capital is found to retain important relevance under dynamic conditions also.

These simplified theories are also valuable in that they enable us to make *comparisons* between actual and conceived developments. They then function as *instruments of analysis*, with the aid of which we discern the special elements that are causally operative in a given case, and trace the complications due to these elements.

Furthermore, simplified theories are in familiar practice often expanded to greater complication through a step-by-step process, e.g. from a barter to a money economy, from a one-commodity to a two-commodity community, and so on. In such a procedure there is usually an implicit ascent to a more general theory covering both the old and the new cases, as explained above. It should especially be emphasized that the transition from a simplified case to a more complicated one does not obviate the necessity for the general theories already discussed. But if we are in possession of a general theory, covering the complicated cases of the real world, is it then necessary to begin with the simpler applications before proceeding to the more complicated real cases? No, from a logical point of view it is not necessary, but it can often be justified on the same pedagogic grounds as those mentioned above. The consideration of simple cases gives the reader the mental training that prepares him for a better understanding of the actual and more difficult cases.

Our reasoning has thus led to the conclusion that both general and simple structures are required in economic theory, but that, for the time being, there is an especial need for generalization of the concepts and assumptions used by theorists.

4. Dynamic versus Static Theory

Before proceeding further, we may illustrate the significance of our thesis by a question that is of primary importance, not only for this essay, but for the whole foundation of economic theory, namely the relation between Statics and Dynamics.

We have already said that the aim of economic theory is to explain the connections between certain given conditions and the corresponding developments. In mathematical phrasing, the object is to determine certain variables as functions of time (or time curves) with the help of equations, based on what is known as to the initial values of these variables and the conditions which determine their fluctuations. A theory of this type must be called *dynamic*. If our definition of economic theory is accepted, it is then impossible to avoid the somewhat perplexing conclusion that *all* economic theory that fulfils its purpose must have a dynamic character.

We have given dynamics here such a broad sense that it also includes the *static* problem.* Properly interpreted,

* Cf. the instructive little work by Rudolf Streller, *Statik und Dynamik in der theoretischen Nationalökonomie*, Leipzig 1926, where (see, e.g., p. 134) an apparently contrary view is supported, namely, that statics represents a higher degree of abstraction than dynamics. This may hold true of the relation between static and special dynamic,

static theory also has for an object economic developments taking place in time, only the variables studied do not change their values with the lapse of time. The corresponding time curves have thus the nature of straight lines parallel with the time-axis. Only one value must therefore be determined for each variable, which of course considerably simplifies the solution of the problem. A community that is thus characterized by a *repetition* of the same economic processes is called a *stationary* community. Thus we may conclude that static theory represents a special application of general dynamic theory for stationary conditions.

The application of general dynamic theory to communities that are not stationary, but *changing* or *evolutionary*, may be called dynamics in a more *special* sense. It is a theory of this type, namely one that cannot be simplified in the same way as the static theory, that is in the first place required for the analysis of the actual problems of the real world.

In relation to special dynamics, statics represents a simplification and general dynamics a generalization, as illustrated by the following scheme:

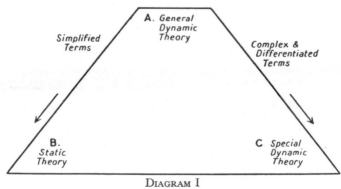

DIAGRAM I

Continuation of footnote from p. 31]
if by abstraction is meant merely the dropping of special complications. But if the abstractions are made with a view to finding the most general structures, then the opinion expressed in the text holds.

In accordance with our previous argument, we should in point of principle begin with (*A*) and from there proceed on different paths, both to (*B*) and to (*C*), when we set out to construct our theoretical system. The usual method, however, is to begin with (*B*) and then continue to (*C*); (*A*) is generally entirely neglected. As a supplement to the exposition given above, we should now point out the disadvantages which seem to be connected with this latter procedure.

In the first place we cannot fully understand the true character of the static simplification, if we do not begin with a broad formulation of the problem. As in mechanics the concept of equilibrium can be defined only on the basis of a theory of forces, so the significance of a reiterating process which, as stated above, is the central concept of the static theory in economics, can be explained only on the basis of a more general theory of economic development. If we begin with the static assumption as an isolated premiss, formulated as "abstraction from the time factor" or something of that sort, we are easily led astray, as is shown by the laborious but not always very successful attempts "to introduce the time factor in the Walrasian system of equations."* Secondly, special dynamic problems are more difficult to grasp in the right way, if our assumptions at the start have been of a static nature. The seemingly very natural construction of a "theory of variations" as a complement to a "theory of equilibrium" is thus not without its dangers, as it easily leads to the idea that the variations centre around a certain equilibrium, an idea that, as is now commonly admitted, is not generally true, even if it can be applied under certain special

---

* As the present author has made a serious effort to work on these lines, in the third part of this book, he has some experience of the difficulties associated with the static method as a first starting point in theoretical analysis.

conditions. Thirdly, also as a basis for the development of a general dynamic theory, the static structures seem to be rather inappropriate, because a theory of that kind must be founded on a *new and broader* basis. When this groundwork is prepared, it is comparatively easy to introduce more special assumptions, either static, or dynamic in the narrower sense.

But, if we thus take it for granted that the systematic exposition of economic theory should begin with general dynamic structures and then proceed to more particular assumptions, we may ask: Have the static premises any very important relevance for the treatment of the particular dynamic problems of the real world? What is the use of this whole body of beautiful doctrines, grouped around the concept of a stationary equilibrium? That is the real problem concerning the relation between statics and dynamics.

In answering this question, we have to examine how far the arguments advanced in the previous section as a justification of simplified assumptions can be used for defending the static premises.

In the first place we can often use the static structures as *approximations* to the real phenomena. This holds true especially with regard to the solution of more special problems. Even in the real world, all factors do not alter continually. There is always a good deal of invariability. In some fields, fairly stationary conditions may prevail for a comparatively long time. Static structures are also very helpful for the explanation and exposition of economic motives, expressed in the planning activity of business men and consumers. Secondly, we need the static structures as *instruments of analysis*. If we can state under what conditions the variables studied do not change, we can better understand the course of their actual fluctuations. Such comparisons between real and hypothetical

34

cases are often very instructive. Finally, if the static structures are only conceived as referring to developments of a certain simple kind, they can with great pedagogic advantage be used as an *introduction* to the treatment of more difficult dynamic problems. We may therefore conclude that in this manner most parts of the traditional static theory can be incorporated in a system of essentially dynamic character.

5. THE STRUCTURE OF GENERAL DYNAMIC THEORY

The study of economics is largely concerned with human actions or the result of human actions. Leaving aside the question whether man can exercise free-will or not, it is of course not possible to determine the causes of his behaviour in the same way as those of the events of the external world. We cannot prove that certain human actions will *necessarily* be the result of a definite situation at a given point of time. We can only state that they do *probably* result from it and that a variation of the data will probably cause the individuals to act differently.

There lies in this a serious limitation to the possibilities of our analysis of historical and practical problems in the economic field. This deplorable inexactitude, however, affects only the application of economic theory, not the theory itself. In the construction of economic theories whose aim, as already indicated, is to determine certain developments on the basis of certain data, all inexactness can be avoided by explicit *assumptions* about all these phenomena which in the real world cannot be definitely determined. We can thus assume that individuals, under given conditions, do act in a certain manner, and the adoption of this assumption makes it possible to determine exactly what results will develop from any given situation.

Such assumptions used in economics concerning human behaviour, should correspond as much as possible to our

35

knowledge of reality. The value of the theoretical structures as instruments in the analysis of the actual problem depends, as we have pointed out above, very much on the realistic character of the assumptions made. Most theoretical controversies on the economic field have arisen over questions of this type. It is sufficient to be reminded of the dispute as to the correctness of the psychological assumptions on which the theory of marginal utility is based. When we are dealing with concrete problems, it is always possible and appropriate to make alternative assumptions in a doubtful case. But when we have to outline the basic constructions that should be most generally applicable, it would be too laborious to develop them along alternative lines. We must then try to work with a few generally acceptable assumptions.

In the following statement of the general dynamic problem we have only made use of *one basic assumption* about the behaviour of the individuals concerned, namely that their actions, for a shorter or a longer period in the future, represent merely the fulfilment of certain plans, given at the beginning of the period and determined by certain principles which it is possible to state in one way or another. These principles should in general state that the plans are made for the attainment of certain aims (for business firms for instance the attainment of maximum net income) and that they are based on individual expectations concerning future conditions, expectations which in their turn are influenced by individual interpretation of past events.

The question whether such planning by the economic subjects is a realistic assumption or not will constitute a test of its suitability. In some important cases the planning is quite obvious. The state and other public bodies furnish us in their budgets with examples of definite plans. Private enterprises usually outline similar plans for their activity though they are generally not divulged; first there is a general plan for a comparatively long period of time and then there are more detailed plans for the immediate future. Even individual consumers do not infrequently draw up some plans for their economic behaviour during a longer or shorter period. In certain other cases our assumption that economic actions are the result of planning activity may seem more difficult to apply. It can hardly be pretended that every individual has a clear conception of the economic actions that he is going to perform in a future period. Nevertheless, in the greater number of cases it will certainly be found that underlying such actions there are habits and persistent tendencies which have a definite and calculable character comparable to the explicit plans already mentioned. We may accordingly without danger proceed to generalize our notion of "plans," so that they will include such actions. Plans are thus the explicit expression of the economic motives of man, as they become evident in his economic actions. The variations among economic motives may be introduced as special assumptions concerning the content of the plans. Our general dynamic assumption will thus be seen to be a fairly good approximation to reality.

The assumption just stated has important consequences for the more definite formulation of the general dynamic problem. The statement of "the given conditions" that represent the data for the explanation of the development can now be made more explicit. If we know (1) the *plans* of the economic subjects concerned at the initial point of time, if we further know (2) how these individuals are likely to *change their plans* in the future under different assumptions, and if we have (3) enough knowledge of *external conditions* to be able to make definite statements with regard to future changes in plans, and the results of the actions undertaken then it should be possible to provide a theoretical construction of the developments that will be the outcome of the initial position. Our basic assumption will thus give a definite character to the data underlying the dynamic problem and to the entire structure of the theoretical system.

The plans of the economic subjects at any given point of time are neither fully consistent with one another nor with the external conditions,* and therefore they must be successively revised.† The construction of the development that results from the endeavours to realize all these successively revised plans, is therefore a complicated problem. Its given factors are the three indicated above, and the general procedure in its solution should be as follows:

Starting from the plans and the external conditions valid at the initial point of time, we have first to deduce the development that will be the result of these data for a certain period forward during which no relevant changes in the plans are assumed to occur. Next we have to investigate how far the development during this first period—involving as it must various surprises for the economic subjects—will force them to revise their plans of action for the future, the principles for such a revision being assumed to be included in the data of the problem. And since on this basis the development during the second

* A good exposition of this problem that is quite in harmony with the ideas developed in this essay, has been given by Professor Hayek in his interesting paper on "Economics and Knowledge," in *Economica* 1937, pp. 33 ff.

† If all the economic subjects in the community considered had a perfect knowledge of the future, the problem of economic theory would be enormously simplified. Such an assumption implies that all plans prevailing at the starting point are based on expectations in conformity with reality, and that they will undergo no change with the lapse of time. The actual development will thus be the same as has been anticipated in all plans, and the only task for the theoretical economist is to describe the content of these plans. In the third part of this book it is shown that this problem can be treated in essentially the same manner as the equilibrium of static theory.

period is determined in the same manner as before, fresh deductions must be made concerning the plans for the third period, and so on.

This is the general scheme for the treatment of a development that takes place in a longer period of time, comprising many such shorter periods. But many methods of abridgment may of course be invented for the determination of such a development. A class of problems of a more formal character is related to questions of this kind.

From this formulation of the problem it follows that the construction of a dynamic process must be based on an investigation into the character of the planning of the economic subjects. And this latter investigation must evidently be founded on certain assumptions regarding technical, institutional and psychological conditions, which of course should as much as possible approximate to reality.

A systematic exposition of a general dynamic theory of economics can therefore conveniently be divided into three parts:

(1) The exposition of the *technical, institutional* and *psychological* conditions with regard to which the economist must make certain definite assumptions in explaining the principles of planning and the effects of the endeavours to ˙realize the plans. The investigation of the relations between input and output (the so-called productivity laws) and of the economic motives of man, his "valuation attitude," etc., may be cited as examples of theories belonging to this branch.

(2) The theory of *economic planning*, dealing with the contents of the plans at a certain point of time and also explaining the principles valid for the alteration of plans with the lapse of time.

(3) The theory of *economic development* that, as has just

39

been said, is to explain the dynamic process on the basis of certain assumptions regarding planning and external conditions made in accordance with the theories developed in the two first parts of the system.

In this connection there is no reason to dwell upon the well-known theories of the first part of the system. We shall therefore proceed directly to the second and third parts, adding to our observations on them some discussion of alternative methods of attacking the theory of price.

6. The General Theory of Planning

(i) *Planning at a Given Point of Time*

In the activity of economic planning two phases can be distinguished: first the intellectual *prognoses* of future developments under alternative assumptions as to the actions of the individual making the plan, now and in the future; secondly the valuation and decision whereby a *choice* between these alternatives is made. The actions of the individual prescribed in the selected alternative represent the "plan" in the strict sense.

In the *first* phase the planner explores the causal relationship between his future actions and the aims he desires to attain. The purpose of this exploration is in the first place to show the consequences of the possible actions between which he has to choose in the immediate future. But these consequences can in general not be fully clarified, if he makes no assumptions regarding his actions during later periods also. Therefore, the analysis should in principle investigate all the relevant paths in the "field of choice" that displays itself to the view of the individual at the given point of time.

Now it should be observed that the actions undertaken by an individual in a certain period may *constrain* his future behaviour in certain respects.* If for example a producer has made a contract to deliver certain goods at a future date, this contract will govern his scheme of production in the meantime. At any given point of time, it can be assumed that the planner has through his previous actions in various ways imposed certain limits on his immediate behaviour. For more remote periods, however, the apparent possibilities of varying his actions are greater. The alternatives to be investigated will therefore ramify to an increasing extent as more distant periods are envisaged.

This would also be true if the anticipations of the individual were "single-valued,"† that is, if he were convinced that he could exactly estimate the course of future events under different assumptions. In general anticipations must be assumed to be increasingly "many-valued," i.e. comprising a greater number of alternative possibilities the more distant the future to which they refer. Therefore, both in respect of the future situation in which the individual is about to act and to the consequences of each path of action, various alternatives with different probabilities have to be taken into consideration. The prognosis in its entirety will thus be a very complicated scheme. The practical solution of the problem implies broadly that in each case a judgment concerning these relative probabilities is first made, and that attention is then con-

* Here a general reference should be made to a recent work of a young Swedish economist, Dr. Ingvar Svennilson, *Ekonomisk Planering* (*Economic Planning*), Uppsala 1938, which contains a very thorough investigation of the theoretical and methodological problems connected with planning. This author has especially been interested in the "intertemporal aspects" of planning, and the question of "the binding of the parameters of action" for future periods, to which we refer above in the text, is examined at length (pp. 31 ff.).

† Cf. A. G. Hart, "Anticipations, Business Planning and the Cycle," in *Quarterly Journal of Economics*, vol. li, No. 2 (February 1937). The clear exposition of the problem given in this paper has been of relevance for the present study in other respects also.

centrated on the most probable alternative, subordinate estimates also being made concerning other less probable alternatives. The crux of the problem will lie in the calculation of the probability values, but this can of course be carried out more or less summarily.

In the *second* phase of planning a valuation of the relative advantages of these different alternatives is made, with due regard to the uncertainty factor in each case. The so-called "valuation-attitude" of the individual, underlying this comparison, can usually be expressed as a system of indifference-curves, displaying both his reaction to the uncertainty factors* and to the combinations of different phenomena between which a choice is to be made. We need not go into the complication of this point here however. It is sufficient to have made it clear that the outcome of the co-ordination of the anticipations described above, and of the individual valuation-attitude, forms the outline of a programme or "plan" governing the future actions of the planner.

The diagram on page 43 illustrates the content of such a plan in a simplified schematic form. The planning is supposed to be undertaken at a given point of time, t_0, and to cover an arbitrary number of future periods, $t_0 t_1$, $t_1 t_2$, etc. The division of the planned development into definite periods has deep-lying grounds in the imperfection of human knowledge. Man cannot continuously register all that happens around him. He can only take account of it *intermittently*, observing the total result obtained for certain time periods, or registering more important events that can be referred to definite points of time. Since the points of registration are taken as the boundary points between the periods, the length of these "individual periods of registration" may vary within wide limits.

The paths of action planned for each period are repre-

* Cf. I. Svennilson, op. cit., chap. 5.

sented by the lines moving along the time-axis in the diagram, their distance to this axis indicating their degree of "advantageousness," as measured in the way prescribed by the individual valuation-attitude. (If a business firm is under discussion, the Y-axis can conveniently be assumed to represent its subjective capital value.) Since the future is

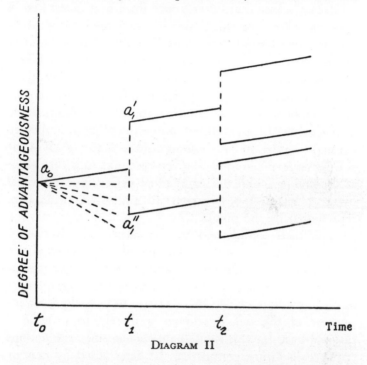

DIAGRAM II

uncertain, the planner has to allow for different possible effects of the actions undertaken in each period (in the diagram only two such possibilities are indicated). These effects are supposed to be registered at the end of each period, and they determine the line of action for the next period. We therefore get an increasing ramification of the system. For more remote periods the scheme must be assumed to become more and more diffused.

43

Since each line of action is the best of the possible alternatives between which the individual (under the given conditions) has to choose, it can be characterized as the upper limit of the field of choice in each case (the dotted lines in the first period). For all other (and lower) alternatives in this field of choice a similar diagram can be drawn whose main divergence from that given here is that the effects of the lines of action selected must be judged to be less advantageous. The line of action chosen for the first period will thus *determine* the planned lines of action for succeeding periods also. But it should be observed that the first line of action is also *determined* by the later ones. For the advantageousness of the selected course cannot be ascertained, unless the process is followed through—under various assumptions as to the result of the actions undertaken in each given case. (The upward slope of the line of action during the first period is conditioned by the expectation of two alternative possible effects, here represented by the points a'_1 and a''_1, and these points are in their turn conditioned by the succeeding alternative lines of action, and so on.) Only by taking account of this whole complex of alternatives and their respective probabilities, can the individual fully realize the consequences of his immediate choice. As a matter of fact, the primary purpose of the whole scheme is merely to provide a rational basis for this immediate choice, since the actions required in future periods can be determined by new or revised plans. Only if the anticipations turn out to be correct and if the valuation-attitude is unaltered, will the original plan retain its relevance for the succeeding periods.

From what has just been said it follows that, if we take a given plan as a whole, there exists a *mutual* interconnection between the present and future actions included in the plan. The equilibrium analysis of traditional static theory can therefore be applied to the present problem, although the question now concerns the *intertemporal* relations between expectations and planned actions, which are included in a certain individual plan.

Plans may be further differentiated with regard to their *degree of definiteness* by making the following distinctions:

(*a*) The actions planned are *unconditioned*, if their realization does not depend on what happens in the intervening period, and they are *conditioned* in the opposite case when they are performed after the realization of a certain condition, either *immediately* or *with a certain time lag*. All alternative planning is concerned with conditioned actions, since the realization of each alternative is dependent on the previous realization of certain definite conditions.

(*b*) The plan is *uniquely* determined, if it indicates what concrete actions the planner is going to perform, and it is determined *between limits*, if a certain choice is left open to the individual. In the former case we may speak of "lines of action" and in the latter case of "field of actions" as the content of the plan.

(*c*) The plan is *unalterable*, if the individual has bound himself in some way or other to perform the planned actions, and it is *alterable*, in so far as the individual is at liberty to substitute a new or revised plan for the old one.*

It can in general be asserted, that a programme of action is in all these respects more definite for the immediate future than for more distant points of time.

We have seen in Diagram II that for the first period the plan comprises only one single line of action. For this period it is thus assumed to be both unconditioned and uniquely determined. The individual is supposed to act immediately, and he must therefore have made up his mind how to act. This description of the situation requires,

* This distinction is of course quite independent of the first, since both unconditioned and conditioned planning can be either unalterable or alterable.

45

however, some modification. Even in respect of the immediate future, the economic subject has not always a definite conception of the actions he is going to perform. Some of them may be determined only in as much as that they will be immediately performed after the realization of certain conditions.* We should therefore add to the unconditioned and uniquely determined actions those that are conditioned but are assumed to be realized without any relevant time lag, when we are describing the content of the plan for a short period immediately following.

All actions planned for later periods are conditioned by certain events which have already happened expressed in the diagram as results of the previous actions of the planner. They are thus conditioned, and can be supposed to be realized either with or without a time lag. It can also be assumed that the lines of action drawn in the diagram, will be replaced by fields of action to an increasing degree for more remote periods. We have made no assumptions in the present case concerning the alterability of the plan. But that it is easier to change a plan for distant periods than for the immediate future—for which the individual, as already said, has bound himself in various respects—is a familiar truth calling for no special comment.

(ii) *Changes in Planning with the Lapse of Time*

So far we have discussed the planning process and the resulting plan, with reference to a given point of time. As time passes the plan will not be retained in its original

* The plan of a shopkeeper, for example, who plans his behaviour for a certain period forward from a given point of time, might contain nothing more than the determination to sell as much as possible of certain goods at a certain price. Since the quantity he is going to sell depends on the demand of his customers, the planned transactions may be said to belong to the *conditioned* category, though following *immediately* after the realization of the condition.

46

form. Though each plan is in principle designed for the entire future, it thus has immediate relevance only for the periods next in time. The actions undertaken in later periods will be determined by new or revised plans. The second and more difficult part of the theory of planning will therefore be concerned with the important question of the principles according to which this *alteration of plans* take place.

Four independent distinctions may be applied to the changes taking place in planning with the lapse of time:

(*a*) If the explanation of planning given above is correct and we may thus characterize it as a combination of anticipation and valuation, we can first distinguish between the changes in planning due to *altered anticipations* and those occasioned by an *altered valuation attitude*. It is hardly necessary to mention that changes of the former type are the commonest, both in actuality and in economic theory. The latter changes are usually of a more irregular character, and hence they present a more difficult subject for theoretical treatment.

(*b*) We may further distinguish between changes occasioned by *economic events* that in some way or other appear in the system of the economist, and other changes of a *non-economic* character which are the outcome either of events not included in the economic system or of mental processes of a more spontaneous kind. This distinction is of theoretical importance, since only changes of the former type can be explained by the economic development which has taken place in preceding periods.

(*c*) We may also draw a distinction between *immediately relevant* changes affecting the actions planned for the nearest periods and other changes *referring only to more remote periods*. Since the plan can be altered many times before these more distant periods are reached, this part of

47

the planning is of importance only in so far as it facilitates the understanding of the plans actually put into practice. The economist is of course primarily concerned with plans of immediate relevance.

(*d*) Finally we may point out that some changes fall *within the framework of the previous plan*, while other changes are not in conformity with it but result in *a new plan*. Of the former changes we can discern two kinds: (i) conditioned actions will become unconditioned through the realization of the condition in question, and (ii) fields of action will be restricted and finally transformed into paths of action. The effect of these processes is merely that with the lapse of time a given plan becomes more determinate in respect of future periods.

On the basis of this classification we may conclude that the economist is primarily concerned with immediately relevant changes in plans (those which are more fundamental than the mere increase in definiteness of earlier plans) when they have their ground in changes in expectations, occasioned by the course of events during earlier periods.

The different links in the chain of events to be analysed are the following: (1) the actual development of the factors relevant to the planner, (2) the latter's view of this development, (3) the resulting changes in his anticipations of future conditions which are of importance for his actions, and (4) the resulting alterations of his plans of action for the nearest period ahead.

The first link in this chain can in the present case be assumed to be known. Only when it is our task to construct a complete theory of development is it necessary for us to determine these data also. With regard to the second link, it should be noted that even in cases where the course of actual development is continuous, it cannot usually be assumed that our planner's apprehension of them also changes without discontinuity. As already pointed out (p. 42) it can be stated as a general rule that individuals register external events which are relevant for their planning only intermittently.

The general deficiency of human knowledge, therefore, has in this case the important result that we must take account of certain discontinuous alterations in the economic subject's view of the past and his anticipations for the future. The interval of time that lies between the points when the individual registers what has happened has been termed his "period of registration."

The relation between the second and third links of the chain, i.e. the influence of registered past events on the expectations of the individual, naturally varies greatly in different circumstances, and hence the economic theorist must make alternative assumptions. It seems suitable here to deal first with three simple cases which may be regarded as typical: (a) the change (e.g. the raising of a price) is assumed to continue at the same rate (an equal rise is expected for the next period), (b) the new conditions are expected to continue (the higher price is expected to remain unchanged), and (c) the change is regarded as temporary, so that in the next period a return to the original position is anticipated (here the rise is assumed to be followed by an equal fall in price).*

Finally, on the question of the influence of anticipations on the plan of action, the circumstance to which we have already alluded must be taken into account—that a

* The term "elasticity of expectations" suggested by Professor J. R. Hicks in *Value and Capital*, p. 205, may perhaps prove useful in this connection. It should be observed that Professor Hicks does not interpret the term as "the ratio of the expected proportional change for the next period to the actual proportional change during the past period," but as "the ratio of the proportional rise in expected future prices of X" (in relation to the price *at the base point*) "to the proportional rise in its current price" (in relation to the same base).

49

plan is usually to some extent binding for a certain time ahead owing to measures that have already taken effect. It may happen, therefore, that events which have been registered affect plans only after some delay. Also, since it is reasonable to assume that the individual will not make frequent alterations in plans that do not refer to current periods but to more distant ones we may conclude that the intervals between relevant changes of plans, that is, the "periods with fixed relevant plans," will usually be considerably longer than the "periods of registration." This conclusion, as we shall see immediately, is not without importance for the construction of a theory of development on the basis of relevant plans.

The considerations set forth here on the general theory of planning have been entirely formal in nature. The question of what plans will be the result of certain given anticipations has not been considered. It is probably impossible to treat this subject more comprehensively in a general way. Instead, it will probably be necessary to distinguish between different categories of economic subjects and between their different valuation attitudes. These more special theories, which of course cannot be discussed here, may be divided into the following three main groups according to the categories of planners concerned:

(1) The planning of *private individuals*, in their capacity of owners of labour and capital and with regard to the utilization of their incomes;

(2) The planning of *business firms*, as owners of capital, aiming (usually) at maximizing net profits in the long run;

(3) The planning of *public bodies*,* covering the whole

* From certain points of view it may be advisable to group together the two last types, perhaps under the general heading of "firms," which can then be contrasted with private individuals. Cf. below, p. 74.

economic policy of the state, which even in a community based on private enterprise is of central importance for the entire course of economic development within the society.*

7. THE GENERAL THEORY OF DEVELOPMENT

As has already been stated in section 5, the problem here is to determine a particular development on the basis of certain data: (1) the initial plans of the economic subjects, (2) how they are likely to change their plans in the future, and (3) the external conditions of relevance for the future changes in plans and the results of the actions taken. We shall confine ourselves to some general comments concerning the nature of the data and what this determination of the development involves.

If we wish to study a development as a result only of the actions of a single economic subject—that is, if we are concerned only with so-called *micro-economic* developments —not much of essential importance need be added to the theory of changes in plans, the main elements of which were outlined in the preceding section. We should require in addition, firstly, certain functions stating the connection between the individuals' actions as planned, and their actual result, and secondly, certain other functions, necessary to determine the relation between this individual development and the total course of events which will exert an influence on the plans for coming periods. An analysis of the individual development as in part determined by the relevant plans belonging to each period, and in part determining the plans for the succeeding

* The great and growing importance of the study of this type of planning for the understanding of the economic development of the present decade has been well described by the Swedish economist Johan Åkerman in his recent work, *Das Problem der Sozialökonomischen Synthese*, Lund, 1938.

periods must clearly be based on a subdivision of the development into periods, having the times when relevant plans are changed as the boundary points.*

The processes studied in economics, however, are generally *macro-economic* in character, that is, they consist of acts and the results of acts carried out by a number of economic subjects, together constituting a *group* of a certain definite character. The variables that are to be determined consist, e.g. of the quantities of services used up in the

* The first Swedish attempt to give a systematic account of the nature of an analysis of development on the lines suggested is contained in Dr. Dag Hammarskjöld's doctoral thesis, *Konjunkturspridningen* (*The Transmission of Economic Fluctuations*), also printed as an appendix to the Report of the Unemployment Commission (Statens offentliga utredningar 1933 : 29). In the simple case when we are dealing with a planner whose acts are influenced only by a certain "strategic factor" in the total development (for a firm, e.g. the net profit), Dr. Hammarskjöld's reasoning may be summarized as follows (cf. op. cit., pp. 53–56): Owing to the fact that the changes in the strategic factor are registered by the acting subject at certain intervals only, the alterations in plans will also take place discontinuously and probably at the same time as the registrations in question. In an analysis of the development, therefore, it will be necessary to make a subdivision according to the periods lying between these points of time when past events are registered and plans are altered. (The choice of periods will thus be determined by the interval of registration.) For each period the strategic factor can be determined as a function of the entire development, i.e. it may be taken as the unknown in an equation covering all the other factors entering into this development. Assuming that the active reactions of the economic subject to this strategic factor are known, his acts and their influence on the entire development during the next period can be determined. With a series of equations covering successive periods of registration and formulated in such a way that, firstly, the acts of the economic subject and their results in each period are expressed as a function of the size of the strategic factor in the immediately preceding period, and, secondly, that the size of the factor itself in the current period is determined as a result of these acts and the other data referring to the period, we evidently obtain a complete analysis of the acts of a certain subject as being on the one hand determined by and on the other hand to some extent determining the total course of the economic development.

production of each commodity, the amounts of goods and services produced and consumed, the prices demanded by entrepreneurs and factor owners and the volume of various transactions carried out at those prices. These macro-economic magnitudes may usually be found by the *summation* of the corresponding micro-economic terms, or, when dealing with prices and other relations, by calculating an *average* of one kind or another.

All these variables can be regarded as functions of time. But it should be observed that they cannot conveniently be determined as continuous functions of time. Some of the actions considered, for example the announcement of prices and sales and other transactions, have, strictly speaking, no time dimension. They must therefore either be correlated with definite points of time or with certain time periods for which the total result is calculated. Other variables, e.g. the amounts of services put into production, have undoubtedly a time dimension. But even in this case only the total result for certain definite periods is usually of interest, and not the continuous variation from moment to moment. In the case of macro-economic phenomena also, the economic development should thus be divided into time periods for which only the *total* results obtained are calculated.* If in certain cases the value of a variable is to be determined with reference to a definite point of time, it seems most convenient to let this point be the *boundary* between two such periods.

A period of this type, the shortest taken into account in any given case (since only the total result and not its distribution within the period is of relevance) may be

* Cf. I. Svennilson, op. cit., p. 8: "The selection of a certain period involves a choice, as elementary variables in the system, of the *totals* (integrals) *for the entire period* of the streams of income and expenditure, between which there must exist certain relations of identity. Only these sums are determined by the assumptions made, whereas the development *during* the period remains undetermined."

called the "period of registration" with respect to the variables studied by the economist. From the point of view of the theorist it is naturally desirable to make these periods relatively long, since the analysis of what happens during each period will then cover a greater number of relevant events. The limit for lengthening the period lies in the fact that the explanation of an economic process is after a certain point dependent on the registration of what has happened, and this registration may relate either to the total result achieved during the past period, or to an event occurring at a definite moment, which is then taken as the dividing point between the periods. Such registration is necessary in so far as it must be assumed to influence the planning and future actions of the economic subjects.

In dealing with micro-economic developments, the "period of registration" in respect to the variables chosen can be made long enough to correspond to the period with fixed relevant plans applicable to the economic subject in question. Here also the period of registration of the variables chosen should not be longer than the interval during which the relevant plans, determining the actions performed during the period, can be assumed to be unchanged. If all the members of the group were to alter their plans at the same time, we should have agreement between the period of registration and of planning for each individual in this case also. In reality, however, the synchronization is very incomplete, and the period during which the relevant plans of all members of the group are retained unchanged, must therefore be taken to be *fairly short*. In the greater number of instances studied we then find in operation a great variety of plans that have been drawn up, not only by public authorities and individual consumers, but also by private and more or less independent entrepreneurs who do not know very much about one another's intentions. One cannot count upon all these plans being kept wholly unaltered during any long period. The attempts to realize the plans must quickly reveal that they are more or less incompatible. The actual course of events cannot correspond to all the anticipations of the individuals about the behaviour of the others. The result must therefore be a modification of some of the plans.

On the other hand it should be noted that it is not necessary to regard the modification of the plans as a continuous process. As stated above, since the decisions to apply new plans can be allocated to certain moments, *some* time must always elapse between these moments in any given case, during which all plans are unaltered (just as a finite period can be regarded as the sum of an infinite number of moments). Our scheme can therefore, even from a strictly logical point of view, be directly applied, as long as the time periods used are made sufficiently short. It should further be observed that, in applying our scheme to practical problems, it is quite a justifiable simplification to assume that the intervals elapsing between alterations of plans are not impossibly short, but long enough to be of practical interest. This represents only a slight modification of what really happens, and it helps us to get a clearer insight into the nature of the economic process.

We now turn to the question of the *data* required for the determination of the variables entering into a macro-economic development, subdivided into time periods of this nature. It will be convenient to distinguish between the development (i) during the first period and (ii) in succeeding periods.

(i) For the determination of the development during the first period we require firstly some knowledge of the contents of the relevant plans, and secondly some knowledge of the external conditions affecting the development.

With regard to the plans, we want to know:

(*a*) The totals of all *unconditioned and uniquely determined* plans that are supposed to be realized during the period. It is, therefore, not necessary to have a knowledge of each individual plan; we can deal in sums (for example the total demand for a certain commodity at a certain price) or averages (e.g. the average selling price of a commodity). How far the summation and averaging may be carried, naturally depends on the degree of differentiation of the variables that are to be determined.

(*b*) The totals of the *unconditioned* plans, valid for the period in question, that are *determined within limits*, as found by an application of probability calculus. Even though the acts of each individual may be supposed to vary within a narrower or wider margin, the probable result of the totality of their acts may be deduced by means of the law of large numbers.

(*c*) The totals of the *conditioned* plans, the realization of which is bound up with some definite condition, derived either from the unconditioned acts referred to above as taking place during the period or else from external factors belonging to the data of the problem (see below). The realization of these plans may be supposed to take place either immediately upon the fulfilment of the condition or, if the latter is realized at the beginning of the period, with a time lag which may not exceed the length of the period.* The conditioned plans must evidently enter into the data as *functions* of the conditions valid in each given case.

To these data concerning the plans we should add the

* A demand curve may be named as an example of conditioned plans. The size of the actual demand will depend on the announced selling price. If this price is established at the beginning of the period, the demand must appear with a time lag smaller than the length of the period, if it is to have relevance for the development during the period.

following, which apply to the external conditions affecting the development:

(*d*) The *relations between the actions* that take place during the period and which are determined as described above, and the *variables* entering into the problem, when there is not identity between the actions and the variables studied, but the latter refer to the *result* of actions. For example, if in a given case the acts consist of certain kinds of inputs of productive services, and the output resulting from these inputs is included among the variables studied, we must naturally know the true relation between input and output.

(*e*) Concerning other ("non-economic") events during the period, enough must be known to make it possible to calculate (on the basis of the functional forms mentioned in (*c*) above) the conditioned actions that follow therefrom. Here we may have to deal with climatic or political conditions. For instance, if we know that the members of the group are prepared to act in a certain way on a sunny day and in a different way on a rainy day, the determination of their actions presupposes knowledge of which alternative is realized.

If all these data are available, it must clearly be possible to determine the variables constituting the economic development during the first period.

(ii) In order to determine the development during subsequent periods, we must have knowledge of the following types:

(*a*) The variables for the first period (determined as just described).

(*b*) The other ("non-economic") events that influence plans and actions during the second period.

(*c*) The disposition of the individuals to alter their relevant plans for the second period in consequence of the factors mentioned in (*a*) and (*b*). The data of (*a*)–(*c*) are

57

therefore sufficient to determine the relevant plans for the second period by the same method as described for the first period, and the actions carried out during this period will then also be determined.

(*d*) The relations between these actions and the variables studied for the second period.

For the determination of the development during a third period, analogous data are required, and so on.

We have now given a general account of the data that must be available in order to enable us to construct unequivocally an economic development, expressed by means of certain variables which change their values with the lapse of time. A theoretical treatment of the problem may of course be facilitated by the use of various simplifying assumptions. Thus if "non-economic" events are neglected and we also assume constant relations between actions and their results, between the unconditioned and the conditioned actions in a certain period, and also between the variables in a period and the plans which will be unconditioned in the next period; for the determination of developments for an indefinite time ahead we require a knowledge only of (1) the unconditioned actions during the first period, (2) the functions necessary to determine the conditioned actions consequential on the unconditioned ones, (3) the functions required for determining the results of the actions, and (4) the functions showing how the unconditioned actions in each period are determined on the basis of the variables from the preceding period.*

* Cf. I. Svennilson, op. cit., p. 11, where it is clearly shown "that certain variables not affected by events occurring during the period but only by earlier events *govern* the development during the new period, while the other variables are functionally dependent on the governing variables. The realized development of the governed variables is assumed to influence the governing variables only intermittently, i.e. by their sum as accrued at the end of the period." The distinction made here between governing and governed variables

It would lead us too far to inquire how the setting of the problem varies under more specific assumptions.* In this connection we may confine ourselves to two observations.

In view of the fact that the scientific treatment of a macro-economic development must, for reasons already put forward, be based on a subdivision of the development into fairly short periods, it is of course impossible for the economist to follow it in detail from period to period. In spite of this, it is quite feasible to give a picture of the course of events during a fairly long stretch of time. If by the analysis of certain selected typical periods, one can determine the directions of movement during these stretches, the character of the intervening periods may also be understood. It may sometimes be necessary to modify the actual character of the periods selected so that they may adequately represent the active tendencies during the phase in question.

In general it is impossible for the economist to give a complete analysis of a complicated course of development in one and the same exposition. He must usually be content to discuss the total developments from some special point of view, i.e. he must make a selection among the variables entering into the development. He must then assume that the other variables connected with those selected are given in one form or another, and must leave their study to other branches of the science. In this way separate treatment can be given to specific economic problems, thus

corresponds to that made by us between unconditioned and conditioned plans and actions.

* Dr. Erik Lundberg, in his book *Studies in the Theory of Economic Expansion*, has given the first exposition in English of Swedish dynamic theory and has also made an important contribution to the theory of economic development, or as he calls it, "Sequence Analysis." Of special interest are the model sequences constructed in his ninth chapter to illustrate the different phases of an expansion under various simplifying assumptions.

permitting a certain division of labour, not only between economics as a whole and the other social sciences, but also between the various branches of economics itself.

8. DISEQUILIBRIUM AND EQUILIBRIUM METHODS IN THE THEORY OF PRICE MOVEMENTS

(i) *The Disequilibrium Method*

The pricing problem is often treated under the assumption of free competition, whereby the prices operating in a certain period can be regarded as the *result* of the operation of certain given demand and supply functions during the period. This construction is quite appropriate when used for the analysis of the *equilibrium* position of a price or a system of prices. But it is not always so appropriate when the pricing problem is analysed from a more realistic point of view. In an actual dynamic case, there is no necessity for equality of demand and supply. But the opposite concept of price as *continuously changing* under the influence of the demand and supply factors is equally not correct. For the analysis of the pricing process a more careful study of its elements is required.

From a dynamic and realistic point of view we must distinguish between *two* kinds of action which are the foundation of the pricing process: firstly those actions whereby prices (referring to specified goods or services of a determined or indetermined amount) are *offered* by the sellers or buyers, and secondly those actions, whereby these offers are *accepted* by the other party (often to a greater or a lesser extent than expected by the suppliers). Both these actions take place at definite *moments* of time (but the offers are valid for a certain period of time or until further notice). The pricing process is thus not a continuous one. If described graphically, the supply and demand prices appear as lines parallel to the time axis, with discontinuous movements at the points when prices are changed. The transactions performed at these prices appear as lines perpendicular to the time axis at those points of time at which the terms have been agreed.

We must now try to indicate how these price phenomena can be most appropriately fitted into our scheme.

In consideration of the fact that an alteration of the prices offered by sellers or buyers is usually combined with, or is the expression of, some modification of the general plan of business, the most natural procedure is to assume that price changes take place at the transition points between periods (as defined above). In accordance with this assumption, *no price movements occur during the periods* themselves. The central pricing problem as it concerns the determination of the prices offered by sellers and buyers, is thus not directly related to what happens during the periods, but to the more complicated events occurring at the transition points between periods.

The announcement of new prices, for example, by certain sellers, will generally induce other firms or persons who for some reason (as buyers or competing sellers) are directly interested in these prices, to modify their own plans of action, and eventually the prices they themselves offer. In applying our scheme we must assume that either these alterations follow the original price changes immediately and can therefore be allocated to the same points of time,* or that they are allocated to a transition point between certain later periods. For our present purpose the first assumption is the more convenient.

* This assumption involves of course a simplification, as in reality some time must always elapse between the moment when a seller alters his price and the moment when a buyer decides for that reason to buy more or less of the article in question. But if no bargains are transacted during this short interval (which is quite a reasonable assumption, as the buyer may be waiting for the new price before he decides how much to buy), this is of no economic importance.

61

The second element of the pricing process, that is, the acceptance (by buyers) of the prices offered (by sellers), can be allocated either to the time period immediately following the announcement of the price offered, or to a later period. If these transactions are not in accordance with the anticipations (of sellers), they will in many cases lead to a fresh modification of the business plans based on the anticipations. But it seems reasonable to assume that these reactions are usually not very sudden. A seller will generally sum up the result of all transactions during a certain period, before he decides to alter the price of what he is selling. Thus if we suppose that transactions of this type always occur *within* a definite period and that the reactions resulting from them are allocated to the end of the period (or to some later date), it will be well in accord with the course of events in the real world.

To sum up the above reasoning, our method is the following: the dynamic process is divided into fairly short time periods, e.g. days; all decisions about the business and consumption plans to be adopted, and all price changes, take place at the transition points between these periods. Within the periods all transactions, by which the prices offered are accepted by the buyers or sellers, are carried out, and the more or less continuous processes of production and consumption take place.

In order to illustrate the significance of our method, as applied to a society with private entrepreneurship, we may complete our analysis with the following example.

The starting-point is the morning of a certain day. It is assumed that all sellers have already announced their prices and that all entrepreneurs and consumers, guided by these prices, by other known circumstances and by their expectations of the future, have taken their decisions as to the necessary modifications of the plans for their own economic activity during the day. Each producer has thus decided what and how much he will produce, which services, raw materials and capital instruments he will buy, and each consumer how he will spend his income. During the day all these plans are carried through as far as possible.

On the evening of the same day, each individual sums up his experiences and reflects upon his actions for the immediate future. The producers and traders look over their stocks and orders. If a producer has received more orders than he expected, he will want to raise his prices. Another producer will, for the opposite reason, lower his prices. The former will perhaps expand and the latter restrict his production. On the morning of the next day, the new prices are announced, plans are modified, and then the process will continue in the same way as on the preceding day.

An analysis of price development on these lines has recently been greatly facilitated by the adoption of the distinction between calculations made *ex ante* and *ex post*, or between prospective and retrospective estimates in Dr. Marschak's terminology. This method has been found to be fruitful and to provide a simple solution of a number of disputed points particularly in the explanation of general price level movements, as determined (among other things) by the relation between saving and investment. We are indebted to Professor Myrdal for having originated the suggestion and indicated its consequences for the analysis of price movements.* The method has since been further

* In this connection the following quotation from Professor Myrdal's work *Der Gleichgewichtsbegriff als Instrument der geldtheoretischen Analyse* (*Beiträge zur Geldtheorie*, ed. Hayek, Vienna, 1933), is of interest: "In the foregoing I have pointed to the discrepancy between Volume of Capital and Total Volume of Real Investment as the distinguishing feature of a Wicksellian process; but this is only valid as long as one is considering the tendencies at work at a given moment of time, in which the quantities in question (Income, Saving, Con-

developed by Professors Frisch and Ohlin,* and by other economists in England and America.

In the detailed study of the relations between important economic concepts in the next essay I have dwelt at some length upon the significance of estimates made *ex ante* and *ex post*. I have tried to give an analysis of a perfectly general nature, international relations being also taken into account. My aim has been to increase the usefulness of the concepts and their applicability to the complicated conditions met with in reality.

(ii) *Two Equilibrium Methods*

The foregoing analysis of the pricing process as a series of disequilibria, rested on the realistic assumption that the prices quoted in the market are regarded as the supply

sumption, Investment, etc.) are represented by price expectations for future periods, discounted to the present period. But if one turns to the actual development during a period, and compares *ex post* the value of the capital accumulated during the period and the value of the real investment used to accumulate it, it will be found that they are equal. This final equality clearly arises from *gains* and *losses*. . . . In a Wicksellian upward process certain gains (the so-called *Ertrags-und Kosten-Gewinne*) are regularly greater than losses, and in so far as they do not give rise to any alteration in consumers' demand, they must be included among savings calculated *ex post*. These therefore receive an increment in the *ex post* calculation in comparison with that made *ex ante*. This increment covers the difference between free capital *ex ante* and invested capital or real investment—which is higher in this case—during the period for which the calculation is made. In a downward process losses predominate, and free capital *ex ante* is larger than real investment *ex post*. The difference in this case is evened out through losses. Here again the result is that the amount of invested capital *ex post* agrees with the real investment during the completed period." (op. cit. p. 247 f.)

* For general references, cf. Bertil Ohlin, "Some Notes on the Stockholm Theory of Savings and Investments," I–II, *Economic Journal*, 1937, pp. 53 ff. and 221 ff. Professor Ohlin's own contribution to the theory is to be found in a report delivered to the Swedish Unemployment Commission, on *Monetary Policy, etc.*, *Essay on the Theory of Expansion* (Statens offentliga utredningar, 1934: 12).

prices of sellers (or in certain exceptional cases as the demand prices of buyers). These prices are, it is true, based on sellers' anticipations of the magnitude of demand at different prices, but the anticipations are often more or less false. It is the deviations between the transactions anticipated by sellers and those actually carried out, and the associated changes in stocks and orders, which are the most important factors influencing the decisions of sellers to alter their prices from one period to the next. The method thus has the advantages of being realistic and of clearly displaying the motive forces behind price movements, namely the excess or deficiency in demand anticipated by sellers when fixing their previous prices.

It is, however, clear that when the process of price formation has proceeded in this manner for a number of periods, a situation may conceivably be established which the sellers see no reason to alter under prevailing conditions. The situation thus constitutes a temporary eouilibrium in a *first* sense—one in which the market price is adjusted to the demand and supply factors as they appear currently in the market. The price is therefore in a sense an independent factor, which can be determined from the supply and demand conditions prevailing during the period, conditions commonly presented graphically by means of certain supply and demand curves conceived as independent of the price to which they lead. These conditions are then regarded as unaffected by the price established in this period.

Not until a subsequent period are costs and incomes affected by the market price established. New demand and supply curves may be required and they in turn will lead up to a new price determined by them, and thus the process may continue from one temporary equilibrium to the next. Under certain conditions a position may conceivably be reached at which we have not only equilibrium

65

between demand and supply brought about by price, but also obtain income and cost relations (on which the curves are based) that agree with the current price. Here we evidently have a temporary equilibrium position in a *second* sense, characterized by *interdependence* between prices and the supply and demand functions during the period. This equilibrium position is therefore of the Walrasian type, although it is not permanent but is valid for the period only. This situation may be conceived to have originated through all buyers and sellers having found by negotiation at the beginning of the period, those prices which satisfy the conditions of equilibrium, due account being taken of the reaction of prices on the cost and income situation and accordingly also of the forms of the demand and supply curves.

The *first* of these two equilibrium methods is the one ordinarily used in the treatment of price formation in a particular market. But it can also be used in an analysis of total conditions directed to the explanation of movements of the general price level, whether this problem is attacked by means of the cash balance approach, or by way of saving and investment. In the latter case, the price level for consumers' goods is conceived as wholly determined by the relation between the purchasing power directed to the purchase of consumption goods and services (= Income — Saving), in relation to the available quantity of such goods and services. This is the method underlying Keynes' well-known Fundamental Equations in his *Treatise on Money*.* In the work already cited Dr. Hammarskjöld

* These equations, as is well known, have been set out in a form in which they are applicable only under very simplified assumptions (among others that "the net increment of investment" which in reality is the value sum obtained by subtraction from the value of gross output of investment goods of the depreciation of the old ones can be regarded as consisting of certain concrete goods). It is not difficult however to express the same line of thought in a completely

66

uses a similar method for analysing a complete dynamic process. He proceeds to transfer the gains arising in each period from the pricing process, to the purchasing power of the next period.*

This method is very useful for the determination of general tendencies in the formation of prices for a some-

general form. Applying the definitions and notations used in the following "Algebraic Discussion" we denote income by E, saving by S, value of real investment by I, all calculated net and *ex ante*, and let B and C indicate the purchases (planned and realized) for productive and consumption purposes respectively, A^b and A^c the corresponding expectations of the producer sellers, P_{0I} the price level of consumers' goods anticipated by sellers, P_{II} the price level for these goods realized during the period, Q the quantity of consumers' goods that was expected to be sold and also actually sold. (This last assumption naturally limits the possibility of applying the reasoning to real conditions). We can then set up the following equations:

$$P_{II}Q = C = E - S$$
$$P_{0I}Q = A^c = E - (A^b - B + I) = E - (I + \Delta^b)$$

(As will be seen in the following essay, we have by definition $E = A^b + A^c - B + I$; Δ^b is defined as $= A^b - B$.)

If we divide the first equation by the second, we obtain

$$\frac{P_{II}}{P_{0I}} = \frac{E - S}{E - [A^b - (B - I)]} = \frac{E - S}{E - (I + \Delta^b)}$$

We thus see how a divergence between saving and investment *ex ante* can bring about a shift in the realized price level in relation to that anticipated by sellers. The expression in brackets denotes what producers expect to sell for productive purposes minus the excess of actual sales over the value of planned net investment (the amount that buyers do not regard as net investment, e.g. replacing worn out capital, thus being deducted), or, as the matter may also be expressed, the value of planned net investment plus the difference between expected and actual sales for productive purposes." It corresponds to what Keynes has called the "cost of investment."

* In *ex ante* and *ex post* terms the assumption may be interpreted as that each period's income *ex ante*, on which the actual demand during the period is based, is assumed to be equal to the income *ex post* of the period immediately preceding, which income includes the gains that arise as a result of the formation of prices during that period.

what longer time ahead. The conclusions drawn by Keynes from his formulae (conclusions which agree in many respects with the lines of thought developed in the second part of the present work) may therefore in general be accepted. But the method involves a certain limitation, arising from the basic assumption that the quantity of consumers' goods sold is independent of the prices received for them. In reality this quantity can at least partially be adjusted to the price through changes in stock holdings. In a realistic analysis of current price movements, therefore, it is more correct to follow the disequilibrium method outlined above.

The *second* interpretation of the concept of temporary equilibrium, according to which a general interdependence is assumed to exist between prices and the demand for and the supply of factors during each short period, would seem to correspond to Marshall's "short period equilibrium."* The significance of this method of conceiving a dynamic process as consisting of a series of such equilibrium positions has recently been very clearly illustrated in Professor Hicks' important work, *Value and Capital*, where it has been extensively used. Since it also underlies the study of the theory of price movements in the second part of the present work, it seems appropriate to indicate its relation to other methods.

The advantage of this method is that the entire static apparatus may be employed in the analysis of a dynamic sequence. It thus bridges the gap between statics and dynamics. The cumbersome *ex ante* and *ex post* terminology becomes superfluous, for the individuals are assumed to have knowledge at the beginning of the period of all the transactions and of the relevant prices valid for the period. On the other hand, this method has an even more limited

* Marshall, *Principles*, v, 2; cf. also Hicks' comments in *Value and Capital*, p. 119 f.

field of usefulness than the previous one, and a narrower range of application to real conditions. In a real dynamic development such equilibria are probably found only sporadically. Especially unrealistic is the assumption that the dynamic development presents an abrupt transition from one such equilibrium position to another. Further weakness lies in the fact that the dynamic element is not overtly present in the equilibrium equation in each period, unless the equation is made so complicated that it also includes anticipations referring to future periods. The dynamic element itself lies in the incompatibility of these anticipations, and this becomes manifest at the beginning of each period when the parties undertake the commitments valid for the period. In other words, during each period there is present a latent disequilibrium, and that is the reason why the equilibrium achieved during the period is found to be only temporary. The driving force in the dynamic process thus lies entirely in the sphere of expectations, and this curtails the usefulness of this method as a basis for the construction of exact model sequences.

These disadvantages, however, are less apparent when we aim at a description only of the main lines of a dynamic development. It then seems to be justifiable to concentrate our study on such possible temporary equilibria in different phases of the development. By comparing such equilibrium positions, as the analysis in Part II will show, we obtain a picture of the essential characteristics of the development that is both simple and clear.

9. A Note on the Pricing Problem in a Community with Centralized Planning

In the foregoing analysis we made no special assumptions as to the political organization of the community considered. We had primarily in mind a community where free entrepreneurship exists since it is the most relevant for us. It may therefore not be inappropriate to add a few remarks on the pricing problem in a community where the productive activities are mainly directed by a supreme Central Authority. This problem presents many interesting features, varying with the degree to which the Authority limits the initiative of the individual members of the community. Some alternative assumptions on this essential point are therefore necessary.

(i) At one *extreme* the organization of both production and consumption is determined by the Central Authority. This means that the members of the community receive their income in kind, or that consumption is controlled in some other way. If incomes are paid in money, the payment may be combined with various licenses to buy specified goods and services at certain definite rates.

The characteristic and very interesting feature of the economic life of such a community is, from our point of view, that for a certain definite period it can be regarded as the result of attempts to realize *one single plan*, that drawn up by the Central Authority for the community's activity during the period in question. In order to explain its working we have to analyse the content of the current plan and the conditions under which its realization is attempted. And if we take a longer period into consideration, we must observe how the plans of the Central Authority are modified from time to time as a result of past experience. The longer period is thus naturally divided into shorter periods during which each plan is kept unaltered. In this case, however, these shorter periods may be of a considerable length, possibly several years. This follows from the fact that there is only one single plan in force and that disappointments can therefore arise only from the influence of unforeseen external events on the conditions of production and consumption. Our general scheme for the treatment of economic development can be applied in the simplest possible manner in such a case.

(ii) The next type of community is that in which the members receive their income in money and have free disposal over it for *consumption* purposes. This freedom of consumers' choice must render the Authority's task of planning more difficult. In the former case its choice between alternative combinations of goods and services to be produced with the given quantity of productive resources, could be based on its *own* valuation of the needs of the consumers. In the present case the planning entails an estimate of how the *consumers themselves* value their needs. On the basis of this estimate the problem of production has to be solved in conjunction with the pricing problem.

If we assume that money incomes are given (as a result of a valuation made by the Authority, of the same kind as that on which the distribution of real incomes was determind in the previous case), the solution of these problems entails, on the one hand that the prices of the different goods and services should be fixed in such a way as to secure equality between demand and supply in each case, and on the other, that the value of the whole output, calculated at these prices, cannot be increased by employing the factors of production in some other way. If these two conditions are not fulfilled, it must be possible to increase the total satisfaction of the consumers (as valued by the Authority, who determines the incomes of the consumers) through a modification of the production plan. Planning is thus concerned with an equilibrium problem of the same character as that treated in static theory. But here the equilibrium refers only to the planning.* It

* There are also other differences between the two cases. In the stationary equilibrium there is a mutual interdependence of the prices of products and the prices of the services of factors determining individual incomes. In the present case, there is no *necessary* relation between the incomes of the individuals and the value of the services rendered by them, calculated on the basis of the value of the products. It is thus possible to assume (as we have done above), that the basis for the distribution of income is determined before the solution of the production and pricing problem. But it is also a possible assumption that the individual incomes are determined in relation to the productive value of the services, as estimated on a marginal analysis. (They need not be equal to these values. If we suppose that the total income of the capital owned by the state is employed in the first place to pay all expenses that would otherwise be covered by taxation and that any necessary increase of capital must also be provided from it, a surplus or a deficit may arise, causing a raising or a lowering of the payments made for services.)

71

seems probable that the carrying out of the plan (even if we disregard the possible occurrence of unforeseen external events) will involve a disequilibrium in several respects, owing to the fact that actual demand will deviate more or less from that anticipated by the Authority.

Whenever the demand is discovered to have been greater or less than was expected, the Authority has to modify its plan of production, if it desires to do its best to satisfy consumers' needs. The duration of each plan will thus be comparatively limited and in any case much shorter than under the previous assumption. This arises from the fact that the activity of planning is no longer concentrated in the Central Authority. The various plans of the consumers are now relevant and must also be taken into account in the solution of the problem. When different plans, drawn up by independent planners, come into operation, the results cannot be satisfactory from all points of view, as the plans are bound to be incompatible with one another to some extent.

In the two cases now examined, genuine monetary problems are absent, if we disregard the possibility of hoarding in the second case. The total money income will in principle be kept equal to the total value of the output available for sale to consumers. The problem is concerned only with the fixing of relative prices so that the total amount of money paid by the state to consumers will flow back as payment for the goods and services delivered to them.

(iii) If we now take a third type of a socialist community, and assume that private *saving* is allowed and that the members of the society can invest money in state securities, or deposit it in the state bank, interest being paid on these investments and deposits, a new problem presents itself. When the Central Authority has to decide how to apportion productive resources between consumption and capital industries for a certain period ahead, it must make an estimate of the probable amount that consumers will save during this period. The sum of this expected private saving, and the saving performed by the state itself should be equal to the planned increase of capital. This means that the total value of the consumption goods offered for sale to consumers should correspond to the non-saved part of their incomes. If the consumers dispose of their incomes in a different way from what the Authority has anticipated, the result will be either a shortage or an excess of consumption goods. This will not necessarily, as in a community with free entrepreneurship, lead to a corresponding rise or fall in the prices of these goods, since they are fixed by the Central Authority, but it will nevertheless represent an important deviation from the plan of the Central Authority and cause it to be modified for the next period.

Thus we see that in this case the Central Authority will have to solve a problem of exactly the same nature as the Central Bank in a community with free entrepreneurship. In both cases the task is to direct the productive resources of the community to production for present and future needs so as to correspond to the consumers' wishes. In both cases the problem must be solved on the basis of an *anticipation* of these wishes. But the practical solution is perhaps a little simpler in the socialist than in the capitalist state, since the distribution of productive resources is carried out by authoritative measures. In the capitalist state the Central Bank must try to direct the activities of entrepreneurs by monetary measures, especially by changes in the rate of interest.

As a result of this investigation it appears that our method of analysing dynamic processes may be particularly appropriate for the study of socialist economics.

ALGEBRAIC DISCUSSION OF THE RELATIONS BETWEEN SOME FUNDAMENTAL CONCEPTS

1. Definitions and Notation

In the following exposition we distinguish between two chief categories of economic subjects: (1) individuals or private households, and (2) "firms," this term being taken in a sense wide enough to cover all ownership of real capital and goodwill included in capital and income calculations. The firms are in their turn mainly owned by individuals who get their income from this "financial capital" and from the remuneration of the labour services sold to firms.

The system of notation is based on the principle that small letters apply to micro-economic phenomena, that is to magnitudes referring to a single private household or to a single firm, whereas capital letters indicate the corresponding macro-economic terms, i.e. sums or averages for a group of individuals or firms, defined in a particular way. Unless otherwise stated, the same micro-economic terms can be applied both to private individuals and to firms.

It should be observed that most of the terms can have negative values. All values referring to periods are assumed to be located at the end of the period; thus they include the interest accrued (or expected to accrue) during the period.

Subscripts on the right are used for time notations. The points of time t_0, t_1, t_2, etc., are denoted by 0, 1, 2, etc., and the periods lying between these points, $t_0 t_1$, $t_1 t_2$, etc., by 1, 2, etc. Such subscripts may indicate either the points of time when the estimate is made ("points of estimate"), or the points or periods of time to which the estimated magnitudes refer. (For certain transactions a further distinction can be made between the time when the contract is made and the time when it is carried out. The term a_{012} indicates for example the estimate at t_0 of the amount of sales contracted during the period $t_0 t_1$, and delivered during the following period $t_1 t_2$. Payment for the goods is assumed to take place at the same time as the goods are delivered; if other payment

74

conditions have been stipulated, a credit is supposed to be given to one of the parties.)

Superscripts on the right denote subspecies of the terms in question. The sign $*$ indicates that the term refers to transactions of the group with other groups, it thus refers to imports and exports or to other relations of an "international" or "interregional" type. The sign $°$ indicates that the term refers to transactions within the group.$*$ Terms without such signs indicate the sum or the average, as the case may be, of terms which have them.† This principle is followed consistently with regard to all superscripts to the right.

Subscripts to the left are used more freely for other purposes. They may, for example, indicate the subject of the estimate or the group to which the estimate refers. Superscripts on the left are principally used for denoting that the terms in question are to be interpreted in a special sense; thus, for example, k = value of capital, ^sk = subjective value of capital, ^ak = accounting value of capital.

The significance of the various terms used in this paper is indicated below in alphabetical order. The definitions there given are generally more fully explained later, but in order to simplify the task of the reader it has been found appropriate to put them together in a list.

LIST OF TERMS

a : sales, either of the labour services of an individual $(a^l = \pi y)$, or the products of a firm $(a^k = px)$; it is assumed that the seller receives the payment for the services or goods sold at the same time as they are delivered,

* This method of notation which has been found very appropriate was introduced by Professor Frisch in his mimeographed lectures (Oslo, 1935) on *Et generelt monetaert begrep-og symbolsystem* (A General System of Monetary Concepts and Symbols). It is expected that this work will shortly appear in revised shape in *Econometrica*.

† The only exception to this rule refers to the superscripts $+$ and $-$, which are used to denote positive and negative items entering into a special term; in that case the term without index is equal to the difference between the positive and negative terms. For example $f = f^+ - f^-$ (net lending and net acquisition of securities is equal to the difference between loans given and securities bought on the one hand and loans taken and securities sold on the other).

if the selling transaction is not combined with a credit transaction.

b: purchases for productive purposes, either in connection with the rendering of labour services (b^l), for the utilization of real capital (b^k), or for carrying out financial transactions (b^h).

c: purchases for consumption purposes, including the "productive consumption" of private individuals for increasing the earning capacity of labour.

d: depreciation of real assets (and of goodwill connected with them), including costs of maintenance and repairs.

e: net income of a private individual or a firm.
e^l: net income from labour, defined as the wages or salary received minus expenses incurred for the work $(= a^l - b^l)$.
e^k: net income from real capital, defined as the difference between sales and productive purchases with addition of the net real investment $(= a^k - b^k + i)$.
e^h: net income from the ownership of securities and of capital lent out, defined as the net amount of dividends and interest paid out in the given period plus the net amount of unrealized interest (which latter item is equal to the excess of net financial investment over net purchases of securities and net lending) with a further deduction for expenses incurred in connection with financial transactions $(= r + j - f - b^h)$. The income that the owners of a firm receive from it must, in order to avoid double counting, be deducted from the firm's own income from financial capital.

f: net result of financial transactions, i.e. excess of lending (including increase in bank deposits, whether on current account or not) over borrowing (f'), and of purchases of securities of all kinds over sales (f'').

g: gains and losses, i.e. instantaneous changes in the subjective value of wealth (as estimated respectively by the entrepreneur or the owner), not directly occasioned by accrued interest or purchases or sales;

g' : income gains and losses, attributable to a revision of the income for the last period;

g'' : capital gains and losses, representing the remainder.

h : net value of financial capital (and of goodwill connected with it), i.e. capital lent out (including bank deposits, and current accounts) in excess of debts (h'), and securities (h''). The capital of a firm is a debit item for the firm itself and a credit item for its owners.

i : net value of real investment, that is, increase in value of real capital due to the excess of net income and productive purchases over sales $(= e^k + b^k - a^k)$.

j : net value of financial investment, that is, increase in value of financial capital due to financial transactions or to an excess of interest accrued over interest and dividends paid out, or else to expenses incurred in connection with the transactions $(= f + e^k - r + b^k)$.

k : value of real capital (and of goodwill connected with it).

l : average number of labourers employed by a firm.

m : holdings of cash, both "home" money, i.e. notes and coin issued by the Central Bank or other authority within the group considered (for which the amount issued is regarded as a negative item), and international money that is gold, notes and coin issued by foreign authorities;

$\dot{m}$: increase in cash-holding.

p : average price of the products of a firm.

π : average price of the services of labour.

r : net receipts of interest and dividends paid out. For a firm the dividends paid by itself to its owners must be included as a negative item.

ρ : rate of interest, reckoned for the period in question.

s : saving, i.e. excess of net income over consumption purchases and taxes paid out of this income during the same period $(= e - c - t)$.

t : taxes paid out of net income and not included in consumption. Subventions and gifts of all kinds can also be

77

included under this head. The receipts of taxes by public bodies and the receipt of gifts represent a negative item in t.

u: gross value of output, including not only finished products but also other goods and services rendered from one department to another within a firm.

v: gross value of input, including not only goods and ser-services purchased, but also those received by one department from another within a firm.

w: net value of wealth $(= k + h + m)$ of a private individual or a firm; in the former case k is zero, and in the latter case h is in general negative, since the amount belonging to the owners of the firm enters as a negative item.

x: quantity of goods and services sold by a firm.

y : quantity of labour services sold by an individual.

γ: excess of income from financial capital (calculated without deduction of the possible expenses connected therewith), i.e. $e^h + b^h$ over taxes and similar payments $(= r + j - f - t)$.

$\eth$: excess of sales over purchases, i.e. "export surplus" $(= a - b - c)$; thus $(\eth + \gamma)$ is the amount available for bringing about an increase of net financial investment.

2. Micro-economic Values

(i) *Relations Valid both for Prospective and Retrospective Values*

We may first state some general relations between the concepts, valid for micro-economic values, which are the results of estimates all made at the same point of time. Values referring to a private household are assumed to be estimated by the householder himself, and values referring to a firm by the planning and leading man of the firm for whom we here use the traditional term "entrepreneur." It is in general of no relevance, whether the values refer to periods or points of time in the future or in the past, from the point of view of the individual making the estimate. The relations stated are thus valid both for retrospective values as estimated at the end of the period considered and for prospective values as

78

estimated at the beginning of the period, which in the latter case, however, must be assumed to be so short that the estimates are single-valued.

The *receipts-expenditures* equation (or *cash* equation) expresses the fact that the monetary receipts of an individual or a firm are equal to disbursements during the same period plus the increase in cash-holdings:

$$a \; + \; r \; = \; b \; + \; c \; + \; t \; + \; f \; + \; \dot{m}$$

Sales	Net receipts from financial capital	Productive purchases	Consumption purchases	Taxes, etc., not reckoned as costs	Net lending and net purchases of securities	Increase in cash

The significance of the equation is quite obvious in the case of a private individual: a denotes his salary or wages earned during the period, r his monetary income from capital, b the (usually unimportant) expenses for his work or for his financial transactions, c his consumption, t the direct taxes paid (other taxes being included in c or b, since they cannot be separately calculated), f the net amount of securities bought plus excess of lending over borrowing, and $\dot{m}$ the increase in holdings of notes and coin. In the case of a productive enterprise we have to observe that r, the income from financial capital, has a negative value during periods when it includes the dividends distributed to the owners as a large negative item. In the case of a bank, r, denoting the interest on accounts, b, including the operating expenses, and f, denoting the changes in capital claims and debts in relation to the public, will be the most important terms. For the state and other public bodies, the term t, now indicating income from taxes, instead of tax payments,* assumes a negative value.†

* As already stated, only direct taxes paid out of the net income and thus not reckoned as costs by the tax-payers, are included under this head. The income of public bodies from other taxes is, a little inappropriately, included under a (sales to the public of services of a collective nature).

† If the state gives subventions to individuals or firms (for example in order to relieve unemployment), they will constitute a positive item in t for the state ($- t$ will thus signify the amount of direct taxes minus subventions) and a negative item in t for the recipients of the subventions (for whom t denotes the direct taxes paid minus subventions received).

79

The equation is thus generally applicable, although the significance and the importance of the various terms may change from case to case.

The concepts of income, saving, and investment have no place in the equation given above, which deals only with purely monetary in- and outgoings. The terms have been chosen with the practical purpose of arranging the economic material in such a way that the results of economic activity during a certain period can be judged in relation to future periods. Unfortunately, full agreement regarding the most suitable definition of the terms has not yet been achieved. Later in this essay we shall make clear which definitions seem to constitute, in the opinion of the author, the most appropriate base for a theoretical analysis. We shall also make a comparison between this theoretical interpretation of the terms and the meaning usually given to them in accounting practice. In the present section, however, we need make no other assumption with regard to the definitions of the three concepts than that they should be *correlated* with one another in the manner shown below. In order that the validity of our exposition may be as wide as possible, we have thus here given it a form so general that it can serve both for theoretical and for practical interpretations of the terms.

We may start with the following equation which shows how the *earning of income* from factors, i.e. labour and real capital, can be calculated:

$$e^{l+k} \quad = \quad a \quad - \quad b^{l+k} \quad + \quad i$$

| Income from factors | Sales | Productive purchases | Real investment |

The net income from factors is thus equal to the difference between sales and productive purchases plus the net amount of real investment, or, as it can also be stated, equal to the difference between the sales proceeds and the amount of productive purchases not involving a net increase in real investment, $a - (b - i)$. The correlation between income and investment is most clearly seen, if we write $e - i = a - b$, which equation indicates that *the difference between net income from factors and real investment is equal to the difference between purchases and sales during the same period.* Every definition of income or of real investment thus entails certain consequences with regard to the definition of the other concept, since the

80

difference between them in a given case should be a constant amount. It is of course theoretically possible to define the terms in other ways. But to do so would make the system less simple, and the theoretical economist would be sinning against his first duty, which is to avoid all unnecessary complications.

The earnings equation has now been stated in a form so general that it can be applied both to the labour income of an individual and to the income of a firm from real capital. In the case of *labour*, however, it can be interpreted in two different senses, depending on whether the i-term is maintained or dropped (i.e. given the value zero).

From a theoretical point of view, the first alternative, which implies a quite parallel treatment of the income from the two factors, seems to constitute a possible and even admissible method. The net income from labour would then, with help of the formula given above, be calculated as the sales proceeds (a), i.e. the salary or wages, minus productive expenses which do not represent "personal investment" increasing the productive capacity of the individual $(b - i)$. Costs for education and occupational training which give rise to such "personal capital" would consequently be included both in i and in b. This method has the advantage that due regard is had to the important capital formation of this type, and further some relations can be stated more simply than is otherwise possible. But when the study is carried on to the relations between income and capital—and our investigation will later (p. 96) reach this point—the parallel treatment of the real capital factor and the labour factor encounters the difficulty that money values are usually calculated only for the former. In general private individuals do not estimate the value of their earning capacity as labourers (in a wide sense), and only if the theorist himself invents such values, will he be able to treat the two factors according to the same scheme.*

In the present case, however, when we have been chiefly concerned to define our terms with the greatest possible conformity to real conditions, even at the cost of some com-

* The reader may find examples on the application of this method elsewhere in this book, since we have found it admissible to use it on two separate occasions (cf. p. 146, and pp. 328–9 ff).

plication in the exposition, we have found it advisable not to include personal capital and its formation in the concepts of capital and investment, since it is not measurable in the same way as real capital. Thus the i-term has to be left out in the equation for income from labour, and consequently the expenses incurred in increasing the earning capacity of labour are transferred from productive to consumption purchases (from b to c).* The equation for income from labour will thus be written:

$$\underset{\substack{\text{Income from} \\ \text{labour}}}{e^l} = \underset{\substack{\text{Sales of labour} \\ \text{services}}}{a^l} - \underset{\substack{\text{Current} \\ \text{expenses for} \\ \text{the work}}}{b^l}$$

With regard to the income from *real capital*, however, the earnings equation must, in accordance with the formula previously given, be written:

$$\underset{\substack{\text{Income from} \\ \text{real capital}}}{e^k} = \underset{\text{Sales}}{a^k} - \underset{\substack{\text{Productive} \\ \text{purchases}}}{b^k} + \underset{\substack{\text{Real} \\ \text{investment}}}{i}$$

We have already pointed out that this formula is so wide that it covers all possible definitions of income and investment that are correlative with each other. The significance of the a- and b-terms will be the same in all definitions since it is here question of unequivocally determined amounts, but the content of the i-term may vary with corresponding consequences for the content of the e-term. In section (iii) we shall return to the question of the manner in which the terms should most appropriately be determined from the standpoint of theoretical analysis. In this connection we need only add some remarks on the relation of the equation just given to accounting practice.

The significance of the equation from this point of view will appear more clearly, if we split up the e-term into the components entering into the profit and loss account of the firm. Since the accounting methods of firms differ greatly

* The dropping of the i-term and the diminishing of the b-term will not necessarily lead to a different result from the other method with regard to the size of the e-term, since the changes may cancel out. The disparity between the two methods will chiefly find expression in the distribution of the income between consumption and saving.

the following exposition can only be illustrative. We assume that the items transferred to the profit and loss account emanate from separate accounts, where they are calculated in a manner indicated by the following equations:

$$
\begin{array}{lll}
& \overbrace{\quad -d \quad} & \\
e' & = u' & - v' & + i' & \text{(Net income from fixed real assets and goodwill)} \\
e'' & = u'' & - v'' & + i'' & \text{(Net income from stock of raw materials)} \\
e''' & = u''' & - v''' & + i''' & \text{(Net income from production department)} \\
e^{IV} & = u^{IV} & - v^{IV} & + i^{IV} & \text{(Net income from stock of finished products)} \\
e^{V} & = a & - v^{V} & & \text{(Net income from selling department)} \\
e^{VI} & = & - v^{VI} & & \text{(Overhead costs not included in other items)} \\
e^{VII} & = v & - u & - b & \text{(Difference between accounted and actual costs)} \\
\hline
e^{k} & = a^{k} & - b^{k} & + i & \text{(Total net income from real capital)}
\end{array}
$$

The u-terms indicate here the various items credited to the special accounts, the v-terms those debited to them, whereas the i-terms represent the differences between the out- and ingoing values of the respective accounts.* The *first* equation thus indicates that the net income calculated from land, buildings, plant, machinery, and other fixed real assets and goodwill is equal to their rental value (u') less allowance for depreciation (d), including costs of maintenance and repairs. The depreciation term is again determined as $d = v' - i'$, where v' indicates costs incurred on the assets plus net purchases of new assets of this type; if v' is greater than i', the cause must obviously be a depreciation of assets. In the *second* equation the stock of raw materials has been treated in a completely analogous manner. The u-term indicates here the value of materials taken from stock and delivered to other departments of the firm, the v-term costs of storage, etc., plus actual pur-

* If the ingoing value is denoted by i^- and the outgoing value by i^+, the special accounts in question will thus be made out in accordance to the following scheme:

Debit Items		Credit Items
i^-		u
v		i^+
e		
$i^- + v + e$	$=$	$u + i^+$

Thus $e = u - v + i$.

83

chases of new materials, and i'' the accounted increase in value of the stock. If the terms u'', v'' and i'' were calculated on the basis of the same prices, they would cancel out, except for the storage costs included in v'' and implying a negative e''. The *third* equation states that the net income from the production department is equal to the value of the finished products (u''') delivered to stock plus the difference between out- and ingoing values of goods in process (i''') minus the accounted costs of production (v'''). It is worth noticing that the prices used in the calculation of u''' and i''' are often substantially lower than the actual selling prices, and that therefore the essential part of the profit appears first in the selling department. The cost term comprises both what has been transferred from other departments of the firm, and the services of workers and of other firms purchased from outside, though not necessarily reckoned at the same prices as those actually paid. The *fourth* equation is of the same character as the second; the net income from the stock of finished products is usually negative, representing certain storage costs. The *fifth* equation tells us that the net income from the selling department is equal to the excess of the actual sales proceeds (a) over the accounted value of the goods sold and taken out of stock (u^{IV}) and over certain selling costs ($v^V - u^{IV}$). The *sixth* equation contains only a negative item, i.e. certain overhead costs that have not been apportioned among the various departments of the firm (e.g. general costs of administration, certain taxes and licences, etc.). And the *seventh* equation, finally, takes account of the fact that the accounted costs, i.e. the v-terms, entering into the other equations, are often calculated on the basis of prices other than the output values, i.e. the u-terms, when it is a question of services and goods transferred from one department of the firm to another, and that they may deviate more or less from those actually paid, i.e. from the cost of services bought from outside. A difference may thus appear between the sum of accounted costs (v) on the one hand, and the sum of output values (u) and the amount of actual purchases (b) on the other. Since the accounted costs are usually calculated at standard prices lower than their actual value, this last item will also in general be negative.

In the example now given we have had a productive enterprise of the ordinary type in view, but our reasoning can be analogously applied also to firms of other kinds. If it is a question of a commercial business, for example, which does not produce but merely distributes goods, we have only to drop the third equation (in some cases also the two first ones), to make the scheme applicable.

The income from *financial capital* can be expressed by a formula similar to that used for real capital and labour:

$$e^h \quad = \quad r \quad + \quad j \quad - \quad f \quad - \quad b^h$$

| Income from financial capital | Net receipts of dividends and interests | Financial investment | Net lending, and net purchases of securities | Certain expenses |

This formula is so wide that it covers both the theoretical definition of income from capital as interest, and the more usual definition of such income as the actual monetary receipts from the capital. In the former case interest not paid out but added to the capital is included both in income and financial investment, this latter concept then being defined in a manner entirely parallel to real investment. As can be seen in the formula above, the financial investment will then exceed the amount of net lending and net purchases of securities with the unrealized accrued interest which thus $= (j - f)$. (If in a certain period the dividends and interest realized exceed the interest earned in the same time, then $j - f$ assumes a negative value.) In the latter case, when this unrealized interest is disregarded in the income calculation, it follows that it should also be excluded from the concept of financial investment which is then limited to net lending and net purchases of securities. In accordance with this view, $j = f$, and thus $e^h = r - b^h$. The negative term b^h refers to certain expenses (for services of various kinds) connected with the financial transactions.

There are no essential difficulties in the application of the formula given above in the income calculation of a private individual. It should merely be observed that r in general has a positive value since it includes not only interests on ordinary loans (representing positive items for the creditors and negative items for the debtors), but also all payments of dividends, interest, etc.* from firms to their owners. If the

* In so far as the payments of the firm are of the nature of a distribution of capital, they should enter as a negative item in the term f in the income calculations of the owners.

85

income from financial capital is interpreted in the broad sense as including unrealized interest $(j - f)$, this item is assumed to be calculated on the basis of the individual's own estimate.

With regard to a firm, however, the income from financial capital can be calculated either in the same way as for a private individual, or with deduction of that part of the income earned by the firm which is included in the income calculations of its owners. The former method is the usual one, but the latter must be applied, when the income calculations are to be used in a study of the macro-economic type. We must then proceed to a summation of all individual income items belonging to a certain group of economic subjects, for example a whole country, consisting both of firms and private individuals. Since in such a calculation of the total income of a group the income that the owners of a firm receive from it should not be reckoned twice, it will be necessary to make a corresponding deduction from the income of the firm. Hence, the income of a firm from financial capital has been defined here as including the income of its owners as a negative item.

The application of the above formula to firms thus implies, according to this principle, that the term r will usually be negative, since it includes the big negative item represented by the disbursements to the owners of the firms. And in so far as the undistributed profits of a firm are included as a positive item in the term $(j - f)$ in the income calculations of the owners, they should also reappear as a negative item in the same term in the firm's income calculation. In this case there is the difficulty that the estimates of these profits, on the part of the owners, may not necessarily coincide with the estimate made by the manager who is responsible for income calculation of the firm. The difference between the estimates will thus enter as a positive or negative item in the total income of the group. In a later section (3 (ii)) when we are dealing with macro-economic relations, we shall return to this point. Here it need only be observed that, in point of principle, the income of firms, calculated in accordance with the system outlined here, should only contain such items as are not included in the calculation for the owner's income. From this it follows that the distribution of total income of a group between firms and private individuals will vary with the concept of income on which the calculation is based.*

If we add the formulae for income from factors and income from financial capital, we finally get the equation for the *total net earnings* of an economic subject:

$$e^{l+k} = a - b^{l+k} + i$$
$$e^h = r + j - f - b^h$$

$$\overline{e = a - b + i + r + j - f}$$

This equation can accordingly be applied both to private individuals and to firms, though in each particular case some of the terms may be zero. The application of the formula to macro-economic magnitudes involves, as has already been mentioned, the difficulty that the income that the owners of a firm receive from it should, to avoid double counting, be deducted from the firm's own income from financial capital. If, in accordance with ordinary practice, we wish to calculate the net income of a firm as including the amount that enters into the income calculations of the owners, we have only to interpret the terms in the equation given here in another way.†
In practice it is usually most convenient, first to estimate the income of firms irrespectively of the income that the owners

* For example, in the case of an ordinary corporation whose whole net income from factors belongs to its owners, to treat the income from financial capital as interest entails the consequence that the e of the firm is zero for all periods, a positive e^k being neutralized by a negative e^h. If f is assumed to be zero, then this negative e^h is balanced by a negative j in periods when no dividends are distributed, and by a negative r (eventually combined with a positive j) in periods when such disbursements occur. If on the other hand income from financial capital is defined as monetary receipts from the ownership of this capital, then $e^h = r$, and in periods when e^k is positive and $r = 0$ or when $e^k > (-r)$, the firm will get a positive e. In accordance with this more traditional method the undistributed profits of corporations are not included in the income of the shareholders, but added to this income as a separate item when the national income is calculated.

† If we dissolve the terms referring to financial capital—using the index ' for terms referring to capital lent out or borrowed and the index " for terms referring to securities, and further introducing the top index + for positive terms and the top index − for negative terms—

receive from them, and then in the summation to make a general deduction for this income.

To the equations now set up for the earning of income we can add two others. For *the use of income,* our definition of saving gives us the following equation, on which no other comment is needed than that saving is here determined in a manner quite analogous to the income concept:

$$\underset{\text{Income}}{e} \; = \; \underset{\text{Consumption}}{c} \; + \; \underset{\text{Taxes, etc.}}{t} \; + \; \underset{\text{Saving}}{s}$$

Finally, if the two equations for the earning and the use of income are set together with the cash-equation, we obtain the following *saving-investment* equation:

$$\underset{\text{Saving}}{s} \; = \; \underset{\substack{\text{Real}\\\text{investment}}}{i} \; + \; \underset{\substack{\text{Financial}\\\text{investment}}}{j} \; + \; \underset{\substack{\text{Increase in}\\\text{cash}}}{\dot{m}}$$

All saving undertaken by a firm or by a private household must thus find expression in an increase either of real investment or of financial investment or of cash-holdings. That the relation between the concepts can be stated in such a simple way must be regarded as an advantage gained through the method of defining them in a correlative manner.

The significance of a difference between saving and real investment in a single economic unit appears clearly from the equation now stated. It can be further elucidated, if this equation is put together with the cash-equation, rearranged, and modified by the addition to both members of the un-realized income from financial capital $(j-f)$:

$$
\begin{array}{c}
a - b - c + r - t = f + \dot{m} \\
j - f = j - f \\
\hline
\underbrace{a - b - c + r}_{\eth} + \underbrace{j - f - t}_{\gamma} = j + \dot{m}
\end{array}
$$

Continuation of footnote from p. 87]
we can rewrite the equation for the income of a firm in the following way:

$$e = \underbrace{a - b + i}_{\substack{\text{Income}\\\text{from real}\\\text{capital}}} + \underbrace{r' + j' - f'}_{\substack{\text{Income from}\\\text{capital lent}\\\text{out}}} + \underbrace{r'' + j'' - f''}_{\substack{\text{Income from shares,}\\\text{etc.}}} - \underbrace{(r'' - + j'' - - f'' -)}_{\substack{\text{The part of the income}\\\text{belonging to the}\\\text{owners}}}$$

If we exclude the last items, referring to the owners, and interpret the terms r, j, f in a corresponding way, we get the formula for the net income of a firm calculated in the usual manner.

88

Thus we can write:

$$\delta \quad + \quad \gamma \quad = \quad j + \dot{m} \quad = \quad s - i$$

| "Export surplus" | Income from financial capital (gross) less taxes | Increase in financial holdings and cash | Excess of saving over real investment |

From this we may conclude that if the sum of the excess of sales over purchases (the " export surplus ") and the financial income (calculated without deduction for expenses for services, etc.) is a positive magnitude, saving must exceed real investment by the same amount, and that this excess must find expression as an increase in holdings of financial capital or of cash. In a later section, when we come to macro-economic relations, we shall have occasion to comment further on the significance of this statement.

The equations given so far may be summarized as follows:

$$e = \underbrace{a - b}_{} + \underbrace{r - f}_{} + i + j$$

with braces: $\underbrace{e^{l+k} - b^h - i}$ over $a-b$ region, $\underbrace{e^h + b^h - j}$ over $r-f$ region, $\underbrace{c + t + \dot{m}}$, $s - \dot{m}$, $\underbrace{c + t + s}$

Finally we have to add the equation for the net amount of *wealth*, owned by an economic subject at a certain date:

$$w \quad = \quad k \quad + \quad h \quad + \quad m$$

| Wealth | Value of real capital | Value of financial capital | Stock of money |

This equation is applicable both to private individuals and to firms, though the terms must be interpreted for them in different senses. As mentioned in the introductory section, all real capital of the relevant type is assumed to belong to " firms " (interpreted in a wide sense). For private individuals the term k will thus be zero. (This assumption does not of course prevent us from conceiving private individuals as possessors of certain capital goods, as for example clothes, furniture, motor cars, and so on, but these items are left out of consideration in this connection. They appear in our system only as consumption purchases.) The wealth of private individuals will therefore mainly be confined to h. For firms, on the other hand, h will in general have a negative value.

89

If the capital held by a firm belongs to its owners, which holds true for most corporations, the firm has no wealth of its own. The positive value of its real capital and its cash-holdings must therefore be neutralized by a negative value of the same size for its financial capital which includes the " debt " to the owners as a large negative item. With regard to money as an object of wealth, it seems to be most appropriate to let the positive items, represented by the cash-holdings of the firms and the public, be balanced by a negative item for the State or the Central Bank, corresponding to the amount of money issued by them. This " home " money is of course reckoned as wealth by the cash-holders, but since it does not add anything to the wealth of the country as a whole and, in so far as it is held by foreigners, obviously represents a negative item in the calculation of this wealth, it should be neutralized by a corresponding debt for the money-issuing authority.*

We have now covered the most important aspects of the relations between the fundamental concepts dealt with here, in so far as these relations are so general that they apply both to prospective and retrospective values, and at the same time to values interpreted both in a theoretical and in a practical sense. The logical procedure would now perhaps be to take up the prospective and retrospective aspects separately. As a matter of fact, the central part of modern economic theory, dealing with marginal analysis, belongs to this field. There is, however, no necessity for us to restate these well-known and beautiful doctrines here. Instead we shall proceed at once to a discussion of the relations between prospective and retrospective values.

(ii) *Relations between Prospective and Retrospective Values*

The equations given above for certain economic magnitudes entering into the budget of a private household or a

* The distinction between financial capital (h) and money capital (m) is therefore more one of degree than one of kind. It is consequently of no essential importance how the line between these two categories is drawn. If, for example, deposits subject to cheque are classified as money, a procedure not followed here but which is very suitable from many points of view, this would not in the least alter the validity of our equations.

single firm were valid for all estimates made at the same point of time, irrespective of how this point of estimate was located in relation to the period or points of time to which the estimated values referred. If we now proceed to a study of the results that may occur through *a shift of the point of estimate,* for example from t_0 to t_1, we can therefore start from a scheme of equations which is obtained by subtracting the values estimated at the former point of time from the values resulting from estimates at the latter point of time. These equations give expression to the relations between the *differences* between the respective estimates.

As a starting point we have written below some equations of this type, referring to estimates made by an economic subject at two different points of time, t_0 and t_1 (the time indices now indicate these points of estimate), concerning his receipts and expenditures during a certain period, and concerning the earning and use of his income during the same period (the index indicating this period is left out). The equations are stated in a form so general that they are *valid for any arbitrary combination of period of event and points of estimate* for which quantities of the single-valued type can be obtained:

$$a_1 - a_0 + r_1 - r_0 = b_1 - b_0 + c_1 - c_0 + t_1 - t_0 + f_1 - f_0 + \dot{m}_1 - \dot{m}_0$$
$$e_1^l - e_0^l = a_1^l - a_0^l - (b_1^l - b_0^l)$$
$$e_1^k - e_0^k = a_1^k - a_0^k + i_1 - i_0 - (b_1^k - b_0^k)$$
$$e_1^h - e_0^h = r_1 - r_0 + (j_1 - f_1) - (j_0 - f_0) - (b_1^h - b_0^h)$$
$$e_1 - e_0 = c_1 - c_0 + t_1 - t_0 + s_1 - s_0$$

We must now make two assumptions which will be maintained throughout this section:

(1) The points of estimate are assumed to be located respectively at the beginning and the end of the period to which the estimated values refer. The reason for making such an assumption is that the two kinds of estimates will then both be of great economic relevance. The prospective estimate, made *ex ante* at t_0 for the period $t_0 t_1$, refers to what the subject is planning to do in the immediate future and should therefore be taken as a starting point in the explanation of the actions actually taken. The retrospective estimate, made at t_1 for the same period $t_0 t_1$, may, on the other hand, be supposed to influence his planning for the next period, and is thus of

immediate relevance for the explanation of the actions under-taken in that period. But in order that the *deviations* between prospective and retrospective values should obtain their full importance, we have to make a further assumption with regard to the length of the period considered.

(2) The period to which the estimated values refer is sup-posed to be so short that the planning of the economic subject is realized in unaltered form with regard to (i) selling prices (p or π as the case may be) and (ii) purchases made for productive and consumption purposes. The assumption (ii) may be expressed:

$$b_0 = b_1$$
$$c_0 = c_1$$

This assumption of equality between certain prospective and retrospective magnitudes has the essential significance that all relevant actions in this field undertaken by the economic subject during the period in question can be directly deduced from the plans given at the beginning of the period. The differ-ences between the *ex post* and *ex ante* values with regard to the other terms retained in the equations will, on the other hand, make evident the manner in which events during the given period (which are mainly the result of the actions of other people), have brought various surprises for the individual and impressed his mind before he has to decide how to act in the forthcoming period. Actions during this latter period are thus directly connected, not only with the *ex post* values of the first period, but also with the differences between them and the *ex ante* values for the same period. An explanation of the relations between the prospective and retrospective magni-tudes, referring to a certain period, will thus constitute one of the missing links that is needed in order to state the way in which the events that have taken place in this period will influence the events occurring during the period immediately following.

In the system of equations given above, our assumption obviously results in cancelling all b- and c-terms. A consider-able simplification is thus achieved. The equations are stated below in their new form—which is thus *valid only for a relatively short period with unaltered planning*—with the addition of the equation for the saving-investment relation:

$$a_1 - a_0 = f_1 - f_0 + \dot{m}_1 - \dot{m}_0 - (r_1 - r_0) + t_1 - t_0$$
$$e_1^l - e_0^l = a_1^l - a_0^l$$
$$e_1^k - e_0^k = a_1^k - a_0^k + i_1 - i_0$$
$$e_1^h - e_0^h = r_1 - r_0 + (j_1 - f_1) - (j_0 - f_0)$$
$$e_1 - e_0 = s_1 - s_0 + t_1 - t_0$$
$$s_1 - s_0 = i_1 - i_0 + \underbrace{j_1 - j_0 + \dot{m}_1 - \dot{m}_0}_{\delta_1 - \delta_0 + \gamma_1 - \gamma_0}$$

We may now proceed to an interpretation of these equations and to an explanation of their significance:

(1) The first equation states that if the sales of a firm or of an individual in a given period have exceeded the expectations of the "seller," this "unexpected increase in sales" $(a_1 - a_0)$ must lead to a corresponding "unintentional increase" either in his net lending $(f_1 - f_0)$ or in his cash-holdings $(\dot{m}_1 - \dot{m}_0)$, if this is not neutralized by an expected change in the terms r and t. The most usual form for the increase in financial investment will in this case be either a credit given to the buyer or a deposit in a bank.

(2) An unexpected increase in the quantity of labour services sold at a given price during a given period $(a_1^l - a_0^l)$ will give rise to a corresponding increase in the retrospective income over the prospective income of the factor owners $(e_1^l - e_0^l)$. If the whole increase in sales is to represent an increase in income, it must of course be presumed that the current expenses for the work have not increased from a retrospective point of view (we have assumed that $b_0 = b_1$) and that the subjective trouble of the labourer is left out of consideration.

(3) For a firm an unexpected increase in sales $(a_1^k - a_0^k)$ will give rise to an increase in income for the same period $(e_1^k - e_0^k)$ only in so far as it is not neutralized by a corresponding decrease in real investment (expressed in a negative value of $i_1 - i_0$), for example a reduction of stocks of finished products, other real investments being unchanged in total amount. A rise in income can thus be accompanied by a decrease in real investment, so long as this decrease is smaller than the simultaneous increase in sales. An excess of retrospective income may also arise, if the real investments made during the period turn out to be greater than the individual making the plan has previously expected (which implies a positive value of $i_1 - i_0$), in so far as this increase is not due

93

to a decrease in sales and takes the form of unsold stocks. The necessary condition for a rise in retrospective income is in both cases obviously either an unexpected increase in the physical productivity of the factors—leading to a greater output for a given input of services and raw materials, etc., or to a smaller input for a given output—or expectations of a rise in the selling price of the products, leading to a rise in the estimated value of what has been produced during the period.

The increase in physical productivity is in some cases directly occasioned by an increase in sales, for example for firms who sell services but have large overhead costs (an increase in traffic will for instance raise the productivity of a railway company and thereby also its net income). Expectations of higher selling prices may of course also be based on an increase in sales. It can thus in general be contended that a greater or smaller rise in income will be the probable result of an unexpected increase in the demand for a product. But, as already stated, this may also occur if no unexpected rise in sales has taken place. An increase in physical productivity may have occurred irrespective of sales, or some favourable event may have given rise to expectations of a future increase in productivity or of a future rise in the prices of the products.

(4) Financial holdings may lead to an increase in the post-calculated income $(e_1^h - e_0^h)$, if either the dividends and interest actually received during the period are greater than was expected $(r_1 - r_0)$ or the unrealized interest $(j - f)$ is greater *ex post* than *ex ante*. Since we are dealing with relatively short periods and since the dividends and interest paid by firms are generally announced some time beforehand, the former case is on the whole more unusual than the latter. An unrealized gain in accrued interest arises whenever an unforeseen increase has occurred in the total value of the financial capital on which the interest calculation is based.

(5) The difference between total income *ex post* and *ex ante* $(e_1 - e_0)$ is equal to the difference between saving *ex post* and *ex ante* $(s_1 - s_0)$, if we disregard unexpected events such as unforeseen taxes, etc. The excess of retrospective income just mentioned is thus, for the period considered, not consumed but saved to its full amount, since the economic subject becomes aware of this increase in income only at the end of the period. This part of the retrospective saving has here been

characterized as "unintentional," since it does not enter into the plan of the individual but represents a pleasant surprise to him. Nor can it strictly speaking be interpreted as the outcome of an increased "propensity to save" (to use one of Mr. Keynes' terms). As we shall see later, the most interesting aspect of this unintentional saving is just that it makes possible an increase in total saving even in the case when the propensity to save remains unchanged. It should, however, be added that for longer periods income gains generally increase the propensity to save for future periods, since they usually bring about a more unequal distribution of income.

(6) It follows from what has just been said that an unexpected increase in retrospective income and savings will find expression in an unintentional increase either in real investment $(i_1 - i_0)$, in financial investment $(j_1 - j_0)$ or in cash-holding $(\dot{m}_1 - \dot{m}_0)$. Since we have learned from the first equation that an unexpected increase in sales must increase either the lending or the cash-holding of the economic subject by the same amount (if we disregard changes in r and t), we can now draw the following conclusions: in so far as the income gain $(e_1 - e_0)$ is greater than the increase in sales $(a_1 - a_0)$ it will be expressed either in real investment $(i_1 - i_0)$ or in accrued interest on financial capital $(j_1 - f_1) - (j_0 - f_0)$; if it is equal to the increase in sales, the whole gain will be expressed in an increase in lending $(f_1 - f_0)$ or in cash $(\dot{m}_1 - \dot{m}_0)$; and if it is smaller than the increase in sales, which is the most usual case, then the difference between them will represent a further increase in lending and in cash, and at the same time the real investment together with the accrued interest on the financial capital will decrease by the same amount.

These unintentional changes in the distribution of the assets belonging to an economic subject will in most cases induce him to undertake certain adjustments in the near future. When the amount held in cash and financial investments has increased, there will in general be a tendency to shift over to real investment. But in the other case, also, when the income gain has found expression as an increase in real investment, the same tendency may appear, since the increase in productivity may stimulate the entrepreneur to enlarge the business.

95

In our reasoning above we have had an expansion in mind and spoken of increases in sales and in income and capital-values. But the propositions laid down can of course be analogously applied to the contrary case of a contraction when sales have diminished and losses are experienced. A tendency to diminish real investment will then be apparent.

(iii) *Relations between Subjective Values**

In the exposition so far we have carefully avoided the use of special definitions of income, investment, capital, etc., which may be theoretically defensible but are not in full harmony with the practical use of the terms. Our propositions have been framed in such a general form in order that they may be valid both for theoretical and practical interpretation of the terms under one important assumption, namely that the terms should be correlated with another. As a consequence of this procedure, our equations have on the whole been limited to the *income* situation of an economic subject. The problems concerned with *capital* values and with their relation to income values have hitherto mainly been neglected, since a fruitful discussion of them is hardly possible, if the meaning of the terms is not more precisely defined. Propositions that are valid for subjective capital values, for example, may not at the same time be applicable to capital values taken in the accounting sense, and vice versa.

In this section we shall complete our exposition of micro-economic relations by adding some remarks on problems concerned with subjective capital values and with special definitions of income, investment, etc., in harmony herewith and which appear to offer an appropriate basis for theoretical analysis. A parallel investigation of the accounting aspect of the same problems is not undertaken here, though some references to and comparisons with accounting practice will be found in the end of the section.

(1) *Subjective Capital Values Estimated at the Same Point of Time.*—Our definition of a subjective capital value corresponds fairly well to what is usually meant by capital value in economic theory: the estimate made by an individual of the

* This section (pp. 96–111), although important, may be omitted by the reader, since it is not referred to in the following exposition of macro-economic relations.

lowest price of an asset he as seller would demand for it or the highest price he as buyer would pay for it. Such values (reckoned in monetary units) being based on individual expectations and individual judgments as to risk-taking, etc., cannot be objectively determined. They may differ both from accounting values and market values, and may vary both with the person who makes the estimate and with the point of time when he makes it. In the following we assume that the owner of the asset is the maker of the calculation, but that, in the case of firms, the owner is represented by the planning and leading man of the firm, the entrepreneur. We shall first assume that the date of calculation is the same in all equations (the index for it can then be left out). The equations are thus valid for any arbitrary date of calculation. If the point of estimate is altered, the values of the terms will change, but the study of the effects of such a shift will be postponed to the later part of this section.

The *value of the real capital and goodwill* belonging to a firm at any given point of time, t_0, can be assumed to be equal to the sum of the discounted values of all future net receipts (calculated as the differences between sales proceeds, a^k, and productive purchases, b^k, for the n periods that the firm is assumed to last), as these are estimated at a particular date, with due regard to the risk factor :*

$$^sk_0 = \frac{a_1^k - b_1^k}{1+\rho_1} + \frac{a_2^k - b_2^k}{(1+\rho_1)(1+\rho_2)} + \cdots + \frac{a_n^k - b_n^k}{(1+\rho_1)(1+\rho_2)\ldots(1+\rho_n)}$$

At a date later than t_0, say t_1, the value of the capital, $^sk_1$, estimated at the same time and on the same base as $^sk_0$, will have increased by the interest accrued during the intervening period, $\rho_1{}^sk_0$, and have diminished by the net amount received by the owner, $(a_1^k - b_1^k)$:†

* If it is assumed that the firm will last for ever but that after a certain future date, t_ν, stationary conditions will prevail (cf. below p. 328), the equation will be modified as follows (the superscript k is left out) :

$$^sk_0 = \frac{a_1 - b_1}{1 + \rho_1} + \frac{a_2 - b_2}{(1 + \rho_1)(1 + \rho_2)} + \cdots$$
$$+ \frac{a_\nu - b_\nu}{(1 + \rho_1)(1 + \rho_2)\ldots(1 + \rho_\nu)\rho_\nu}$$

† The same equations are also used below, p. 329.

97

We thus obtain

$$^sk_1 - {^sk_0} \quad = \quad \rho_1 {^sk_0} \quad - \quad a_1^k \quad + \quad b_1^k$$

Increase in value of the real capital	Accrued interest	Sales of output from the capital	Productive purchases connected with the use of the capital

(Value at the end of the period)

The *value of the financial capital* owned by a private individual or a firm can be estimated in an analogous manner. We have only to substitute ^sh for ^sk, r for a^k and $(f + b^h)$ for b^k in the equations just given for the value of real capital:*

$$^sh_0 = \frac{r_1 - f_1 - b_1^h}{1 + \rho_1} + \frac{r_2 - f_2 - b_2^h}{(1 + \rho_1)(1 + \rho_2)} + \ldots + \frac{r_n - f_n - b_n^h}{(1 + \rho_1)(1 + \rho_2)\ldots(1 + \rho_n)}$$

For the increase in value during the period $t_0 t_1$ of such a capital we can analogously write:

$$^sh_1 - {^sh_0} \quad = \quad \rho_1 {^sh_0} \quad - \quad r_1 \quad + \quad f_1 \quad + \quad b_1^h$$

Increase in value of the financial capital	Accrued interest	Dividends, etc., paid	Net lending and net purchases of securities	Net expenses incurred

(At the end of the period)

Since the change in the *wealth* of an individual from one point of time (t_0) to another (t_1) must be equal to the sum of the changes that can be estimated for the real, financial and money capital held by him at the same time, we obtain

$$w_1 - w_0 = k_1 - k_0 + h_1 - h_0 + \underbrace{m_1 - m_0}_{\dot{m}_1}$$

* The value of a bond, for example, whose annual yield is r and which after t years is redeemed with $f-$ (representing a sale of the bond from the side of the bondholder), is, if we reckon with an unchanged rate of interest, ρ:

$$^sh = \frac{r}{\rho}\left(1 - \frac{1}{(1 + \rho)^t}\right) + \frac{f_t^-}{(1 + \rho)^t}$$

If we drop the f-term, the formula expresses the capital value of an annuity, lasting t years. If we let t increase to infinity, then the negative term in the parenthesis will be zero, and the formula will be simplified to $\dfrac{r}{\rho}$.

If we put this equation together with the equations given above for $({}^s k_1 - {}^s k_0)$ and $({}^s h_1 - {}^s h_0)$, we can write:

$$ {}^s w_1 - {}^s w_0 = \rho_1({}^s k_0 + {}^s h_0) - \underbrace{(a_1^k - b_1^k)}_{(e_1^k - i_1)} - \underbrace{(r_1 - f_1 - b_1^h)}_{(e_1^h - j_1)} + \dot{m}_1 $$

or, substituting s for $(i + j + \dot{m})$,

$$ {}^s w_1 - {}^s w_0 = s_1 + r_1({}^s k_1 + {}^s h_0) - e_1^{k+h} $$

| Increase in wealth | Saving | Accrued interest on capital | Income from capital |

(Both real and financial)

This equation tells us that if an individual at a given point of time calculates the change in the subjective value of his wealth during a given period, this change must be equal to the saving calculated for the same period *plus* the difference between the interest accrued (or expected to accrue) on the estimated capital values during the period in question and the calculated income from this capital. This statement is valid for all definitions of income and saving that are correlated with one another.

From this, however, we can immediately conclude that if income from capital is defined as the interest accrued (or expected to accrue) on this capital during the period in question, it will be possible to state the relations between the capital and income values in a simplified manner.

(2) *Income from Capital as the Current Interest on Subjective Capital Values.*—We thus reach the following definitions:

$$ {}^s e_1^k = \rho_1 {}^s k_0 $$
$$ {}^s e_1^h = \rho_1 {}^s h_0 $$

and in accordance therewith

$$ {}^s i_1 = \rho_1 {}^s k_0 - a_1^k + b_1^k $$
$$ {}^s j_1 = \rho_1 {}^s h_0 - r_1 + f_1 + b_1^h $$

If we compare these equations with those just given for the changes in the value of real and financial capital and wealth, we find that

$$ {}^s i_1 = {}^s k_1 - {}^s k_0 $$
$$ {}^s j_1 = {}^s h_1 - {}^s h_0 $$
$$ {}^s s_1 = {}^s w_1 - {}^s w_0 $$

99

The content of these equations* is not very sensational. That the real investment undertaken in a certain period should give rise to a corresponding increase in the value of the real capital, that a certain financial investment should bring about an increase in the value of the financial capital of the same size, and that the amount of saving should be equal to the increase in wealth, corresponds fairly well to the common-sense conception of these terms. But it is not always

* Other equations may also be added. With regard to the *depreciation* term, for example, take the equation previously (see p. 83) set up:

$$d = v' - i',$$

characterizing the depreciation as the excess of all costs laid down on the assets (including purchases of new goods) over the net investment in these assets. (Depreciation is here interpreted in a wide sense, including costs of maintenance and repairs.) Thus the content of the d-term was made dependent on that of the i-term, but both terms can be defined in an arbitrary way, if their sum is kept equal to the v-term which can be objectively determined. We have intentionally used such an incomplete definition of the terms in order that the validity of our equations should not be unduly limited. Since we have now introduced a special definition of investment, we can also make our definition of depreciation more complete. Applying the investment formula given above to depreciating assets (k'), we can write

$$^s i = \rho k' - u' + v'$$

If we put the value of i given here, in the equation just stated for d and if we further compare it with the equation previously given for the change in value of real capital, we obtain

$$d = u' - \rho k'$$
$$= v' - (k_1' - k_0') = k_0' - k_1' + v'$$

Thus we find that depreciation of fixed real assets and other durable goods takes place whenever the value of the services rendered by them has surpassed the simultaneous increase in value occasioned by the accrued interest, and that the amount of depreciation thus corresponds to the net decrease in value of these goods with the addition of all purchases and other costs belonging to this category. It should be observed that, in this statement, the capital values are assumed to be estimated at the same point of time. If we want the depreciation term in relation to the actual change in the capital values ($k_{00} - k_{11}$), we have to make a deduction for the eventual capital gains and losses.

realized that these rather simple and clear statements do as a matter of fact presuppose that, if we are dealing with subjective capital values, income from capital is to be defined as the interest accruing on that capital during the period in question, and that the concepts of real and financial investment and of saving are defined in harmony therewith. When we have here proposed such definitions, our essential purpose has been to simplify the relations between the economic concepts as much as is possible without diminishing their applicability to the phenomena of the real world.

(3) *Subjective Capital Values Estimated at Different Points of Time.*—So far our investigation has been limited to capital values estimated at the same point of time (i.e. to series such as: w_{oo}, w_{o1}, w_{o2}, etc., or such as: w_{10}, w_{11}, w_{12}, etc.), the first subscript denoting the point of estimate and the second the point of time to which the capital value relates. As in section (ii), we may now drop this assumption and take account of the effects of an actual shift of the point of estimate, for example from t_o to t_1, thereby comparing capital values resulting from successive points of estimate. In the same manner as before we shall then assume that the expectations and the valuation attitude of the person making the estimate have changed once only during the period $(t_o t_1)$ lying between the points of estimate, this period thus being relatively *short*. As a consequence we can assume that the equations and the reasoning developed in section (ii) hold true in the present case also. While the previous reasoning, however, was conducted in somewhat general terms, we may now proceed to an application to subjective capital and income values.

We have first to introduce the following definitions:

For capital values estimated at the same point of time as that to which they refer (w_{oo}, w_{11}, w_{22}, etc.) we shall use the term *actual* capital values.

The difference between an actual subjective capital value and the latest anticipated value deviating therefrom referring to the same point of time ($^s w_{11} - {}^s w_{o1}$, $^s w_{22} - {}^s w_{12}$, etc.) is called *gain* or *loss*.

The part of a total gain or a loss that can be attributed to a difference between the retrospective and prospective income for the last income period ($^s e_{11} - {}^s e_{o1}$, $^s e_{22} - {}^s e_{12}$, etc.) is called *income gain* or *loss*.

101

The remainder of the total gain or loss, $({}^sw_{11} - {}^sw_{01}) - ({}^se_{11} - {}^se_{01})$, etc., is called *capital gain* or *loss*.

With regard to the length of the income period, we assume either that it is so short that it corresponds to the period lying between the points of estimate $(t_0t_1, t_1t_2,$ etc.$)$, or that it corresponds to the income period reckoned with in practice, that is, a year. The distinction between income and capital gains and losses can therefore be made on two alternative lines: it can be based on *current income* or on *annual income*.

We may first set out some equations which are independent of the distinction between current and annual income. Introducing the signs g', g'' and g respectively for income, capital and total gains and losses, we can split up the definitions given above in the following way (when a single time index is used, the point of estimate is referred to):

$$g'^l = e_1^l - e_0^l = a_1^l - a_0^l \qquad \text{(Income gains from labour)}$$

$$g'^k = e_1^k - e_0^k = a_1^k - a_0^k + i_1 - i_0 \qquad \text{(Income gains from real capital)}$$

$$g'^h = e_1^h - e_0^h = r_1 - r_0 + j_1 - j_0 - (f_1 - f_0) \qquad \text{\small(Income gains from financial capital)}$$

$$\overline{}$$

$$g' = e_1 - e_0 = i_1 - i_0 + j_1 - j_0$$
$$+ \underbrace{a_1 - a_0 + r_1 - r_0 - (f_1 - f_0)}_{\dot m_1 - \dot m_0} = s_1 - s_0$$

$$g''^k = k_{11} - k_{01} - (i_1 - i_0) \qquad \text{(Capital gains from real capital)}$$

$$g''^h = h_{11} - h_{01} - (j_1 - j_0) \qquad \text{(Capital gains from financial capital)}$$

$$0 = m_{11} - m_{01} - (\dot m_1 - \dot m_0)$$

$$\overline{}$$

$$g'' = w_{11} - w_{01} - (s_1 - s_0)$$

$$g^l = m_{11} - m_{01} - (a_1^k - a_0^k) + f_1 - f_0 - (r_1 - r_0) \qquad \text{\small(Total gains from labour)}$$

$$g^k = k_{11} - k_{01} + (a_1^k - a_0^k) \qquad \text{(Total gains from real capital)}$$

$$g^h = h_{11} - h_{01} - (f_1 - f_0) + r_1 - r_0 \qquad \text{\small(Total gains from financial capital)}$$

$$\overline{}$$

$$g = w_{11} - w_{01}$$

The equations given here for income gains are broadly the same as those contained in the system presented on p. 93. Only we have here dropped the t-term—supposing that $t_{11} = t_{01}$, i.e. that the anticipated taxes are realized—in order to simplify the exposition. In the equations for capital gains these are characterized as unforeseen increases in the value of real and financial capital* over and above the increase directly occasioned by investment. The equations for total gains are obtained by the addition of the equations for income and capital gains.† (In order to simplify the summing up of these three equations we have, however, substituted the value contained in the cash-equation on p. 93 for $a_1^l - a_0^l$.)

The aim of these equations is to illustrate the way in which the various gains (and losses, representing negative gains) arise, and how they find expression in an increase in wealth. As we are here using the terms income and capital in a sub-jective sense, income and capital gains usually accompany one another. But in some cases, for instance, when an unfore-seen increase in sales or in dividends or interest is received from a financial asset, the income gains are primary in rela-tion to the capital gains. In other cases when the value of the assets has increased as a consequence of higher anticipations of monetary receipts in the future, the capital gains are primary; the income gains arising only as a reflection of the capital gains, and taking the form of a retrospective increase in accrued interest. It should be observed that the income gains also find expression in an increase in the value of wealth. The explanation of this is that this part of the retrospective income of which the economic subject is first conscious at the end of the period represents "unintentional savings" as we have called it above.

The distinction between *entrepreneurial* gains and *windfalls*

* In practice, of course, cash-holding can also give rise to gains or losses. An unforeseen change in the purchasing power of internal money will thus bring gains or losses to the cash-holders, if their wealth is estimated in a monetary unit of constant value. And if the cash is held in foreign money, any unforeseen change in the exchange rates will occasion such gains and losses. These cases, however, are on the whole less important, and are here left out of consideration, in order that our exposition may not become too complicated.

† In section (ii) we did not use the term income gains and losses, since it seems advisable to reserve the application of this term to a subjective interpretation of the income concept. The exposition given there was couched in more general terms, in order that it should be applicable also to other concepts of income, especially to income in the accounting sense.

explained elsewhere* has not been taken account of in the equations given here. The entrepreneurial gain arising when a person has a new idea on the planning of his business is in general mainly of the nature of a capital gain, whereas windfalls tend to appear primarily as income gains. In this connection it is worth noticing that the special kind of entrepreneurial gains which we have called *investment gains* should not be confounded with the excess of retrospective over planned investment $(i_{11} - i_{01})$ appearing in the equations above. As an anticipative item, the investment gain arises already with the *planning* of the investment, which can be assumed to be undertaken in a period *preceding* that during which the investment is realized. The gain finds expression in the increase in capital value in relation to previous estimates that has occurred during this period as a consequence of the planning. The investment gain thus already belongs to the past when we come to the period when the investment is realized; it is neither included in the planned investment (i_{01}), nor in the increase in the capital value expected as a direct result of the investment† $(k_{01} - k_{00})$. The unforeseen increase in retrospective investment should, in so far as it represents a gain, in general be classified with the other category of gains—windfalls.

(4) *The Distinction between Income and Capital Gains and Losses Based on the Concept of Current Income.*—We may now add some further remarks on the significance of the distinction between income and capital gains. The term "income gain" has been applied to the difference between a retrospective and a prospective estimate of the income for a given period. If income from capital is interpreted in the subjective sense as the interest accruing (or expected to accrue) on subjective capital values, then the income gain resulting from the ownership of capital during a given period is equal to the difference between the

* In a paper to be published in *Economica*.

† If the investment is planned at t_0 and realized in the period $t_0 t_1$, then $(k_{00} - k_{-1,0})$ represents the investment gain ($k_{-1,0}$ representing the value of the capital as it was anticipated before the planning) ; the planned investment and the increase in value expected as its result is equal to $(k_{01} - k_{00})$; finally $(k_{11} - k_{01})$ represents the windfall gain or loss, occasioned by a difference between what has been realized and what was expected with regard to the investment.

retrospective and prospective calculations of the interest for that period. We may now assume that the period lying between the points of estimate is the same as the income period, and that this period is relatively short. This implies that the income is interpreted as the current interest on the subjective capital values referring to the beginning of each short period. For this interpretation of the concept of income we have introduced the term *current income*.

If we apply this definition of income to our present problem, then we can substitute

$$\rho_0 k_{00} + b_0^k - a_0^k \qquad \text{for } i_0$$
$$\rho_1 k_{10} + b_1^k - a_1^k \qquad \text{for } i_1$$
$$\rho_0 h_{00} + f_0 + b_0^h - r_0 \qquad \text{for } j_0$$
$$\rho_1 h_{10} + f_1 + b_1^h - r_1 \qquad \text{for } j_1$$

in the equations given in the system on p. 102.

We thus obtain (observing that $b_1 = b_0$) the following equations for *income gains*:*

$$g'^l = a_1^l \quad - a_0^l$$
$$g'^k = \rho_1 k_{10} - \rho_0 k_{00}$$
$$g'^h = \rho_1 h_{10} - \rho_0 h_{00}$$

$$g' \ = a_1^l - a_0^l + \rho_1(k_{10} + h_{10}) - \rho_0(k_{00} + h_{00})$$

With regard to labour there is thus no difference, but with regard to capital the income gain is represented by the difference between the retrospective and prospective estimate of the interest on the capital value at the beginning of the period.

For *capital gains* we obtain in the same way the following equations of which the third merely expresses the fact that the amount of cash-holding at t_0 does not change by a shift of the point of estimate to t_1:

$$g''^k = k_{10} \quad - k_{00}$$
$$g''^h = h_{10} \quad - h_{00}$$
$$0 \ = m_{10} - m_{00}$$

$$g'' \ = w_{10} - w_{00}$$

* In order to make the exposition simpler we speak only of "gains" but the reasoning can of course be analogously applied to "losses" which can be treated as negative gains.

A capital gain thus finds expression in an enhancement of the value of an asset at the beginning of a given period, when this value is recalculated at the end of the period on the basis of the better knowledge then obtainable.

It is of interest to put the income and capital gains, connected with the ownership of real or financial capital, in relation to one another. If the rate of interest is the same *ex ante* and *ex post*, we get the simple formula:

$$\frac{g'^{k+h}}{g''^{k+h}} = \rho \quad \text{or} \quad g'^{k+h} = \rho \cdot g''^{k+h}$$

With our present definitions, *income gains are thus simply the accrued interest on the corresponding capital gains.* This simple relation between the concepts makes the task of the theorist a little easier than when he is working with other concepts of income, which give rise to more complicated relations. In fact, if the income and capital values stand in a fixed relation to one another,* the theorist can take either of them as a starting point when he wants to solve a dynamic problem.

In conclusion we may just add a table, showing the relations between capital values at the beginning and at the end of the period.† In studying this table, the actual values at the beginning of the period (k_{oo}) should be taken as starting point. At this moment the individual is supposed to make a prospective calculation of his investment during the coming period (i_o) which, as he then views the case, will give rise to a corresponding increase in capital value at the end of the period (k_{oI}). However, when this point of time is reached, he finds that he has been mistaken, the actual value of the capital

---

* If the rate of interest valid for the period in question is not the same *ex ante* and *ex post*, then the income gain will include not only the interest on the capital gain, calculated on basis of the rate *ex ante*, but also some interest on the whole capital value, corresponding to the difference between the rates *ex post* and *ex ante*, in accordance with the following formula:

$$g'^{k+h} = \rho_o g'' + (\rho_I - \rho_o)(k_{Io} + h_{Io})$$

However, when it is question of relatively short periods, as in our reasoning above, such differences between retrospective and prospective rates of interest may be regarded as exceptional cases that can be neglected even in an analysis aiming at conformity with reality.

† The method of graphic representation used here has been taken from a mimeographed manuscript *On Investments* by Dr. Marschak.

CHANGES IN WEALTH
CALCULATED "EX ANTE" ($\rightarrow$) AND "EX POST" ($\leftarrow$)

REAL CAPITAL

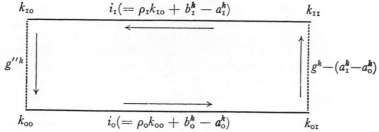

k_{10} $i_1(= \rho_1 k_{10} + b_1^k - a_1^k)$ k_{11}

g''^k $g^k - (a_1^k - a_0^k)$

k_{00} $i_0(= \rho_0 k_{00} + b_0^k - a_0^k)$ k_{01}

FINANCIAL CAPITAL

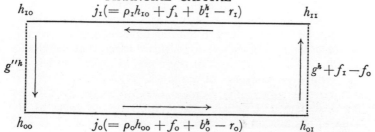

h_{10} $j_1(= \rho_1 h_{10} + f_1 + b_1^h - r_1)$ h_{11}

g''^h $g^h + f_1 - f_0$

h_{00} $j_0(= \rho_0 h_{00} + f_0 + b_0^h - r_0)$ h_{01}

CASH-HOLDING

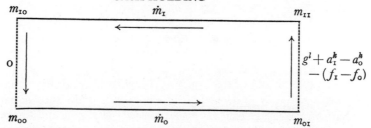

m_{10} $\dot{m}_1$ m_{11}

0 $g^l + a_1^k - a_0^h - (f_1 - f_0)$

m_{00} $\dot{m}_0$ m_{01}

TOTAL WEALTH

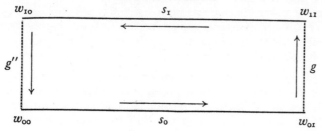

w_{10} s_1 w_{11}

g'' g

w_{00} s_0 w_{01}

being not k_{01} but k_{11}. If the latter value is higher than the former, due regard being taken to changes in the amount of capital through unforeseen sales, the difference may be characterized as a (total) gain. The way from k_{00} to k_{11} thus described is the one actually taken by the individual. When he reaches the latter point, however, he may return by the retrospective path to the starting point. He will first recalculate the investment made during the period. The result of this calculation in relation to what was expected gives him an income gain. He then obtains a new value for the capital at the beginning of the period, the difference between this value and the initial one representing the other part of the total gain, which we have called the capital gain.

Analogous reasoning can be applied to the changes in financial capital. The changes in cash-holding have been added in order to make the system complete. It is easily seen that the change in total wealth is the sum of the changes experienced in the three different categories of resources.

Since the sum of the changes that occur on the forward looking path $(w_{00} \rightarrow w_{01} \rightarrow w_{11})$ must be the same as the sum of changes on the retrospective path $(w_{11} \rightarrow w_{10} \rightarrow w_{00})$ we finally get the following equations:

$$k_{11} - k_{00} = i_o + g^k - (a_1^k - a_0^k) \qquad\qquad = i_1 + g''^k$$
$$h_{11} - h_{00} = j_o + g^h + f_1 - f_0 - (r_1 - r_0) \quad = j_1 + g''^k$$
$$m_{11} - m_{00} = \dot{m}_o + g^l + a_1^k - a_0^k - (f_1 - f_0) + (r_1 - r_0) = \dot{m}_1$$

$$w_{11} - w_{00} = s_o + g \qquad\qquad\qquad\qquad\qquad = s_1 + g''$$

The *actual changes* in the value of the wealth of an individual from one point of time (t_o) to another (t_1) are thus equal both to the *sum of prospective saving and the total gain* and to the *sum of retrospective saving and the capital gain*, the difference between the retrospective and the prospective saving representing the other part of the total gain, namely the income gain. This holds true for a longer period also as long as the calculation implies a summation of the results for such relatively short periods as have been treated here.

(5) *The Distinction between Income and Capital Gains and Losses Based on the Concept of Annual Income.*—If instead we assume that the period for which the income is calculated is relatively long, for example a year, whereas the period lying between

the points of estimate is relatively short, as above, for example a day, we get another distinction between income and capital gains. How far can the equations set up above be applied also to this interpretation of the concepts?

We assume that the period lying between the points of estimate as before is $t_0 t_{\mathrm{I}}$, but that the income period is $t_{-\mathrm{I}} t_{\mathrm{I}}$. The relevant magnitudes will then be those shown in the following graph:

$w_{\mathrm{I},\,-\mathrm{I}}$	s_{IO}		w_{IO}	s_{II}	w_{II}
$g''_{\mathrm{I},\,-\mathrm{I}}$			g''_{IO}		g_{II}
$w_{0,\,-\mathrm{I}}$	s_{OO}		w_{OO}	s_{OI}	w_{OI}
$t_{-\mathrm{I}}$			t_0		t_{I}

The total gain arising from a shift of the point of estimate from t_0 to t_{I} is the same as before, but it is now split up into income and capital gains in the following way:

$$\underset{\substack{\text{Total gain}\\(g_{\mathrm{II}})}}{w_{\mathrm{II}} - w_{\mathrm{OI}}} = \underset{\substack{\text{Income gains}\\\text{referring to}\\\text{period } t_0 t_{\mathrm{I}}\\(g'_{\mathrm{II}})}}{s_{\mathrm{II}} - s_{\mathrm{OI}}} + \underset{\substack{\text{Income gains}\\\text{referring to}\\\text{period } t_{-\mathrm{I}} t_0\\(g'_{\mathrm{IO}})}}{s_{\mathrm{IO}} - s_{\mathrm{OO}}} + \underset{\substack{\text{Capital gains}\\(g''_{\mathrm{I},\,-\mathrm{I}})}}{w_{\mathrm{I},\,-\mathrm{I}} - w_{0,\,-\mathrm{I}}}$$

(Capital gains reckoned on the basis of current income.)

In other words, the income gains now include not only the excess of retrospective over prospective saving during the short period between the two estimates $(s_{\mathrm{II}} - s_{\mathrm{OI}})$ but also the difference between the calculation made at the first point of estimate of the saving performed earlier in the year, and the new calculation of this saving made at the later point of estimate $(s_{\mathrm{IO}} - s_{\mathrm{OO}})$.

If the line between income and capital gains is drawn in this manner, the distinction corresponds fairly well to the common sense concept of the terms.* For theoretical pur-

* The practical significance of the distinction may be made clear by a concrete example. We assume that the traditional yield of some securities has been 5 monetary units and their capital value 100 units immediately after the payment of the dividend and then

poses, on the other hand, this interpretation of the terms seems to be less satisfactory. When we are dealing with dynamic analysis and have to calculate income, saving and investment for short periods, for example days, we cannot appropriately include the income gains arising on a certain day through new estimates of the income earned during previous days, in the income, saving and investment referring to the day of estimate. In these magnitudes we can include only so much of the income gain ascertained on the day in question as related to the income earned during that day. And thus we come back to the distinction based on the concept of current income, explained in the preceding paragraph.

(6) *Comparison with Accounting Values.*—To the analysis given above of the relations between subjective income and capital values we may finally add a few remarks on the relations between income and capital values in the accounting system.

The book values put on the assets of a firm have no direct relation either to subjective or to market values, except when guided by certain legal provisions requiring that they may not in general exceed market values; account thereby being taken also of losses which may be realized in the future. Their purpose is generally to state the results of the year, though in some special cases they may also be used to form a basis for a consideration of the financial position of the firm. Therefore, they stand in a definite relation to the items in the profit and loss account, as shown below ($^a g''$ here denotes capital gains and losses in the accounting sense)

$$^a k_1 - {}^a k_0 = {}^a i + {}^a g''^k$$
$$^a h_1 - {}^a h_0 = {}^a j_1 + {}^a g''^h$$
$$m_1 - m_0 = \dot{m}_1$$

$$\overline{{}^a w_1 - {}^a w_0 = {}^a s_1 + {}^a g''}$$

Continuation of footnote from p. 109]
successively rising to 105. If then, a short time before the dividend is paid out, it is announced that the yield now and in the future will be raised from 5 to 7 units, the value of the securities will rise from 105 to 147, if it is calculated on the same basis. The total gain is thus 42 units, and of this sum only 2 units, representing the unexpected increase of the dividend for the last income period, has the character of "income gain." The remainder 40 units, representing an increase in the discounted value of the future yields, is a "capital gain."

These equations are substantially the same as those holding between subjective capital values and *current* income, as set forth in par. 4, p. 108. The main difficulty with regard to their application relates to the determination of the capital gains and losses ($^{a}g''$), which ought not to be included in the income calculation for the year. In some cases they are the result of an "extraordinary" writing up or (more usually) down of the accounted values of certain assets, in other cases they are caused by a realization of fixed assets resulting in a higher or lower value than the previous book values. How the line is drawn between such capital gains (and losses) and ordinary profits is a matter of convention. If certain gains are regarded as profits it follows that they ought also to be included in calculations of investment and saving for the period concerned. Since in practice there are no fixed rules, and since in addition the principles governing the valuation of assets, including their appreciation and depreciation, vary greatly, accounting values form no sure foundation for a theoretical discussion.

3. Macro-economic Values

If we observe a certain group of economic subjects, either firms only or private individuals only or both firms and individuals, and if we sum up (or calculate averages for) all the micro-economic magnitudes implied in the equations given above, we get magnitudes relating to the whole group. We shall now proceed to an investigation of the relations valid for these total categories.

The problem before us may be regarded as the central one of dynamic economic theory. The following analysis has no further pretension than to give an introduction of the most elementary kind to its study. We have therefore contented ourselves with general formulations, avoiding all special assumptions that would have limited the validity of the results. In consequence we have not made use of the special definitions of income, investment, etc., used in some parts of the previous sections. Our definitions are of so general a nature that they cover both these theoretical definitions and other of a more practical character. The problems relating to capital values have also, for the most part, been left out of account.

The exposition follows the same lines as that dealing with

micro-economic magnitudes. We thus begin with relations between magnitudes based on estimates undertaken at the same point of time. In the case of total categories, however, we have here to make a distinction between relations that are generally valid and those only valid for estimates *ex post*. Among the latter, those of relevance for the calculation of the national income are discussed in a special section. In the last section we shall treat rather briefly the relations between the prospective and retrospective estimates of values referring to a very short period, with special reference to the relation between saving and investment.

(i) *Relations valid both for Prospective and Retrospective Values*

Since all relations valid in each single case must also apply to the sums and averages relating to a group of economic subjects, we can first restate all the equations given in section 2, but now with capital letters indicating that the concepts relate to such a group, defined in some way or other. In defining the concepts at the earlier stage we have indeed had this later summation (or averaging) in view, and therefore carefully paid attention to the claim that the definitions should be fit to use in a macro-economic analysis also. We thus assume all these equations as given for the group that is to be the subject of our study (though we do not rewrite them here).

In this connection we need only add some remarks concerning the question of what the position of the group considered in relation with other groups implies with regard to the interpretation of the equations. For, in order that our reasoning should be applicable to real conditions, we have neither made use of the simplifying assumption of a closed community, nor restricted the compass of the term "group" in other respects.* As a matter of fact, our reasoning will be formally valid for any group of economic subjects, however defined. It is thus not necessary for the group to be a country or a part of a country, it may also be, for example, all firms and individuals belonging to a certain line of production, or some other similar category. But as we shall see later, the

* As we have said elsewhere, the transition from the general case to the simplified one is very easy, but not so the transition in the other direction.

practical importance of our reasoning will be greater, if we think of the group as being a country.

To start with, we may dissolve the receipts-expenditure equation into two, one equation relating to transactions within the group (including terms with the index $^\circ$), and the other to transactions between this group and other groups (these terms have the index *) :*

$$A^\circ + R^\circ = B^\circ + C^\circ + T^\circ + F^\circ + \dot{M}^\circ$$
$$A^* + R^* = B^* + C^* + T^* + F^* + \dot{M}^*$$
$$\overline{A + R = B + C + T + F + \dot{M}}$$

The calculation of these magnitudes implies that, for each member of the group under review, all economic transactions undertaken are divided into two categories: those referring to members of the same group, and those referring to members of other groups. The equality between monetary receipts on the one hand and monetary expenditure and the increase in cash† on the other, must of course also be valid for each of

* In a more thorough-going analysis of the problem of groups it might be necessary, as is shown below in section (iv), to carry the specification of the terms further and also to introduce subcategories.

† It should be observed that $\dot{M}^\circ$ indicates the increase in the cash-holdings of the group members resulting from transactions within the group during the period considered and M^* such an increase resulting from transactions with other groups. Hence M° denotes the amount of cash held by the group members at a certain point of time originating in internal transactions and M^* the amount of cash-holdings originating in transactions with other groups. If a Central Bank or other money-issuing authority belongs to the group, the money issued by the bank should, as previously stated, be regarded as a negative item in the calculation of the cash-holdings of the bank. This negative item, $M-$, can be divided in two parts: $M^\circ-$, representing the debt of the bank to the cash-holding group members, and M^*-, representing the debt of the bank to members of other groups possessing money issued by the bank. From a retrospective point of view, $M^\circ(= M^{\circ+} - M^\circ-)$ must therefore be zero, and $M^*(= M^{*+} - M^*-)$ must correspond to the amount of foreign money held by the group members with deduction of the money issued by the group but held by members of other groups. If there is no money-issuing authority in the group considered, all cash-holdings of the group members must ultimately have their origin in transactions with other groups.

these two categories. If we rewrite the second equation in the following form, the reader will recognize the traditional equation of international payments:

$$A^* - (B^* + C^*) + R^* + (-T^*) = F^* + \dot{M}^*$$

Exports Imports	Income from capital abroad	Gifts, etc., from abroad*	Net lending to abroad and net import of securities	Net import of gold and cash
⎣_____ Export surplus _____⎦				

The distinction between internal and external magnitudes can be carried through similarly with regard to income and financial investment: E° thus indicates the net income from resources within the group and E^* the net income from resources abroad, J° financial investments within the group and J^* those being made abroad; analogously H° is concerned with the financial relations between the group members at a certain point of time, and H^* with financial relations with members of other groups. The term real investment (I) and the term real capital (the value of which is indicated by K), on the other hand, are here applied only to internal magnitudes, since all investments and assets abroad can be assumed to be of the financial type. Similarly there is no reason to apply the distinction with regard to saving (S).

The earning of income equation previously given may therefore be restated in the following way:

$$E^\circ = A - B^{l+k} + I + R^\circ + J^\circ - F^\circ - B^{h\circ} \quad \text{(Home-produced income)}$$
$$E^* = \qquad\qquad\qquad\quad R^* + J^* - F^* - B^{h*} \quad \text{(Income from abroad)}$$

$$E = A - B + I + R + J - F$$

$$\underbrace{\qquad\qquad}_{E^{l+k} - B^h} \quad \underbrace{\qquad\qquad}_{E^h + B^h}$$

Income from factors (with deduction for expenses for financial transactions)	Income from financial capital (expenses not being deducted)

It should be observed that the equation for the home-produced

Continuation of footnote from p. 113]
In this case also M° must therefore be zero. Since the total amount of cash held by the group members cannot be changed through transactions within the group, it follows that, retrospectively, $\dot{M}^\circ$ is also zero.

    * The term T represents the payment of taxes, subventions, gifts, etc.; $(-T)$ will thus mean the receipt of such payments, with regard to international relations in the first place gifts received from abroad.

income which comprises all income emanating from internal resources (labour and real capital, and financial capital implying claims and debts within the group), also includes terms that refer partly to transactions with other groups (A and B^{l+k}). Only dividends and interest received from financial capital invested outside the group (R^*) are here counted as income from abroad, possibly with addition of accrued but not yet realized interest on such investments ($J^* - F^*$) and with deduction for expenses incurred abroad in connection with the financial transactions (B^{h*}).

Further we may restate the use of income equation

$$E = C + T + S$$

and the saving-investment equation

$$S = I + J + M$$

which are the same as before, though it should be noted that the terms C, T, J and M now contain both internal ($^\circ$) and external (*) items.

In order to simplify the exposition we shall now, as we did in the case of the micro-economic relations,* introduce special signs for the excess of sales over purchases (Δ)† and for the excess of income from financial capital over taxes and similar payments (Γ). Thus we define

$$
\begin{aligned}
\Delta^\circ &= A^\circ - B^\circ - C^\circ & & & \Gamma^\circ &= R^\circ + J^\circ - F^\circ - T^\circ \\
\Delta^* &= A^* - B^* - C^* & \text{and} & & \Gamma^* &= R^* + J^* - F^* - T^* \\
\hline
\Delta &= A - B - C & & & \Gamma &= R + J - F - T
\end{aligned}
$$

If we rearrange the receipts-expenditure equations in the same manner as the equation for international payments given above, and then to both members add the unrealized income from financial capital ($J - F$), we get equations that, with use of the new signs, can be written:‡

$$
\begin{aligned}
\Delta^\circ + \Gamma^\circ &= J^\circ + \dot{M}^\circ \\
\Delta^* + \Gamma^* &= J^* + \dot{M}^* \\
\hline
\Delta + \Gamma &= J + \dot{M} = S - I
\end{aligned}
$$

* See above, p. 88.

† The same sign has been used by Professor Frisch in the stencilled lectures previously cited. ‡ Cf. above, p. 89.

These equations make clear how a difference between saving and real investment arises and what it signifies. They are applicable both to prospective and retrospective magnitudes, though, as we shall see in the next section, a certain simplification is possible in the case of retrospective values. The discussion of these equations is postponed to section (iv) where we shall be concerned with the relations between prospective and retrospective values.

Finally we can combine the use of income equation with the saving-investment equation in the following way:

$$E = C + T + S \quad = C + I + \mathcal{J} + \dot{M} + T = C + I + \Delta + \Gamma + T$$
$$\underbrace{I + \mathcal{J} + \dot{M}}_{\Delta + \Gamma} \qquad\qquad\qquad \underbrace{R + \mathcal{J} - F}$$

The total income of the group members appears here as the sum of their consumption and real investment, plus some other terms which may be stated *either* as the net amount of financial investment and the increase in cash plus taxes and similar payments, *or* as the excess of sales over purchases plus the net income from financial capital. As shown in section (iii), one of the methods of calculating the national income is based on these equations.

All the equations set up in this section are valid both for prospective and retrospective estimates. When applied only to the latter estimates, some of the internal terms will be zero and the equations accordingly simplified, as will be shown in the next section.

(ii) *Relations valid only for Retrospective Values*

From a retrospective point of view, the sum of total sales within the group during a given period (A°) must be equal to the sum of total purchases similarly defined ($B^\circ + C^\circ$); thus $A^\circ - B^\circ - C^\circ = \Delta^\circ = 0$. We can further conclude that the positive and negative items must cancel out in respect of payments within the group of interest and dividends (R°); of taxes, gifts, etc. (T°); and with regard to all financial transactions occurring within the group (F°). Finally, since all money issued within the group is regarded as a negative item for the money-issuing authority, the positive and negative changes in cash-holdings, connected with transactions between the group members, must neutralize one another (thus $\dot{M}^0 = 0$).

So far the effects of a change of the point of estimate to the end of the period considered are quite clear. It is more difficult to make an accurate statement of the effects on the estimates, made respectively by the creditors and the debtors, of the accrued but not yet realized interest on financial capital. Expectations relating to the relations between the group members, may show certain deviations from one another, with the result that the sum of all positive and negative items $(\mathcal{J}^0 - F^0)$ may be a positive or negative magnitude. Similarly the corresponding estimates made at the end of the period, which are of course influenced by the transactions and other events that may have occurred during the period need not coincide. On the whole, however, it can perhaps be assumed that the deviations between the retrospective estimates of the creditors and debtors are smaller than those between the prospective estimates and that therefore the net sum $(\mathcal{J}^0 - F^0)$ is smaller *ex post* than *ex ante*.

The question now raised is not without importance for the fundamental construction of the theoretical system. As the system has been outlined here, the financial capital on which the interest should be calculated is not restricted to ordinary loans, contracted on fixed terms. It includes also all the ownership of firms which in their turn are assumed to possess the whole of real capital. As previously explained, the owners of the firms are thus regarded as creditors and the firms themselves as debtors. The estimates made by the former of what the firms will probably earn or of what they have earned during the period in question should consequently be included as positive items in the term $(\mathcal{J}^0 - F^0)$, and the corresponding estimates made by the responsible managers of the firms should be included as negative items. Only if there is a close relationship between the owners and the managers of the firms, can it be assumed that these positive and negative items will cancel out. Otherwise they will not: $(\mathcal{J}^0 - F^0)$ will be positive if the owners are more optimistic than the managers, and it will be negative in the opposite case. As we have just suggested, the retrospective value of the term will, however, probably be smaller than the prospective value.

This difficulty is only connected with the application of the

117

concept of income as including not only monetary payments but also unrealized interest. A method of evading it is therefore to use a more practical interpretation of the term, implying that these unrealized items relating to the financial capital are left out of account. As previously stated,* the income from financial capital would then be restricted to R, and financial investment $(\mathcal{J})$ would coincide with financial transactions (F). We must be aware, however, that this method also leads to certain difficulties, when applied to relatively short periods, for example days. A shareholder who receives the annual dividends of a corporation on a certain day but who spreads out the consumption of this sum over the whole year is, according to this method, performing saving on the day when the dividends are paid and dissaving on all other days. The corporation, on the other hand, is saving during the whole year with the exception of the day on which the dividends are paid. It is true that these peculiarities disappear when we sum up the income, including savings, of the shareholders and the corporation. The total income of these economic subjects, whether reckoned day by day or not, will correspond to what the manager calculates to be the profit of the firm. (On the day when the dividends, R, are distributed, R is included as a positive item in the income of the shareholders and as a negative item in the income of the firm and will thus disappear when these incomes are summed.) And the total saving will be equal to the excess of this total income over the total consumption (of the shareholders, if the corporation has no consumption of its own) and the taxes paid out of the income. This method of calculation is therefore certainly applicable to macro-economic analysis. But since the expectations of the shareholders with regard to the earning capacity of the firm and with regard to the dividends to be received from it in the future are wholly left out of account, the method is insufficient if it is desired to study to what extent changes in these expectations will lead to changes in total consumption.

In the following analyses we have kept to the more general income formula in which unrealized interest $(\mathcal{J} - F)$ is included. On the other hand, we have made the assumption that this item in so far as it refers to transactions within the group is zero from a retrospective point of view. In this

* See above, p. 85.

118

way our exposition will not be much more complicated than if it were based on the practical concept of income. And the transition to this latter method is very easily performed: we have only to omit the term $(\mathcal{J} - F)$ or let its value be zero, and the equations can then be interpreted according to that method. If again we wish to apply the theoretical concept of income, our exposition will be a good starting point for the analysis. Some slight modification of the results only will be required in cases where the retrospective value of $(\mathcal{J}^o - F^o)$ cannot be assumed to be zero.

The above statements can be expressed by the following equations which are thus valid only *ex post*:

$$
\begin{aligned}
A^o &= B^o + C^o & \therefore \qquad & \Delta^o = 0 \\
R^{o+} &= R^{o-} & \therefore \qquad & R^o = 0 \\
T^{o+} &= T^{o-} & \therefore \qquad & T^o = 0 \\
F^{o+} &= F^{o-} & \therefore \qquad & F^o = 0 \\
\dot{M}^{o+} &= \dot{M}^{o-} & \therefore \qquad & \dot{M}^o = 0 \\
\mathcal{J}^{o+} - F^{o+} &= \mathcal{J}^{o-} - F^{o-} & \therefore \qquad & \mathcal{J}^o = 0 \\
& & \text{and thus} \quad & \Gamma^o = 0
\end{aligned}
$$

If we now introduce these values into the equations given in the previous section, the result, valid only for retrospective values, will be as follows:

The earnings equation:

$$E = A - B + I + R^* + \mathcal{J}^* - F^*$$

The use of income equation:

$$E = C + T^* + S$$

The saving-investment equation:

$$S = I + \mathcal{J}^* + \dot{M}^*$$

These two last equations combined:

$$E = C + I + \mathcal{J}^* + \dot{M}^* + T^* = C + I + \Delta^* + \underbrace{\Gamma^* + T^*}_{R^* + \mathcal{J}^* - F^*}$$

The equation explaining the difference between saving and investment:

$$\Delta^* + \Gamma^* = \mathcal{J}^* + \dot{M}^* = S - I$$

If we apply this last equation to a country, we can conclude that the sum of the export surplus and the net income from capital abroad (minus gifts and similar payments to other countries) is equal to the net amount of financial investment made abroad (plus the import of cash), and that this amount represents the excess of total saving over total real investment.

With regard to capital values, it can be assumed, for reasons analogous to those stated above, that all claims and debts within the group cancel out and that the financial capital invested in internal securities is neutralized by a corresponding negative item representing the debt of firms to their owners. And as already explained, the total holdings of internal money by the members of the group will also be cancelled out by a corresponding debt of the money-issuing authority. Our assumptions are thus:

$$H^{o+} = H^{o-} \qquad\qquad H^o = o$$
$$M^{o+} = M^{o-} \qquad\qquad M^o = o$$

The equation of wealth is accordingly written

$$W = K + H^* + M^*$$

implying that the total wealth belonging to the group considered is equal to the value of the real capital and the net value of the capital invested abroad, plus the holdings of foreign money minus the holdings abroad of money issued in the group.

Finally, we need only add the remark that if, in the equations just given, all terms with the index * become zero, the simpler equations then obtained are *valid for a closed community ex post*:

$$E = A - B + I \quad \text{(The earnings equation)}$$
$$E = C + S \quad \text{(The use of income equation)}$$
$$S = I \quad \text{(The saving-investment equation)}$$
$$W = K \quad \text{(The wealth equation)}$$

(iii) *Consequences relating to the Calculation of the National Income.**

We may now proceed to indicate the consequences of our equations in estimating the national income of a country.

* The reading of this section is not necessary for the understanding of the following section.

Starting from the earnings equation given above, but omitting unrealized interest on capital invested abroad ($\mathcal{J}^* - F^*$) which is usually disregarded in such a calculation, we can define the national income in the following way:

$$E = A - B + I + R^*$$

In practice, various methods can be used for the calculation of this aggregate income. In the following equations which can all be reduced to the general equation just stated we shall describe the four most important of these methods.* The choice between them will in general depend on the character of the statistical material that is available for the calculation.

(1) Method based on taxation statistics:

$$E = \underset{\substack{\text{Asserted taxable income} \\ \text{(double counting eliminated)}}}{\Sigma(a - b + i + r - \epsilon)} + \underset{\substack{\text{Difference between} \\ \text{total and} \\ \text{taxable inco}^{--}}}{\Sigma\epsilon}$$

Starting from incomes as assessed for taxation purposes, we have first to make certain corrections for the double counting implied (if for example both the company and the shareholders are assessed for the same income). Then certain additions should be made for income items (ϵ) not included in the taxation statistics. In some cases other modifications may also be necessary, in order to bring the assessed income into conformity with the definition of the national income, on which the calculation is based. (Modifications are here assumed to be included in ϵ.)

(2) Method based on earning statistics:

$$E = \underbrace{A^k - B^k + I + R^* - B^h}_{\substack{\text{Profits and interest} \\ \text{(net)}}} + \underbrace{A^l - B^l}_{\substack{\text{Wages and salaries} \\ \text{(net)}}}$$

When applying this method, we can first estimate the total income of all firms (taken in the wide sense) from real capital; if we then add the net amount of interest from abroad (R^*) with deduction for *all* expenses (B^h) connected with financial

* Cf. Lindahl, Dahlgren and Kock, *National Income of Sweden*, 1861–1930, Part One (Stockholm Economic Studies, No. 5A), London, 1937 (P. S. King & Son), pp. 5 ff., where a more extended account is given of the methods outlined here.

transactions, we get the total amount of interest and profits. (Alternatively we can sum up the net amounts of profits and interest received by the various firms and individuals and then make corrections to eliminate the possible double accounting which arises when the dividends of the firms reappear as income of the shareholders.) We have further to calculate the total amount of wages and salaries earned by the inhabitants of the country from which a deduction then should be made for all expenses incurred in connection with their work. The sum of the two amounts now defined is the national income.

(3) Method based on production statistics:

$$E = \underbrace{A^k + I''' + I^{\text{iv}}}_{\substack{\text{Value of output}}} - \underbrace{(B' - I')}_{\substack{\text{Depreciation} \\ \text{of fixed} \\ \text{real assets}}} - \underbrace{(B'' - I'')}_{\substack{\text{Value of} \\ \text{raw materials} \\ \text{used up}}} - \underbrace{(B''' - A^l)}_{\substack{\text{Value of services} \\ \text{received from} \\ \text{other firms}}} + \underbrace{R^\bullet}_{\substack{\text{Income} \\ \text{from} \\ \text{capital} \\ \text{abroad} \\ \text{(net)}}}$$

In this equation the I-term has (in the same manner as on p. 83) been divided into four components, referring respectively to fixed real assets (I'), raw materials (I''), goods in process (I''') and finished products (I^{iv}), and the B-term (including B^k, B^l and B^h) into three components: purchases of fixed real assets (B'), of raw materials, etc. (B'') and of services rendered by labour or by other firms (B'''). The sum of what has been sold by a firm, and of what it has invested in goods in process and in finished products corresponds to the value of the output of the firm. The amount of fixed real assets purchased (including costs of maintenance and repairs) that does not represent net investment corresponds to the depreciation of these assets. In the same manner the difference between the amount of raw materials purchased (including costs of storage, etc.) and the net investment in raw materials corresponds to what has been used up in the productive process. And if we deduct the labour services from all services purchased we get the services received from other firms. The difference between these positive and negative items relating to a given firm represents the contribution to the national income made by the factors (real capital and labour) employed by that firm.* The sum of these net amounts is equal to

* It should be observed that the negative items (the B-terms) refer not only to the firm itself but also the persons employed by the firm (expenses of the labourers for their work, etc.).

the home-produced part of the national income. It is in general convenient to make statistical estimates of the positive and negative items for different branches of production and thus to calculate the contributions made by them to the national income.* To the home-produced income then the net amount of interest and dividends received from abroad should be added, if we wish to get the total income received by the inhabitants of the country.

(4) Method based on consumption and investment statistics:

$$E = C + I + F^* + M^* + T^*$$
$$ = C + I + \Delta^* + R^*$$

| Consumption of inhabitants | Net real investment in the country | Export surplus (in a wide sense) | Income from capital abroad |

These equations are somewhat simpler than those set up in the previous section, since the unrealized interests on financial capital are disregarded here and F therefore can be substituted for J. In the last equation, the home-produced income appears as the sum of the total consumption of the inhabitants and the net real investment within the country with the addition of the export surplus. This equation can also be deduced directly from the earnings equation as follows:

$$E^\circ = I + A^* - B^* + A^\circ - B^\circ$$
$$0 = C - C^* - C^\circ$$

$$\overline{}$$

$$E^\circ = C + I + \Delta^*$$

It should be observed that C here denotes the total consumption of the inhabitants, including what they consume abroad (C^{*J}) but excluding the consumption of foreigners visiting the country (^JC). But the second of these items is included in A^* and the former in C^*; the latter thus enters as a positive and the former as a negative item in Δ^*. We can

* This method has been applied in the calculation of the national income of Sweden, in the work referred to above. The most difficult part of the estimate relates to the calculation of the negative items for which in general no statistics are available. In the Swedish estimate, this calculation was based on a detailed classification of all goods and services available in the country (production + imports − exports), according as they are destined for different productive purposes or for consumption.

therefore transform the consumption of the inhabitants into the inland consumption, if we merely adjust the calculation of the export surplus correspondingly:

$$E^o = \underbrace{C + {}^fC - C^{*f}}_{\substack{\text{Inland} \\ \text{consumption}}} + \underbrace{I}_{\text{Investment}} + \underbrace{\Delta^* - ({}^fC - C^{*f})}_{\substack{\text{Export surplus excluding} \\ \text{inland consumption of} \\ \text{foreigners and consumption} \\ \text{abroad of nationals}}}$$

This formula is in general easiest to apply, since the distinction between nationals and foreigners is not usually made in the statistics of consumption.

With regard to investment, two calculations should be made: first an estimate of all new producers' goods available in the country during the given year (production — export + import), secondly an estimate of what has been used up of these goods during the year, that is, the depreciation of the durable goods, the amount of raw materials used up, etc. These estimates can be based on the same statistical material as the calculation of the national income in accordance with the third method. The difference between the two methods lies in the fact that in the third method the national income is regarded as "the aggregate of the contributions of the different production processes, each calculated as the difference between some credit items (the value of commodities and services produced) and some debit items (the value of services received from other production processes and the consumption and depreciation of capital goods)," whereas on the fourth method these positive and negative items are "split up and combined in such a way that the national income appears as an aggregate of values which, for each category of goods and services, indicate the excess of production over and above what is used up for productive processes."*

Our characterization of the four methods of estimating the national income has been based on variants of the same income equation. From this it follows that in a given case they should all lead to the same result, as long as the terms entering into them are calculated according to the same principles, and if all errors in the interpretation of the statistical material can be eliminated. In practice it is of course impossible to avoid errors, and, therefore, the results obtained will deviate to a

* *National Income of Sweden*, 1861–1930, Part One, pp. 15–16.

greater or less degree. In the comparisons of the national income of different countries, it is, however, still more difficult to eliminate differences arising from the fact that the basic income idea is interpreted in different ways. As a matter of fact, the equations here given can be interpreted in accordance with all possible income definitions. Especially in the cases of the interpretation of the I-term and of the distinction between the B- and C-terms, one has to choose between various alternatives concerning which no agreement has been reached. These questions have not been treated here. Our intention has not been to make a contribution to the income discussion, but only to show the connections between the various methods of estimating the national income, when it has been defined in a particular manner.

(iv) *Relations between Prospective and Retrospective Values*

(1) *The Assumptions and their Consequences.*—We have above in section 2 (ii) discussed the micro-economic relations between the prospective and retrospective values relating to such a short period that equality between them can be assumed as far as concerns selling prices and all purchases both for productive and for consumption purposes. Proceeding to macro-economic relations, we shall maintain these basic assumptions.

In the macro-economic case, however, they should be interpreted in a somewhat modified sense. Since the members of a group do not change their plans simultaneously, the time interval during which the plans of all members are unchanged must of course be much shorter than the time interval during which the plans of a single planner are kept unaltered. Now our reasoning will certainly not lose its importance, even if the period taken into consideration is *very* short. But in order that the length of the period may not become too short to be plausible, we shall assume, not that all individual plans are kept entirely unchanged, but that the resulting sums (or averages) of the individual values only show negligible change during the period considered. In this way our reasoning may in general be applied to such relatively short periods as days.

The assumptions underlying the following investigation are thus that average selling prices are kept unaltered during the period considered, and further that there is equality between the total amounts planned and realized with regard to all

125

purchases undertaken by the group-members, that is, if we now introduce the subscript $_0$ for the prospective and the subscript $_1$ for the retrospective values,

$$B_0^o = B_1^o \quad \text{and} \quad C_0^o = C_1^o \quad \text{(Purchases from members of the group)}$$
$$B_0^* = B_1^* \qquad\qquad C_0^* = C_1^* \quad \text{(Purchases from other groups)}$$

$$B_0 = B_1 \qquad\qquad C_0 = C_1$$

With regard to the retrospective values it can further be stated (as indicated in section ii) that

$$A_1^o = B_1^o + C_1^o \quad \text{or (since } \Delta = A - B - C \text{) that } \Delta_1^o = 0$$

From this it follows that

$$A_0^o - \Delta_0^o = B_0^o + C_0^o = B_1^o + C_1^o = A_1^o \qquad \therefore \qquad -\Delta_0^o = A_1^o - A_0^o$$
$$A_0^* - \Delta_0^* = B_0^* + C_0^* = B_1^* + C_1^* = A_1^* - \Delta_1^* \quad \therefore \quad \Delta_1^* - \Delta_0^* = A_1^* - A_0^*$$

$$A_0 - \Delta_0 = B_0 + C_0 = B_1 + C_1 = A_1 - \Delta_1^* \quad \therefore \quad \Delta_1^* - \Delta_0 = A_1 - A_0$$

In these equations we have a starting point for analysing the causes and effects of a deviation of actual sales from what has been expected by the sellers at the beginning of the period. We have only to combine them with the equations set up previously for the difference between saving and real investment ($\Gamma = R + J - F - T$, i.e. income from financial capital less taxes, etc., as before):

$$\Delta_0 + \Gamma_0 = S_0 - I_0$$
$$\Delta_1^* + \Gamma_1^* = S_1 - I_1$$

(2) *The Causes of Unexpected Changes in Sales.*—In the first place we must make clear what are the consequences of a difference *ex ante* between saving and real investment. The answer to this question is given, if we rewrite the first of the above equations as follows:

$$I_0 - S_J + \Gamma_0 + \Delta_0 = 0$$

and then add
$$- \Delta_0^o = A_1^o - A_0^o$$
and
$$\Delta_1^* - \Delta_0 = A_1 - A_0 \qquad\qquad \text{respectively.}$$

We then obtain the following two equations:

$$I_0 - (S_0 - \Gamma_0 - \Delta_0^*) = A_1^o - A_0^o$$
$$I_0 - (S_0 - \Gamma_0 - \Delta_1^*) = A_1 - A_0$$

126

From these we can conclude that a certain disproportion between the net amount of real investment planned for a short period forward and the net amount of saving planned for the same period can be regarded as a *cause* of the deviation of the actual sales within the group from what has been expected by the sellers for the same period. An increase in the planned investment must, *ceteris paribus* (that is, if the terms S_o, Γ_o and Δ_o^* or Δ_1^* are not altered), lead to the consequence that realized sales will be larger than expected sales. On the other hand, an increase in the planned saving without a corresponding increase in the planned investment (or of the terms Γ_o and Δ_o^* or Δ_1^*) must bring it about that the actual sales will not fulfil the expectations of the sellers.

The conclusions now drawn are of course dependent both on our definitions of the terms and on the assumptions made in this section, implying that a relatively short period is taken into consideration. If for the moment we confine ourselves to a *closed community*, in order to simplify that part of our reasoning a little, we have

$$\text{by definition*} \qquad I_o = \quad E_o + B_o - A_o - (R_o + J_o - F_o)$$

$$\text{by definition} \quad - S_o = - E_o + C_o + T_o$$
$$\text{by assumption} \quad o = \quad A_1 - B_o - C_o$$

$$\overline{I_o - S_o = \quad A_1 - A_o - \Gamma_o}$$

As can be seen already from the equations given previously, an excess of planned real investment over planned saving (with deduction for the term Γ_o) only signifies that prospective purchases exceed the expectations of the sellers (and that thus Δ_o is a negative magnitude). Only under the assumption that purchasing plans are realized, will the excess of realized over expected sales appear as a logical necessity. Since this

* These definitions are in accordance with those given in the list of terms at the beginning of this paper. Thus the definition of investment is obtained in the following way:

$$I = E^k + B^k - A^k$$
$$o = E^l + B^l - A^l$$
$$o = E^k + B^k - (R + J - F)$$

$$\overline{I = E \ + B \ - A - (R + J - F)}$$

assumption, however, merely signifies that the period considered must be taken sufficiently short, it does not remove us from reality. Our reasoning can therefore be applied to real cases also as long as the terms are interpreted in the manner indicated.

Therefore we can also conclude that if in a given case the total sales in a country have exceeded the expectations of sellers (and if this is not caused by an unexpected increase in foreign demand), then the total planned investment must have been greater than the total planned saving (possibly modified in respect of the Γ_o term) during a certain short period, and that, on the other hand, an excess of saving must have existed in the contrary case when actual sales within the country fall short of expectations.

After this digression we shall return to a study of the equations in the general form given above. It can be gathered from them that, in a comparison between real investment and saving *ex ante*, certain deductions should be made from the saving, if the definition given here is used. If we substitute $(\Gamma_o^{\circ} + \Gamma_o^{*})$ for Γ_o, we can distinguish between three such items:

(1) Γ_o°.—If the prospective calculations of the positive and negative items included in the internal income from financial capital less taxes, etc., are biased in a positive or negative direction so that Γ_o° is not zero, these errors may be compensated by a change in the planned saving in the same direction. For example, if an individual mistakenly thinks that he will get a big income from financial capital but at the same time decides to save this extra income, his consumption will be the same as before, the effects of his wrong estimate being neutralized by the corresponding increase in planned saving; from a retrospective point of view, both the extra income and the extra saving will have disappeared.* Errors of this kind, however, will probably be most frequent in estimates of accrued but unrealized interest. If such interest is left out of account, in accordance with the practical concept of income, the value of Γ_o° will approximate to zero.

(2) Γ_o^{*}.—This term represents mainly the prospective income from capital abroad. If such income is saved and at the same time invested outside the group or taken home in the form of cash, it is of no relevance for the real investment

* Cf. E. Lundberg, op. cit., p. 146.

planned within the group. In this case it should therefore be deducted from the total saving of the group members. Similarly if the income in question is brought home to the group by means of an import of goods or services, it should be omitted in this connection since it will then be included (as a negative item) in the export surplus (Δ^*) appearing in the equation as a separate term.

(3) Δ_o^* or Δ_r^*.—The first terms indicates the "prospective export surplus," that is, the difference between the sum of what the members of the group hope to sell to other groups during a certain period, and the total amount of purchases that they intend to make from these other groups during the same period. The latter term represents the "retrospective export surplus," that is, the actual excess of exports over imports. If an expected export surplus (implying that $A_o^* > B_o^* + C_o^*$) is neutralized by a corresponding excess of planned saving over planned real investment (implying that $A_o > B_o + C_o$), then it will obviously not disturb the equilibrium of *internal* transactions (implying that $A_o^o = B_o^o + C_o^o = A_r^o$). But in that case it will in general not be possible to realize at the same time equality between *total* sales *ex ante* and *ex post*, since unexpected changes in the foreign demand may occur (implying that $A_r^* \gtrless A_o^*$). A saving-investment relation that affords equality between total categories in such a case, must entail inequality between the internal categories (implying $A_o^o \lessgtr B_o^o + C_o^o = A_r^o$).

Thus we find that the equilibrium conditions, affording equality between the prospective and the retrospective estimates of the sales during a given period, can only be stated as alternatives as follows:

(a) For *internal* sales: $S_o - \Gamma_o = I_o + \Delta_o^*$
(b) For *total* sales: $S_o - \Gamma_o = I_o + \Delta_r^*$

In a closed economy this difficulty will of course disappear; both equations will then be reduced to: $S_o - \Gamma_o = I_o$.

(3) *The Effects of Unexpected Changes in Sales.*—So far we have only dealt with the causes of a deviation between the estimates of the sales proceeds, made *ex ante* and *ex post*. When now proceeding to a study of the *effects* of such a deviation, we may, to start with, combine the equation for the saving-

investment relation *ex post** with our equation for total sales *ex ante* and *ex post* in the following manner:

$$0 = \quad S_1 - I_1 - \Gamma_1^* - \Delta_1^*$$
$$A_1 - A_0 = -S_0 + I_0 + \Gamma_0^* + \Delta_1^*$$

$$\overline{A_1 - A_0 = \quad S_1 - S_0 - (I_1 - I_0) - (\Gamma_1^* - \Gamma_0)}$$

If $(E_1 - E_0 - T_1 + T_0)$ is substituted for $(S_1 - S_0)$ and the term Γ is dissolved into its components $(R + J - F - T)$, the last equation will be transformed into:

$$A_1 - A_0 = E_1 - E_0 + I_0 - I_1 - (R_1^* + J_1^* - F_1^*) + (R_0 + J_0 - F_0)$$

Substituting instead $(J + \dot{M})$ for $(S - I)$ we may also write:

$$A_1 - A_0 = J_1^* + \dot{M}_1^* - (J_0 + \dot{M}_0) - (\Gamma_1^* - \Gamma_0)$$

The significance of the last bracket of the first and third of these equations, and of the last two brackets of the second equation is merely that total saving, total income and total investment may be influenced by unexpected changes in the income from financial capital less taxes. It is admissible however, to disregard changes of that kind here, since, under our assumptions,† they are not directly caused by the increase in sales. Nothing of importance will therefore be neglected, if we base the following exposition on the simpler equations which relate to a *closed community* and to an application of the *practical concept of income* (which, as mentioned above, enables us to make the assumption that $\Gamma_0^0 = 0$):

$$- \Delta_0 = I_0 - S_0 = A_1 - A_0 = S_1 - S_0 + I_0 - I_1$$
$$= E_1 - E_0 + I_0 - I_1$$
$$= \underbrace{J_1 + \dot{M}_1 - (J_0 + \dot{M}_0)}_{0}$$

* See above, p. 126.

† Among these assumptions the one implying that $\Gamma_1^0 = 0$ is, as mentioned above, not always quite realistic, since deviations may occur between the retrospective estimates of the income of a firm, made by the managers and the owners respectively, with the result that the term $(J_1 - F_1)$, included in Γ_1, may have a positive or negative value. In such a case, causal connections may of course exist between the transactions that have taken place during the period and the value of Γ_1^0.

In the first line the manner is shown in which a certain excess of real investment over saving *ex ante* that can be regarded as the cause of the unexpected increase in sales, disappears in the retrospective values. As a consequence of the increase in sales, either an increase in savings or a decrease in real investment must occur, so that equality *ex post* between the two terms is realized. We have previously used the term "unintentional" for such changes in retrospective values. The unintentional savings are made possible by an unexpected increase in income which is thus equal to the difference between the unexpected increase in sales and the unexpected decrease in real investment. We can further conclude that these changes will be connected with an increase in the sum of financial investment and of cash-holdings, in relation to the amounts planned at the beginning of the period. If the value of $(I_0 - S_0)$ is positive, then $(J_0 + \dot{M}_0)$ must have the corresponding negative value. *Ex post* both J_1 and $\dot{M}_1$ are zero in a closed community, and they must therefore, taken together, have increased in relation to the prospective values by an amount equal to the excess of real investment over saving *ex ante* or to the unexpected increase in sales.

In this connection two questions present themselves: (1) If the net amount of planned real investment is greater or smaller than the net amount of the savings planned for the same period, but the retrospective values of the terms are equal, should we say broadly that investment has adapted itself to the saving, or that saving has adapted itself to investment? (2) How is the amount of money held outside the banks influenced by a disparity between the real investment and the saving planned for a certain period forward? If we split up the term $\dot{M}$ into $\dot{M}^p$, the change in the cash-holdings of the public and firms other than banks, and $\dot{M}^b$, the change in the cash-holdings of the banks, can we say anything about the retrospective value of the term $\dot{M}^p$?

The above equations do not give the answer to these questions. As a matter of fact, they can be answered only on the basis of further assumptions. Here we can only indicate the general lines of the solutions.

(4) *Is Saving or Investment the Primary Phenomenon?*—With regard to the first question, we may, to start with, draw some

conclusions from our reasoning above in section 2 (ii) concerning micro-economic values. We there dealt with the effects of an unexpected increase in sales, and this exposition can therefore be applied to the case where the planned real investment, for the community as a whole, has been greater than the planned saving. In this case, an unexpected increase in income and saving will occur, firstly, if the productive factors have been better utilized as a consequence of the increased demand, and, secondly, if this has given rise to a more optimistic idea of the earning capacity of the firm.* This applies, for example, to a firm which has fulfilled some new orders by diminishing its stock but, at the same time, is planning an increase in production or in selling prices. Therefore, an unintentional increase in income and savings may also occur in cases in which the unexpected increase in sales has resulted in a corresponding decrease in stocks. To the same extent as retrospective income calculations for the period considered are thus affected, total retrospective saving (representing the sum of intentional and unintentional savings) will tend to adapt itself to total planned investment.

On the other hand, if the increase in sales caused by an excess of total planned investment over total planned saving, has been attended by a contraction in stocks not leading to any noteworthy increase in income, the result will, for the period taken into consideration, be an unintentional disinvestment instead of an unintentional saving. To the same extent, total investment *ex post* (including this unintentional disinvestment) will show a tendency to adapt itself to total planned saving.

In a concrete case, both these tendencies may be in operation, so that an initial difference between investment and saving *ex ante* for a short period forward is bridged over by a mutual adaptation of both terms as calculated *ex post*. It thus depends on the relative strength of the tendencies, which factor is most affected. It may even occur that one of the tendencies predominates to such a high degree that the unintentional changes in investment and saving work in the

* As we have shown in another section (2 (iii)), based on the theoretical concept of income, a certain part of the total gain that is the result of the revaluation of the assets of the firm, can in such a case be attributed to the income earned during the latest short period which here is taken into consideration.

same direction, although one of them is the greater. If, for example, investment plans in operation during a certain period amount to a greater sum than saving plans, the resulting increase in sales may lead to such a high retrospective calculation of the actual investment carried out in the period that it exceeds the prospective investment. (This seems to be a very plausible result if the retrospective calculation has been based on a more optimistic view of the future.) In this case the unintentional increase in savings must of course include not only the difference between prospective investment and saving but also the difference between retrospective and prospective investment, for the equality *ex post* between the two factors to be realized.

So much can be said with regard to the development during a given short period of time.

To this a more general remark may be added. If we consider the development over a sequence of several short periods during which there is a recurrent excess of planned investment over planned saving, a recurrent adaption of total real investment to total saving will only be possible up to the point where stocks are exhausted. If a longer period is taken into consideration savings must therefore adapt themselves to the amount of investment. From this point of view the amount of investment is thus the primary phenomenon.

In this connection it should be noted that if a longer period is taken into consideration, the adaption of saving to investment is not brought about only in the way just described, through *unintentional* changes in savings. It will also, and probably to a much greater extent, be due to *intentional* changes, in the sphere of planned "voluntary" saving, and related to the *redistribution of income* which will occur when a more permanent deviation between the planned amounts of saving and investment gives rise to a shift in the general price level. This is a somewhat important point for the analysis of cumulative processes, but since it has been sufficiently discussed elsewhere,* we need only mention it here.

However, if we carry our reasoning one step farther, we must nevertheless admit the quintessential truth of the common opinion that savings on the whole are primary in relation to investment. As a matter of fact, the amount of real investment

* See below, pp. 173 ff.

planned for a certain period forward, is dependent on the rate of interest, and this rate might be regulated by the banks in such a manner that the planned investment corresponds to the planned saving. It is true that actual monetary policy shows many deviations from this rule and that the whole trade cycle phenomenon can be regarded as a demonstration of the manner in which the equality *ex post* between investment and saving is realized by means of unintentional saving and dissaving. But in the long run a certain tendency for the rate of interest to adapt itself to the amount of planned saving could probably be noticed.

(5) *The Cash Holdings of the Public.*—If we now take up the other question, of the way in which total cash-holdings outside the banks will change in consequence of a deviation between savings and real investment *ex ante*, we must base our reasoning on assumptions with regard to financial investment. Hitherto our only assumption has been that all purchases of goods and services planned for the period, will be realized during the period. As a matter of fact, the best starting point for a study of the changes in the cash-holdings seems to be an analogous assumption with regard to the financial transactions carried out between the public (including firms) on the one hand and the banks on the other. Disregarding other financial transactions taking place outside the banks, we may thus assume that the banks adapt themselves to the wishes of the public with regard to the volume of loans and deposits, and that therefore all transactions between the public and the banks are carried out in accordance with the planning of the public at the beginning of the period considered, that is (if we split up J into J^p and J^b in the same way as M) that $J_0^p = J_1^p$.

The consequences of this assumption can easily be shown by the following equations if for the difference between saving and investment *ex ante* we write a, relating only to the public and to firms, and for the planned increase of the cash-holdings outside the banks we write β.

	Ex ante: $S_0 - I_0 = \mathcal{J}_0 + \dot{M}_0$	Ex post: $S_1 - I_1 = \mathcal{J}_1 + \dot{M}_1$
Public and firms (p)	$a = (a-\beta)+\beta$	$0 = (a-\beta)+(\beta-a)$
Banks (b)	$0 = 0 \pm 0$	$0 = (\beta-a)+(a-\beta)$
	$a = (a-\beta)+\beta$	$0 = 0 \pm 0$

The term $\dot{M}_1^p$ thus has the value $(\beta - a)$ or, as it can also be written, $(\dot{M}_0^p + I_0 - S_0)$.

We can therefore make the following statement: If in a closed economy the public (including firms) realize their plans in relation to the banks for a short period forward, other financial transactions being disregarded, total cash-holdings outside the banks must increase by an amount equal to the sum of the planned increase in the cash-holdings and the excess of planned real investment over planned saving. This latter item represents the unintentional increase in cash-holdings.

Actually, however, firms and individuals may to a certain extent counterbalance the unintentional increase in their cash-holdings by *new* transactions with the banks. The actual result will thus depend on their behaviour in this respect, and in a more detailed study of the question, the theorist must therefore make further alternative assumptions. But since the unexpected increase in sales, that has taken place during the given period, will probably increase intentional cash-holdings during coming periods, the conclusion that an excess of real investment over saving *ex ante* gives rise to a tendency for cash-holdings to increase, seems on the whole to be founded on realistic assumptions.

(6) *Concluding Remarks.*—We have in this section, as previously with regard to the micro-economic values, mainly restricted our analysis to expanding processes, which have their origin in an initial excess of investment over saving. The equations set up are, however, also valid for the opposite case where there exists an excess of planned saving over real investment and our reasoning can therefore on the whole be analogously applied to the contracting processes then arising.

Finally we should remind the reader of the assumption, valid for this whole section, that prices are kept unaltered during the short period under consideration. When we have here spoken of changes in sales, we have thus had in view only changes in the quantities sold by firms (X) and by private individuals (Y) during the period in question, as is shown by the following (simplified) equation:

$$I_0 - S_0 = A_1 - A_0 = P(X_1 - X_0) + \Pi(Y_1 - Y_0)$$

Price changes belong to a category of problems connected with the transition from one period to another. These problems have not been treated in this paper, the purpose of which has only been to clear up some elementary relations between prospective and retrospective values associated with a given period, as an introduction to further studies of the relations that may exist between such values over a sequence of short periods. Thus the interesting and important economic problems begin just at the point where this study breaks off.

The theoretical treatment of these other problems referring to the development during a longer period of time must be based on assumptions with regard to the relations between the retrospective values of one short period and the prospective values referring to the next one, that is, on assumptions as to the influence of the actual course of events on the expectations and planning of the economic subjects. Since these reactions may vary between wide limits, the assumptions must often be stated as alternatives. The main difficulty for the theorist in this field lies in the choice of realistic assumptions, such that a close approach to actual economic problems is secured.

PART II

THE RATE OF INTEREST
AND THE PRICE LEVEL

CHAPTER I

INTRODUCTION

1. Simplifying Assumptions, and Plan of the Essay

The present essay is for the greater part a study in pure theory, so we shall find it advisable to follow the traditional method of starting with relatively simple cases. Moreover some simplifying assumptions as to the organization of the monetary system will be maintained throughout.

We may start with a society where the monetary system has the following simple character amenable to theoretical analysis:

(1) The monetary system operates in a *closed economy*. We may therefore neglect the complications arising from international transactions.

(2) A *free currency* is assumed to be established. The factors determining the general price level are most easily brought out if it is assumed that the Monetary Authority can follow a completely autonomous policy, with no obligation to keep the currency on a parity with gold or any other commodity, and with a perfectly free hand to carry out its credit policy.

(3) All granting of bank credits is *centralized* under the Monetary Authority or the Central Bank—which has also the sole right of creating legal tender. This assumption, which may most easily be imagined to be satisfied by the nationalization of the banking system, facilitates the study of the effects of monetary policy, since it is then possible to disregard the complex of problems concerned with the influence of a Central Bank on other banks.

(4) The credit system is assumed to be so developed

139

that there are *no cash holdings*. We accordingly assume that short-term credits are freely granted between individuals and that any other direct payments which still require to be made are financed by book transfers between banking accounts, on which full interest is paid.*

These assumptions will greatly facilitate our exposition but, as will be indicated in chap. v, sec. 5, our results would not be substantially influenced, if more realistic assumptions were used instead.

The rest of this chapter will be devoted to a brief account of the factors determining changes in the price level. We shall find that we require a treatment differing in several respects from the traditional Quantity Theory. The later chapters will be devoted to a discussion of one of these factors, namely the loan rate of interest. In chapter ii we shall make a fuller analysis of the cumulative process, which, according to Wicksell, sets in when the loan rate becomes abnormal. For the purpose of this analysis, we shall assume an initial state which is comparatively simple in nature, namely a stationary equilibrium. But this convenient assumption will not diminish the general validity of our conclusions to any serious extent. The problem of the differentiation of interest rates, especially for short and long term loans, will next be introduced. Chapters iv and v examine the role of the rate of interest as an instrument of monetary policy. We shall there study the dynamic process, which arises when changes in primary factors occur. It will be assumed that the price level is regulated according to certain alternative principles, the merits of which have been discussed in an earlier work on the aims of monetary

* All sight deposits in the Central Bank are assumed to bear the same interest, whether they are subject to cheque or not. The circumstance that some or all of these deposits are chequing accounts is assumed to have no influence on the level of short-term interest rates. Consequently no special accounts are kept for cash purposes.

policy.* The last chapter contains an attempt to clarify the Wicksellian concept of a "normal loan rate of interest."

2. THE BASIC EQUATION FOR THE PRICES OF CONSUMERS' GOODS

The laws governing changes in the price level are usually studied by taking the mechanism of payments itself as the starting-point. This leads to the so-called Quantity Theory, connecting changes in the value of money with the quantity of means of payment. The connection between these two factors is important in several respects, and the quantity theory will therefore always remain a significant part of the theory of money. But it does not lead up to an explanation of changes in the value of money which is both satisfactory and generally valid. This is most clearly apparent when we realize that the theory fails entirely under the simplified assumptions upon which our treatment of the monetary problem is based (see previous section), and which imply *inter alia* that there are no cash holdings in the community. A theory of the value of money which has any claim to generality should be in a position to explain changes in price levels in a community of this kind also. The problem must therefore be attacked from some other starting-point.

As it happens, such a starting-point may be found in the general theory of price. It is true that the problem of price has usually been treated under stationary assumptions, and has then included only relative prices in a given state of equilibrium. But if the theory is extended to dynamic conditions, it must include the treatment not only of the relative prices in each period, but also of the price relations *between* the different periods included in

* *Penningpolitikens Mål* (*The Aim of Monetary Policy*), Malmö, 1929. Cf. below, chap. iv, sec. 1, note.

the dynamic process. If an average for these "inter-temporal"* price relations is worked out, an expression is found for the relative position of the price level in different periods. In this manner it should be possible to arrive at a theory of changes in the value of money. Such an attempt will be made in the following.

In explaining the factors determining changes in the price level, it is convenient to start from the fact that in each period the portion of the total nominal income that is not saved is equal to the total quantities of goods and services consumed during the period, multiplied by their prices. This may be expressed in the form:†

$$E\,(1 - s) = PQ,$$

where E denotes the total nominal income, s the pro-portion of this income which is saved, P the price level for consumption goods and Q the quantity of such goods in a certain period.

P is thus a price index number of goods and services *consumed*, the different prices having been weighted by the total consumption of each category of goods. (The goods produced by their own producers and accordingly not entering into exchange are included, contrary to the usual procedure in formulating the equations of exchange.) Thus P stands for the average price level of consumption as a whole during a certain period. We have taken this equation as our starting-point for the very reason that it would enable us to define the price level in this manner. As shown in a previous work,‡ this method of defining the concept of a price level seems to be the one with most

* Cf. F. A. Hayek, "Das intertemporale Gleichgewichtssystem der Preise und die Bewegung des 'Geldwertes'," in the *Weltwirt-schaftliches Archiv*, 1928, pp. 33 ff.

† This equation corresponds to "the use of income" equation given in Part I, p. 120, and to equation (7) in Part III, p. 329.

‡ *Penningpolitikens Mål* (*cit*), pp. 11 ff.

real importance. The formulation of the two norms for monetary policy, the application of which will be discussed below, is also based on this notion of the price level. In the following, when we speak of the "price level" without any further qualifications, we shall therefore mean this average price level for all goods and services consumed. It is true that the concept is not unequivocally determined, since different methods may be applied in weighting the various prices. These differences can be neglected here, since our conclusions will on the whole remain valid, independently of the precise manner in which the index numbers are constructed, so long as the quantities consumed are used as weights.

Q, which denotes the total quantity of goods and services consumed, weighted by their prices, is dependent on the determination of P. For PQ must be equal to the money value of total consumption in the period in question. Q therefore also includes consumption of goods and services that are not exchanged but nevertheless have an exchange value.

The left side of the equation, $E(1-s)$, denotes the non-saved, that is, the consumed portion of the total nominal income. The determination of this portion is independent of our definitions of income and saving, so long as saving simply means the difference between income and consumption. The exact meaning to be given to the concept of income is, however, of some importance for a successful analysis. In this work we shall attempt to employ a definition of income that is not in common use, but which seems to offer certain advantages from a theoretical point of view.

3. A New Definition of Income

As has been explained in more detail elsewhere,* there

* Cf. *Economic Essays in Honour of Gustav Cassel*, pp. 399ff, and *National Income of Sweden, 1861–1930*, Part I, pp. 2ff.

are, from the theoretical point of view, only two fully consistent concepts of income. The first is that of a stream of *services* obtained during a given period from economic resources of all kinds, the second is that of a stream of *interest* on the capital values of these resources arising from the economic value of the time factor. In the first case we must say that unconsumed services invested in capital goods are to be treated as *negative services* by those capital goods. The logical result of this position, which has been upheld by Professor Irving Fisher, is that net income equals consumption. In the second case net income will be equal to consumption plus the net increase of capital values due to accrued interest. The usual concept of income is a compromise between these two, some of its elements being streams of services, and some being changes in the value of resources. In the following we cannot employ the first definition since we want to be able to speak of "saved income" in the sense of "unconsumed income." We shall therefore endeavour to make use of the second definition in its pure form.

In doing so, we find ourselves faced with the problem of the length of the period to which the income is to refer. This difficulty may be overcome by defining income as the current interest in every short period, on the capital values then prevailing, as estimated by the owners at the moment of time in question. The income for a longer period can be regarded as the sum of these current interest streams.* If capital resources produce services during the period, the value of the resources will be increased only by the difference between the estimated income as defined above and the value of these services.

* [It should be noted that this view, according to which income is measured *ex ante* as it arises at each moment, reduces the deviations between *ex ante* and *ex post* calculations and the difficulties connected therewith to a minimum. Cf. *supra*, pp. 104 ff.]

Such an increase in capital values will then constitute saved income. Negative saving or capital consumption arises when the value of the services rendered exceeds the value of the current interest.

Other changes in capital values, due to unexpected events modifying estimates of such values, are defined as Gains and Losses. They are excluded from income in the sense used here. Only the interest on these changes in capital values enters into the income calculation for the following periods.*

The definition of the income of an individual as the current interest on all capital values belonging to him, including the capital value of his own activities, is comparatively easy to apply to external capital resources, including land, but not labour. The capital values here referred to must be regarded as estimates by the owner on the basis of his anticipations of future yields. In this calculation, on account of uncertainty factors every expectation of future returns must be written down with due regard to the probability attaching to the yields as estimated by the individual, and to his own valuation of these probabilities. To obtain the capital value each anticipated yield must be discounted at the interest rates that are valid for the particular individual up to the time in question, and these discounted values must be added together. The income will then be the short term interest on this capital value.†

* [Our definition of income as *prospectively* estimated interest avoids the necessity of splitting up these total gains and losses into "income gains and losses," as distinguished from "capital gains and losses," a distinction that becomes indispensable when it is a question of *retrospective* estimates of income and of their relations to the prospective estimates. Cf. *supra*, p. 101.]

† We denote by $a_1, a_2, a_3 \ldots$ the total net returns (positive or negative) to be expected from a capital good during successive future periods, as they are valued by the individual in question with due regard to the estimated probabilities of different alternatives, and by $r_1, r_2, \ldots$ the expected rates of interest for loans running from

In the case of income from human labour, however, this definition differs from the traditional view, since it is not customary to calculate a capital value for such labour. The wages received by a factory worker are commonly regarded as income, although they may consist in part of the amortization of the capital which the worker represents. Nevertheless, it is possible and, from some points of view appropriate, to employ similar or analogous reasoning to the analysis of the income from labour.* This method will in particular cases give results which differ positively or negatively from those obtained by the usual method, but for the community as a whole these differences will tend to cancel out.

In conclusion it will be well to stress the point that our definitions are *not* of basic importance for the analysis of the factors determining changes in the price level. This problem can obviously also be analysed with the aid of other definitions of the basic concepts. Hence the validity of the real content of our conclusions will not depend upon the acceptance of the definition of income given here.

4. PRIMARY CAUSES OF CHANGE IN THE PRICE LEVEL

Starting from our basic equation we may lay down that a change in P must be connected with a change in the expression $E(1-s) / Q$. In other words: a change in the price level for consumed goods (and services) presupposes that the nominal income allotted to consumption has been altered relatively to the quantity of consumption goods.

Continuation of footnote from p. 145]
each period to the next one. The current income from this capital good will then be:

$$E = r_1\left(\frac{a_1}{1+r_1} + \frac{a_2}{(1+r_1)(1+r_2)} + \frac{a_3}{(1+r_1)(1+r_2)(1+r_3)} + \cdots\right)$$

* [Cf. *supra*, p. 8.]

Our next problem is to find out which of these changes should be regarded as primary from the point of view of price stabilization, and what are the causes of such changes. A primary cause is likely to influence directly one or more of the factors entering into the pricing equation given above. Primary effects then give rise to secondary effects, which, owing to the interconnection of the said factors, will spread also to those which were not at first in any way affected by the primary cause.

In certain cases the primary cause may directly give rise to a change in the price level which may be followed by changes in the other factors in the equation as they adapt themselves to the new price level. The change in the price level is then *primary* in relation to the changes in the other factors.

Again, in other cases the primary cause may, in the first place, influence the other factors in the equation, but their changes may bring about a subsequent alteration in the price level. In these circumstances it may be said that the change in the price level is of secondary character and that it has been caused by the altered relation between the monetary demand for consumption goods and their supply.

5. The Case of Perfect Foresight

If for the moment we assume that the future is completely foreseen by all, changes in the price level will fall into the first of the above categories. For they are primary in the sense that the individual anticipations of coming price developments are to a certain extent the causes of the actual developments themselves. The other factors in the equation adjust themselves to this anticipated development of the price level.

It must now be asked whether ideas concerning future

price developments must have a certain definite character in order to turn out correct under given conditions, and whether, therefore, any general rules can be laid down for changes in the price level under the assumption that the future is completely foreseen. This question must be answered in the negative, if the simplifying assumptions made here are fulfilled. The price level may show any kind of variation whatever from one period to another, so long as these variations are generally foreseen. This is because anticipated changes in the price level have no economic relevance, since they neither influence the relative prices of factors of production and consumption goods, nor the extent and direction of production. A shift in the price level that is foreseen by everybody early enough can be taken into account in all contracts for the future. When the contracts are concerned with transactions, and both the buyer's and the seller's actions take place at the same future moment, the price can be fixed in terms of the price level at that future time. (For instance, wage contracts can be fixed in relation to a definite cost of living index number.) If the payment for a certain service is to be made at a time different from that at which the service is rendered, any change in the price level that may have taken place meanwhile can be taken into account by modifying the interest accrued during the period, in accordance with the change in the value of money. This may most simply be done by raising or lowering the rate of interest that would have been in force with an unchanged price level by the percentage of the rise or fall in the price level during the period in question. (If the interest rate at an unchanged price level would have been 5 per cent, and the price level rises by 2 per cent during the year, the rate of interest for the year would thus be 7 per cent.) Measures of this type, which do not alter the supply of consumption goods in the various periods, will evidently lead to a total demand for these goods during each period such that the anticipated change in the price level—which includes a *proportionate* adjustment of all prices—will come into operation.*

What has just been said concerning the unequivocal determination of changes in the price level by future anticipations, when these are universal and everything else of economic relevance is completely foreseen, cannot be extended by analogy to other economic problems, for instance to that of the relative prices of the various commodities in a certain period. In order for an expectation of *relative* prices at a particular future date to be capable of realization, it must satisfy certain definite conditions, so that it shall be consistent with the general price development

From this it follows that under the assumption just made the Monetary Authority must follow a purely passive interest policy. For the price development is the primary factor, unequivocally determined by general anticipations, and the rate of interest must adjust itself to this anticipated price development, if the system is not to break down.† The Monetary Authority, therefore,

* Cf. *infra*, p. 336, and *Penningpolitikens Mal* (*The Aim of Monetary Policy*), p. 5, note. The statement there made concerning the impossibility of a deliberate reduction of the price level by more than a few per cent per year, corresponding to the rate of interest at an unchanged price level, is not valid under the special assumption made here, that there are no cash holdings in the society. For in this case there is nothing to prevent the general application of a *negative* rate of interest.

† If a certain price development has first been anticipated and later it becomes certain that the Monetary Authority will apply an interest rate different from that corresponding to this development, the new interest rate would immediately exert an infinitely cumulative effect on the price level, with catastrophic results. Such an assumption is, therefore, contrary to our supposition that the future is completely foreseen.

149

cannot directly regulate the price level through its interest policy, but it can do so indirectly by influencing the primary determining factor, i.e. general anticipations. For if it starts by laying down a definite norm for the price level as an end to be realized, and if the members of the community become assured that the price level will actually follow this norm, because the Monetary Authority would oppose any other programme, then expectations concerning the future will give rise to exactly the price development desired by the Central Bank. The only active measure of monetary policy in this case will thus be to establish a norm for the value of money.

6. THE CASE OF IMPERFECT FORESIGHT

Under real conditions, when the future is not completely foreseen, the problem of changes in the price level becomes more complicated. For reality differs from the conditions assumed above in three respects: (1) the actual developments differ more or less from what individuals have expected; (2) uncertainty itself influences people's ways of looking upon the future, so that their expectations assume the character of probability judgments, which may differ from one individual to another in the same situation (pessimistic or optimistic views); (3) different individuals react differently to the same probability (different valuations of risks and chances, due to differences in personal qualities or economic situation).*

Although, as a result of these complications, it is

* A treatment of the problem of price determination that takes account only of the first of these complications is to be found in the essay, *The Place of Capital in the Theory of Price*, pp. 338 ff. With regard to the two latter points the reader is referred to Myrdal, *Prisbildningsproblemet och föränderligheten* (*The Pricing Problem and Change*).

impossible to express a dynamic process in a single system of simultaneous equations as before, it is nevertheless possible to take the basic equation in the foregoing section as our starting-point. For in spite of these realistic assumptions it is still true that a change in the price level must be accompanied by a changed relation between the total demand for consumption goods: $E (1-s)$ and the supply of the latter: Q.

It is now no longer possible, however, to regard the actual development of the price level as determined in the last resort by the expectations of individuals concerning this development, with the consequent adaptation of the other factors entering into the equation. As has been said above, ideas regarding the future have the character of probability judgments based on different alternatives, and these judgments vary individually. The actual price development is accordingly not, as in our former case, primarily determined and known through the anticipations of individuals in the initial period. We have therefore to undertake a more thorough investigation of the problem of how primary changes influence the factors entering into our equation.

Among these primary causes measures of monetary policy form a special group. According to our basic assumptions (see section 1), the Monetary Authority is at liberty to carry out a completely autonomous monetary policy, and its actions can therefore be regarded as primary causes from the point of view of price determination. Since actual price developments are now not unambiguously determined by and are not the direct result of the anticipations of individuals, but appear as the result of a number of co-operating primary causes, the Monetary Authority has now quite different opportunities of influencing the price level.

Other primary causes to be taken into account here

are concerned with the functions determining the demand for consumption goods, the supply of productive services, and the result of the co-operation of productive services. These causes are partly of an external and objective nature, as for instance when there has been a change in population, natural resources, or general productivity, and partly of a psychological nature, i.e. changes in the ideas and valuations of individuals.

Now it is not inconceivable that one of these primary causes may first give rise to a change in P, followed later by changes in the other factors, so that the equality between the consumed part of the nominal income and the exchange value of consumption is maintained. When analysing a closed community,* it is thus possible to conceive of some kind of general maximum or minimum price legislation, accompanied by an administrative organization which ensures enforcement. Alternatively all producers of consumption goods may be thought of as agreeing upon certain definite prices for their products, without regard to whether demand will vary in relation to supply. P is then determined primarily, and the other factors adjust themselves to P.

But, such cases are exceptional. As a rule the primary events influence initially one or more of the other factors of the equation. Insofar as the result is a changed relation between the demand for and supply of consumption goods, the shift in the price level is *caused* by the changes in the factors in question. By this we do not mean that P is normally an entirely passive element. But in the first place it should be observed that P, especially in the case of temporary changes, has a tendency to remain

* Our present discussion is based on this assumption. Under real conditions, when a country has international relationships and its price level is connected in many ways with foreign price levels, examples of events that begin by affecting P can be multiplied indefinitely.

unchanged, owing to inertia in the process of price determination. It tends therefore to resist the influences of the other factors. Thus, the force of the effect of the primary events on P is weakened. Further it should be borne in mind that a change in P usually brings in its turn a change in the other factors, which sometimes goes in the same direction as the original change, and sometimes in the opposite direction. These secondary effects lead to a fresh change in P. This in its turn influences the other factors, etc. If the secondary effects have the same direction as the original ones, the changes are cumulative. In the opposite case they tend to become weaker and weaker, until an equilibrium state is reached. These interrelations among the determinants of prices, however, do not invalidate the general rule that a *change* in P can usually be regarded as having been caused by some change in the other factors.

7. The Way in which Income, Saving and the
   Quantity of Consumers' Goods are
   influenced by Primary Causes

We must therefore investigate more closely in what way these factors—nominal income, saving and the supply of consumers' goods—are affected by primary causes.

(1) Among the measures of monetary policy influencing total nominal *income* (E), the regulation by the Monetary Authority of the interest rates charged for bank credit requires our attention first. For these rates are of fundamental importance for the interest rates according to which individuals calculate their income. Long term rates are of importance for calculating capital values, and short term rates determine the size of the income obtained from these capital values during the current period. When all interest rates are changed in the same direction, the

effects on income tend to cancel out. For instance, if rates of interest fall, capital values will rise, but the effect on income during the period is counteracted by the fact that the income from higher capital values is calculated according to a lower rate of interest.* The regulation of interest rates by the Monetary Authority may also include a more or less thoroughgoing differentiation of rates in various respects. They may for instance be varied according to the duration of loans or deposits, or according to the kind of surety given and the use to be made of the loan. The entire process of making stipulations concerning credit facilities is of importance as a determining factor for the interest rates which individuals will apply in their income calculations. Finally it should be noted that in the real world the pronouncements of the Monetary Authority as to its programme will influence the ideas of individuals regarding the future, and thereby also their income calculations.

The total nominal income of a community for a certain period depends on such monetary measures, on the quantity of capital assets, by which we mean here all factors of production (natural resources, produced capital goods, and the individuals themselves), and on conditions affecting production and the expectations and valuations of the individuals. It should be especially emphasized that a change in income may arise solely through a change in the *ideas* of individuals concerning future productivity and prices. An altered *valuation* of risks and changes can in itself influence capital values and, thereby, nominal income also.

(2) *The ratio of savings to income*, that is to say the distribution of the income of the community between consumption

* We shall return in the next chapter (especially in sec. 2) to the problem of the influence of changes in interest rates on income in different cases.

and saving in a certain period, may also be directly connected with and dependent on measures of monetary policy. A change in the rate of interest may influence the proportion of income saved by different persons in different directions, but these do not necessarily cancel out. In what follows we shall start from the assumption (as yet not satisfactorily proved) that a higher rate of interest tends to be accompanied by an increase in total net saving, and *vice versa*, although there may be exceptions to this rule. Besides these primary effects, a change in interest rates may also exert a secondary influence on saving, *via* changes in other economic factors, above all in the distribution of income. It should be noted that these secondary influences may work in the direction *opposite* to that of the primary ones, so that the final net result of the altered interest rate may not be as stated above. Differentiation of interest rates of various types is also very relevant to the quantity of savings. It should especially be noticed that stipulations concerning the security for loans may limit the possibilities of obtaining loans, so that in certain cases persons, who desire to consume all the income that accrues to them as interest on capital owned by them, are unable to do so owing to lack of credit, and are forced to save a certain portion by letting the interest be added to the capital.* (This form of saving might be called "forced saving."†) Finally it should be added that the Monetary Authority (in co-operation with the Government) is in a position to

* For instance, the owner of a newly-planted forest, which will not be cut down before a distant period of time, is entitled to regard himself in the present as the recipient of income from the capital value of the forest, an income, which finds expression in the rise in the capital value through the growth of interest. But if he is unable to obtain a loan on his forest property, and has no capital which he can consume, he will be unable to consume this income and will be forced to save it.

† This is not of course the usual meaning of the term.

influence the total savings of the community by financial policy.

Among primary causes that influence saving, but are not of a monetary nature, changes in the size and distribution of the national income, and in the psychological attitude of individuals with regard to the balancing of present and future should be noted. The latter depend in part on their valuation of similar needs now and in the future, and in part on their views regarding the future possibilities of providing for those needs. Here it is unnecessary to investigate more closely the variations in saving in different cases. It will be sufficient to note that on our definitions of income and saving we should in certain instances class as negative saving, i.e. as consumption of capital, what is usually regarded as consumed income, and *vice versa*.

(3) Finally, the quantities of *consumption goods* (Q) offered for sale in a certain period (the total of which depends partly on the output of production and partly on changes in stocks during the period), may also be directly influenced by monetary policy. A change in interest rates affects offers of consumption goods directly by causing changes in the proportion of these goods held in stock, and in the long run by giving rise to adjustments of production in respect of the balance between present and future output. A reduction in the short term rate soon leads to increased stocks, since it reduces interest charges on holding them. This gives rise to smaller offers of consumption goods. Conversely, a higher interest rate leads to a reduction of stocks and increased offers of goods. Adjustments in production are caused by the altered relation between the prices of capital and consumption goods brought about by the change in the long term interest rate. This changed price relation is an immediate consequence of the altered interest rate, but the adjust-

ments in production to which it gives rise can only take effect by degrees, on account of frictions. A reduction in long term interest rates thus raises capital values, and by this means attracts factors to capital producing industries so that the supply of consumption goods is reduced (until the newly produced capital goods mature and produce consumption goods, when the supply of consumption goods will rise once more). From this it follows that effects of changes in interest rates on offers of consumption goods work in the same direction, whether the influence is exerted directly by way of stocks or gradually through adjustments in production.

But of course, both production and stocks of consumption goods also vary for other reasons. Especially noteworthy are fluctuations in output arising from altered conditions of productivity. In this case also the psychological outlook of individuals is of great importance. Thus the belief in a certain change in price levels influences both stocks and the more or less capitalistic direction of production, and once again the effects work in the same direction. A general feeling that the price level will rise causes increased stock holding and a more capitalistic type of production, and the quantity of consumption goods will be reduced for both reasons.

If every primary cause influenced only one of the factors entering into the expression $E(1-s) : Q$, while the others remained unchanged, the analysis of changes in the price level might be carried out quite simply. From the survey already given, however, it appears that both monetary policy and other primary events influence several and usually all of these factors either immediately or after a certain period of time. Sometimes the change in the expression $E(1-s)$ has the same direction as the change in Q, in that case the influences on the price level neutralize one another to some extent. In other cases, the changes may go in the opposite direction, and their influence on the price level be cumulative. The causal connection then becomes more complicated, and a more penetrating analysis is required in order to clarify the final influences of the various factors on the price level.

8. THE METHOD ADOPTED IN THE ANALYSIS

It is impossible to make a satisfactory analysis of the factors influencing the price level if it is confined to a single period. For the most important effects of an alteration of the rate of interest, for instance, do not appear until after a comparatively long period of time. Its influence can therefore only be described by studying a complete *dynamic process*, or, more correctly, by comparing the different processes which arise at different interest levels under conditions that are identical in other respects.

In order to simplify the analysis, it must further be assumed that during the periods under observation no further changes take place. This condition is most simply fulfilled by taking as the starting-point a stationary equilibrium where the rate of interest in force keeps the price level unchanged. If in this situation a change in rate of interest is assumed to take place, it gives rise to a dynamic process.

In order to analyse such a dynamic process, we imagine it to be subdivided into periods of time so short that the factors *directly* affecting prices, and therefore also the prices themselves, can be regarded as *unchanged in each period*. All such changes are therefore assumed to take place at the transition points between periods. The development of prices can then be expressed as a series of successive price situations.

We assume further, that in each of these short periods of time individuals have full knowledge of the prices ruling during the period, and that they allow their actions concerning supply and demand to be determined by these prices, which are therefore consistent with their actions. The price situations will then be *equilibrium* states in the sense that there will be equality between supply and demand during the period.

The formation of prices can in this way be expressed in a system of equations for each period.* Changes in the various prices and in the price level from one period to another will depend on the changes in the factors determining prices, which are assumed to take place in the transition between the different periods.†

Since an account of the entire series of price situations in a given dynamic process would take too much space, we shall confine ourselves in what follows to a few typical situations. The conditions determining prices in these situations will be explained as the result of the process that has taken place in the time between the typical situations chosen. As a rule we shall describe these different typical situations by employing alternative underlying assumptions. For the effects of a change cannot be unambiguously determined, since they depend on the nature of the original state, and the reactions of individuals in different situations. In order not to confine our exposition to assumptions which are altogether too

* As has already been stated, it is more difficult here—in contrast to the case when the future is completely foreseen—to combine the equations valid for each period into a unified system. Owing to the changes that take place in some cases, anticipated only as probabilities, a new system of equations has to be set up for each period.

† I have attempted to apply this method of treating the pricing problem under dynamic assumptions in the paper on the pricing problem already cited. Cf. *infra*, pp. 318 ff. and 338 ff.

special on the one hand, and on the other in order not to weaken it too much by using indefinite assumptions, we shall consequently find it convenient to make our statements more precise by using alternative assumptions.

THE CUMULATIVE PROCESS CAUSED BY LOWERING OR RAISING THE LEVEL OF INTEREST RATES

1. General Assumptions when the Rate of Interest is lowered

The most important means at the disposal of the Monetary Authority for influencing the price level is the regulation of the rates of interest on bank loans and deposits. Interest rate policy may include both an adjustment of the general interest structure upwards or downwards, and a differentiation of interest rates in various respects. In the following we shall attempt to furnish a separate analysis of each of these types of policy.

The bearing of the level of interest rates on prices will accordingly form the subject of this chapter, and for the moment the differentiation of interest rates will be neglected. The condition we require may be most simply conceived by assuming that the same rate of interest applies both for short and long term loans and for loans and deposits—with modifications depending on the different risks attached to the various loans. For the rates of interest on short term and on long term loans to coincide it must be assumed that the Monetary Authority gives and receives credit for long periods as well as for short, for instance by buying and selling bonds. The consequence of maintaining the same interest rate on deposits as that on loans with no element of risk, will be that the Monetary Authority will receive no income from its activities as a credit agent. The costs of administration must therefore be covered by public grants.* The granting of credits is assumed to be entirely free and unrestricted. The terms of credit are the same for all and are not changed by an alteration in the rate of interest. This rate will therefore be the only factor determining the extent to which credits are granted.

Let us first take the case of a stationary equilibrium suddenly disturbed by a lowering of interest rates, which is expected to endure. The process of development which follows will depend on what assumptions are made as to the productive organization of the community and the expectations of entrepreneurs. In sections 2–5 we shall assume that initially all productive resources are fully employed and that all individuals believe that the existing prices of consumption goods will be maintained. If a price change should occur, the new prices in every period will be expected to continue in the future. In the later sections these assumptions will be dropped.

In the course of a development occasioned by lowering the rate of interest we may distinguish three phases. By varying our assumptions we obtain alternative forms of these phases.

2. The Immediate Effects

The immediate result of a lowering of the interest rate will be an increase in all capital values, which will of course be proportionally greater for relatively long term investments than for relatively short term ones. Since the lower rate of interest will be used in the calculation of the net return on these capital values, total nominal income (which, in order to simplify the argument, we take here

---

* The reader will recall that according to the general assumptions given in chap. I, sec. 1, there are no cash holdings in the community, and that therefore the Monetary Authority has no income of the nature of interest on the bank notes in circulation.

as identical with this net return in its widest meaning) will be slightly lower.*

At the same time a redistribution of income in favour of borrowers but against lenders will have taken place (leaving out of account old loans at rates fixed for long periods). Although saving may be decreased as a direct result of the low rate of interest, the redistribution of income in favour of entrepreneurs having debts will be an influence in the opposite direction. Hence it is difficult to say whether there will be an increase in net savings or not. Thus if the effects of the lowering of the rate of interest were limited to those that we have suggested, the

* If the rate of interest is assumed to be the same for all future periods, the equation given in the note on p. 146 will become:

$$ E = r\Big(\frac{a_1}{1+r} + \frac{a_2}{(1+r)^2} + \ldots + \frac{a_n}{(1+r)^n}\Big) $$

Starting from this equation we may describe the relations between alterations in the rate of interest and total income, when other factors remain unaltered.

E is the sum of terms, which vary in different directions when r changes. It is evident that $r\,\dfrac{a_t}{(1+r)^t}$, the general term referring to an arbitrary future date, whose distance from the present is t, varies in the same direction as the rate of interest, if $t < \Big(\dfrac{1}{r} + 1\Big)$, and in the opposite direction, if $t > \Big(\dfrac{1}{r} + 1\Big)$. Hence E varies in the same direction as r, if the positive terms which come before and the negative terms following the term where t changes from less to a greater value than $\Big(\dfrac{1}{r} + 1\Big)$, are together sufficiently important relatively to the remaining terms. Under the opposite assumptions, E and r will vary in opposite directions.

If all the a's are equal, it can generally be laid down that income will vary in the same direction as the rate of interest, but in a proportion relative to the change in the interest rate, that is less than 1 and approaches 0 as n increases. If a is the permanent return on an everlasting capital good ($n \to \infty$), income will be independent of changes in the rate of interest.

163

only effect on the price level of consumption goods would be a tendency for it to weaken slightly.

The alteration in the profitability of investments of different types will, however, cause a tendency both towards an increase of stocks and towards an alteration of production in favour of longer investments. For the further examination of the development it is convenient to make certain alternative assumptions.

3. Further Development: Alternative A: Full Employment and Rigid Investment Period

We may first assume that for technical reasons neither stocks nor the production of capital goods can increase. The latter assumption would be realized in conditions where production was rigid in respect of the period of investment so that factors could not be transferred from consumption to capital goods industries, and there was no possibility of increasing productive services, for example, through the existence of unemployed resources.

Under these assumptions, production in both types of industry will continue in the same lines as before, in spite of the rise in the prices of capital goods occasioned by the lowering of the interest rate. Entrepreneurs in the capital-producing industries will endeavour to increase their activity, but this will merely result in a rise of the prices of the factors engaged in these occupations. This increase will continue until both the advantage of higher output values and the advantage of lower interest costs, accruing to entrepreneurs in these lines, are fully neutralized. (It will be remembered that we are assuming that even after a shift in prices between consumption and capital goods the new prices are expected to remain unaltered.) In short, the increase in income which primarily affected entrepreneurs with debts will now to some extent be passed on to the workers and other owners of factors in the capital producing industries. In the consumption goods industries, on the other hand, the advantage of lower interest costs will be neutralized by the higher prices which now have to be paid for capital goods used in these industries, and there will therefore be no margin for an increase in the prices of factors. Both entrepreneurs and factor owners will thus in general find their position unaltered.

The total nominal income of the community will be, however, just as in the first period, slightly decreased, since the rise in the incomes of factor owners in the capital-producing industries is a little more than balanced by the lower returns to lenders. The situation will evidently be very similar to that in the first period except for the fact that the increase in workers' incomes will be a force tending to produce negative saving (since according to our assumptions, there was no net saving initially). If this negative saving is assumed to offset the decrease in total nominal income, the total demand for consumption goods will undergo no change, and, as the supply of such goods will also be the same as before, their price level may conceivably be unaltered.

We have constructed this highly artificial case to illustrate the point that a lowering of the rate of interest does not necessarily occasion a price rise, under the assumptions made here. Such a rise in prices will not set in unless there has been a reduction in the supply of consumption goods or an increase in the demand for them, caused by a larger total income, brought about through anticipations of high prices, or by a diminished degree of saving. In the case considered, saving will possibly have diminished, from zero to a negative amount, but this may have been counteracted by the simultaneous decrease in total income.

Emphasis on this point is perhaps not uncalled for, since it has been insufficiently noticed in the pioneer analysis of the relation between the rate of interest and the price level put forward by Knut Wicksell. When Wicksell proceeded to illustrate his theory that a cumulative process is occasioned by a loan rate of interest that is too low or too high, he made use of a numerical example based on the same simplifying assumptions as those made in this section.* The analysis developed above shows, however, that such a simplified case is not a good starting-

* See *Interest and Prices*, pp. 136 ff. In the case considered Wicksell assumes stationary conditions at the starting point, a one-year productive process which, owing to technical conditions, cannot be lengthened or shortened, full employment of all factors, expectations that the prices established in each period will remain unaltered in the future, etc.

[The cumulative process that is supposed to arise in this community can, somewhat schematically, be described as follows. At the beginning of a certain period the output to be expected at the end of the same period is for some reason increased in a certain degree. Since the entrepreneurs reckon with unchanged prices, they can now pay more for factors, and competition between them will force them to do so, when they have correspondingly increased their bank loans. The total money income devoted to the demand for consumption goods is thus raised even before the increased output has been brought to market. The consequence is a rise in prices with corresponding gains for the entrepreneurs. All this can be assumed to happen at the beginning of the first period. At the beginning of the next period the increased output of consumption goods is available. But at the same time the prices of factors are raised again, since entrepreneurs base their calculations for this period on the new prices reached in the first period. The total money income of the second period is thus equal to the output of the first period, calculated at the new prices. It is therefore possible to reach equilibrium between demand and supply at existing prices. But this possibility of attaining stationary conditions is not realized, because entrepreneurs will in the second period consume the gains made in the first. The monetary demand for consumption goods will thus exceed the value of the goods available, calculated at the prices of the first period, and as a consequence there will be a new rise in the price level at the beginning of the second period, with corresponding new gains for entrepreneurs, etc. The process can thus continue *ad infinitum*.]

point for an examination of the relation between the loan rate of interest and the price level. If we consider a community with a rigid investment period and further assume that the supply of saving in the community is inelastic in respect to changes in the rate of interest, we must conclude that it is impossible to determine a natural or real rate of interest which is independent of the loan rate. Whatever rate of interest is established for loans in such a community, wages and other factor prices will be adapted to this rate, with the result that stationary conditions can be maintained, if we disregard the fact that unforeseen changes may under certain conditions destroy the equilibrium. The absolute height of the loan rate of interest is thus of great importance as determining the distribution of output between capitalists and factor owners. But it does not necessarily exercise any influence upon movements of the general price level.

[As a matter of fact, the case considered by Wicksell in this connection is of importance as showing rather the *opposite* to what he has himself in mind, the fact, namely, that cumulative processes may arise which are relatively independent of the rate of interest. Processes of this type will occur, if the following conditions are fulfilled: firstly, unforeseen changes must have given rise to certain entrepreneurial gains (or losses); secondly, these gains are assumed to be added to consumers' demand in the next period, thus occasioning new gains for the entrepreneurs in this period. These gains are then passed on to the next period, and so on.* In a general analysis of the

[* Cumulative processes of this type have been analysed by Dr. Dag Hammarskjöld (cf. *Konjunkturspridningen* (*The Transmission of Economic Fluctuations*, Stockholm, 1933, Statens Offentliga Utredningar 1933: 29, see especially pp. 19 ff.). The general method adopted by this author in the treatment of a dynamic process implies that the gains and losses arising in a certain period are added to income in the next period, when the demand for consumption goods is calcu-

effects of lowering the loan rate of interest it is, however, not necessary and not even appropriate to make both these assumptions. The different character of the assumptions made in this respect explains the want of agreement between our analysis and that given by Wicksell.*]

The critical remarks advanced above against a particular part of the Wicksellian analysis do not, of course, detract from the value of his theory under more realistic assumptions, when due regard is also paid to the influence of the rate of interest on the capitalistic character of the productive processes. Wicksell himself already in his earlier work and still more in his later writings realized the importance of this factor for his theory of cumulative price movements.† The following exposition is thus in full harmony with Wicksell's ideas.

lated as the difference between total purchasing power and total saving. The term "saving" is, of course, interpreted in another sense (more in harmony with the terminology used by Professor Robertson) than that used in the present study. Cf. Erik Lundberg, *Studies in the Theory of Economic Expansion*, pp. 77 ff., where a short account is given of Hammarskjöld's theoretical investigations.]

[* Though Wicksell is analysing the case of increased productivity with unchanged loan rate, it is easy to construct an analogous treatment of the case discussed above, where the loan rate is assumed to fall, productivity being unaltered. In this case primary gains for the entrepreneurs would arise, if the income of factors were paid in advance, but the income of the capitalists at the end of the period. The result of the fall in the loan rate at the beginning of a particular period would then be that the total demand for consumption goods during the period in question would consist of the (unchanged) income of the capitalists, from the previous period, and the (just increased) income of factors, for the current period. The lag between the changes in the two income streams is thus a condition for the increase in total demand which gives rise to the gains. In our analysis it has been assumed that no such lag exists.]

[† In his *Lectures*, vol. ii, pp. 194 ff., Wicksell gives a description of the effects of a lowering of the loan rate below the equilibrium rate with full employment, an analysis which is unsurpassed in its admirable conciseness. Perhaps we may be allowed to quote here the following central passages: "If the banks lend their money at

4. Alternative B: Full Employment and Non-Rigid Investment Period

We may now drop the assumption of technical rigidity in the organization of production, while retaining that of full employment. The lowering of the rate of interest will then produce on the one hand an increase in stocks, and on the other a reorientation of production in a more capitalistic direction. The result of these disturbances will be as follows:—

Firstly, the increase in stocks, caused by the lower level

materially lower rates than the normal rate as above defined, then in the first place saving will be discouraged and already for that reason there will be an increased demand for goods and services for present consumption. In the second place, the profit opportunities of entrepreneurs will be greater than before, and the demand for the services of labour and land, as well as for raw materials already in the market, will thus increase in the capital goods industries to the same extent as it had previously been held in check by the higher rate of interest. Owing to the increased income thus accruing to workers, landowners, and owners of raw materials, etc. (the extra profits of the entrepreneurs need not to be considered here, as they arise at a future time and then correspond more or less to the diminished interest received by bank depositors), the prices of consumption goods will now also begin to rise, the more so as the factors of production previously available in these branches are now withdrawn for the purposes of production of capital goods. Equilibrium in the market for goods and services will therefore be disturbed. As against a demand increased in two directions there will be an unchanged or even diminished supply, which must result in an increase in wages, rents and in prices. . . . On the basis of these new prices the future is then judged. Entrepreneurs who so far have been able to offer workmen, owners of raw materials, etc., higher prices simply because they themselves could borrow money at a lower rate. . would now, even if the bank rate were raised to the previous normal level, on the average be able to offer the same high price, because they have reason to expect the same increased prices for their own products (or rents or freights, etc.) in the future. If, therefore, the banks maintain the lower rate of interest, it will again act as a tempting extra profit to entrepreneurs and, by competition between them, force up still further the prices of labour and materials and, indirectly, of consumption goods also, and so on."]

169

of interest rates (even if people believe merely that existing prices will be maintained), will occasion a *temporary* decrease in the supply of consumption goods. If the productive organization is for the time being assumed to be unaltered, this decreased supply will bring about a rise in the price level of consumption goods during the period when stocks are being built up, and it will subsequently remain at this higher level. After the alteration in stocks has been carried through, the supply of consumption goods will be the same as initially and money incomes (as is developed later) may be assumed to adapt themselves gradually to the higher price level. If the proportion of income saved is unaltered, the total demand for consumption goods may at this level of prices correspond to the supply, and in this case there will be no disequilibrium. If the effect of the lowering of the rate of interest on the supply of consumption goods is limited to the increase in stocks, the result will thus merely be a non-recurrent and non-cumulative rise in the price level.

Of greater importance, however, is the change in productive organization, consisting in a lengthening of the investment period which is now profitable owing to the lower rate of interest. Factors of production will be transferred from the direct production of consumption goods to the production of capital goods, the relative prices of which have increased. And in the capital goods industries the newly constructed equipment will be more durable than the old while the productive process will itself occupy a longer period. How the total money income in this first stage will be affected by this alteration it is not easy to say. An indisputable result is, however, that the supply of consumption goods will be successively reduced. This must soon bring about a rise in their price level, in so far as the total demand for consumption goods is not correspondingly reduced. But since there are no reasons for assuming that it will be, and indeed the contrary seems more likely (since the workers who now have higher money incomes save relatively little), a rise in the prices of consumption goods seems unavoidable. Under the assumption that existing prices of consumption goods are expected to continue in the future—which assumption we shall drop later—the immediate effect of the rise in the prices of consumption goods will be a rise in the prices of capital goods, since capital values are partly determined by the anticipated prices of consumption goods. This fresh increase in capital values, which will be somewhat retarded but not reversed by the tendency of prices to fall on account of the greater production of capital goods, will cause a corresponding increase in incomes for the owners of the factors in these lines. The total nominal income will thus rise in about the same degree as the price level of consumption goods has increased. The increase in incomes will, however, not be evenly distributed over the whole community but will be greatest for borrowing entrepreneurs who make an extra gain at the expense of capitalists (capital lenders) who have unaltered incomes. Since this increase in income (which we can hardly suppose to be neutralized by a rise in saving) will cause a stronger demand for consumption goods, the supply of which is not greater but smaller than before, a *further* rise in the prices of consumption goods must take place. Then we have a new rise in incomes, which in its turn will cause a fresh rise in the price level of consumption goods, and so on. Under these assumptions it is thus correct to say that the lowering of the rate of interest occasions a *cumulative* price-rise.*

* Cf. E. Heckscher, "Verkan av för låg räntefot" ("The Effects of an Abnormally Low Rate of Interest"), *Ekonomisk Tidskrift*, 1921, No. 12 (Nationalekonomiska Studier tillägnade Prof. K. Wicksell), pp. 49 ff., where under certain simplifying assumptions the process

If there were no time lag in the effects and counter-effects of rising capital values and prices of consumption goods, prices would soar upwards to an indefinite extent, as soon as the initial disequilibrium between the demand for and supply of consumption goods has set the process in motion.

Under more realistic assumptions, the lowering of the

is described approximately as follows: The immediate result of the lowered interest rate is assumed to be that prices of capital goods are doubled, while their level for consumers' goods is unaltered. Productive forces will accordingly be transferred from the manufacture of the latter to the capital goods industries. As a result, capital goods will fall and consumers' goods rise in price in comparison with the preceding phase. "This will continue until the apparatus of production has been reorientated in such a manner that the prices of capital goods and of consumption goods are in equilibrium once more. This will be the case when the reorientation has been completed with due regard to the fact that demand, through the larger volume of credits or the lower rate of interest, is to a greater extent than formerly directed towards capital goods." (*Ibidem*, p. 52.) The lower rate of interest would according to this view give rise to higher prices of both capital and consumption goods, but this process is *not cumulative*, but will even in time be changed into a (small) decline in the prices of capital goods. (The fact that the lower rate of interest will probably cause a certain diminution of voluntary saving is here disregarded.)—If this analysis is to be correct, it must be assumed that the determination of prices of capital goods is not influenced by the higher prices of consumers' goods. Their prices must instead then be based on an expectation that consumers' prices during the future periods when the capital goods mature as consumption goods will lie at the same level as before the reduction of the rate of interest, or still lower. Heckscher has not stated that this assumption, which probably holds true in reality only under exceptional circumstances, underlies his reasoning. Without it, the process must be that described above in the text. Even if it were conceived that the increased supply of capital goods might cause a temporary drop in their prices in comparison with the high level reached immediately after the reduction of the rate of interest, the direction of the price movement would soon change once more. As soon as price calculations were re-made on the basis of the higher prices of consumers' goods, the cumulative process described above in the text would be in full operation.

172

rate of interest will cause only a gradual price rise, at least at first. This is because the time lag hinders the increase in capital values from causing a corresponding rise in the prices of consumption goods. On account of the stickiness of wages, workers' demand for consumption goods will increase only slowly. And entrepreneurs who experience the largest increase in incomes, may be assumed to save a large part of it for investment in openings which have now become profitable. The time lag works in a less degree in the opposite direction: a rise in the prices of consumption goods will cause a more immediate rise in capital values, so long as it is not considered to be only temporary. Hence the price curve for consumption goods will lag behind the price curve for capital goods and the total price rise will, as we have just said, pursue a more moderate course.

5. ALTERNATIVE B (*continued*) : THE ADJUSTMENT OF SAVING TO INVESTMENT

The saving required to enable production to become more capitalistic has been called "forced saving." And from the point of view of the community as a whole the expression contains the element of truth that, as a result of the redistribution of factors consequent on the lower rate of interest, there must be a corresponding restriction of consumption. But from the point of view of the individual, the saving is in large part quite voluntary. Under a monetary economy every individual is free to consume as much of his income as he likes, the only limit being his credit standing. Only if he refrains from consumption because he cannot obtain credit is it possible to speak of "forced saving" from the point of view of the individual.*

This is a problem that has been rather unsatisfactorily

* Cf. *supra*, chap. I, sec. 7.

discussed. How can a lowering of the loan rate of interest which is generally supposed to have a tendency to decrease (voluntary) saving, thus cause an increase in total saving?

The solution appears to be, that while a lowering of the interest level might possibly diminish the propensity to save if the distribution of incomes were unaltered, it occasions a redistribution of incomes such that those with a relatively strong disposition to save find their incomes increased, at the expense of those whose disposition to do so is relatively weak. The capitalist lenders who may be supposed not to have a strong incentive to save, since they are guaranteed a perpetual income, find their real incomes reduced, partly through the lower rate of interest, and partly also because the real value of their incomes is reduced by the rise in prices. Even workers who, on account of their relatively small incomes cannot save much, find their share of the national dividend decreased. On the other hand, entrepreneurs find their incomes increased and have a strong incentive to apply it to further capital investment. The income that comes to the entrepreneurs at the cost of the rest of the community will thus tend to be saved to a greater degree than would otherwise have been the case. The shift in the distribution of income thus increases total saving to such an extent that it more than counteracts the decline in the propensity to save due to the lower loan rate of interest.

The change in the distribution of income is not a primary consequence of the lowered rate of interest, if we neglect the reduction in the nominal incomes of capitalists mentioned above. It is principally a secondary effect, since it is directly brought about by the rising prices caused by the lowered interest rate. The rise of the price level reduces real income for all persons with contractual earnings (in so far as these contracts are not based on a price index) in favour of other recipients of income. In every case given, the shift in the price level will be sufficiently large to cause such a change in the distribution of incomes that total saving in the community will correspond to the value of real investment, the extent of which is primarily determined by the rate of interest.

The statement commonly met with that the quantity of saving directly determines the amount of real investment is thus, strictly speaking, not quite correct, as long as monetary policy is autonomous. The causal connection should instead be described by saying that the rate of interest, by determining the price relation between capital and consumption goods, makes the production of the former remunerative to a certain definite extent. The required saving will then take place, voluntarily in greater part, and the causal element will rather be the alteration in the distribution of income due to the shift in the price level.*

[If we drop the assumption that a temporary equilibrium is reached in each period (which assumption, as indicated in chap. I, sec. 8, is the basis of the method applied in this study), and instead regard the dynamic process as consisting of a series of *disequilibria*, the analysis given above must be modified as follows. As a consequence of the lower rate of interest, there will in some periods be an excess of planned investment over planned saving. This implies (as is shown in Part I above) that the actual demand for goods and services will surpass the expected demand, with the probable result that the incomes of entrepreneurs, as calculated *ex post*, will exceed their anticipations. This additional income constitutes the

* This shift of prices from one period to the next is of course necessary if, as has been assumed above, prices are to be in equilibrium in each short period, so that demand and supply in every individual case, and hence also for all consumption goods, are exactly equal.

175

"unintentional" saving for such a period. (For this "unintentional saving" the term "forced saving" does not seem to be very appropriate.) As a consequence of the increased demand and resulting increase in income and saving *ex post*, it can be assumed that prices are raised and that the income expectations of entrepreneurs for the next period will reach a higher level. They will thus constitute the base for an increase in the planned saving for this next period (in relation to that of the previous period). If in this period also planned saving is insufficient to meet the demand of investors, the amount lacking will, in the same manner as before, be procured by new "unintentional" saving. In the following period income expectations and planned saving will again increase, and so the process can continue. On this method also, the redistribution of incomes will thus give rise to an increase in voluntary saving. The analysis given above in the text is therefore in full harmony with the results obtained with the aid of the more realistic method. As a matter of fact, it does not seem to be very difficult to pass over from the first to the second method, and thus to interpret the analyses of this study in the terms of the *ex ante—ex post* analysis.]

6. ALTERNATIVE C: UNEMPLOYED RESOURCES AVAILABLE

We shall now drop the assumption that initially there are no unemployed factors. Even if there are unemployed resources, an expansion of capital production is usually required to bring about a general price rise, if purely psychological factors are disregarded. But in contrast to the previous case, this larger production of capital goods may take place without a corresponding restriction in the production of consumption goods.

To illustrate this point we may take the practically

important case of unemployed labour. Suppose that to start with there exist unemployed labourers, in the sense that the supply of labour at current wage rates is greater than the demand for it by entrepreneurs.

(*a*) If such unemployment is confined to industries producing *consumption goods* and no transfer of factors to longer investments is possible on technical grounds, the process will work out in the manner indicated above in section 3, unless psychological factors initiate a rise in prices. The consequence of the lower rate of interest will be a redistribution, but not a rise in total income, since the factors engaged in capital production could not be augmented. Nor will the demand for consumption goods as a whole increase, if saving is unaltered. With unchanged prices for consumption goods, entrepreneurs producing them will have no incentive to demand a greater quantity of labour. Unemployment will then not diminish and production will continue as before, apart from the disturbances caused by the alteration in relative prices.

An expansion in the production of capital goods may, however, take place, if factors belonging to these industries are unemployed, and also if productive resources can be transferred from the industries producing consumers' goods. In both cases a process will set in which will deviate more or less from that described above in section 4, depending on the character of the assumptions made.

(*b*) If we first assume, as in our last example, that factors cannot be transferred from different branches of production, but that there is unemployment in the *capital goods* industries only, the higher prices of these goods will reduce unemployment. The total nominal income of the community will then rise, with a corresponding increased demand for consumers' goods and higher

177

prices for them, since their supply will by our assumption be unchanged.*

Whether prices will rise quicker or slower than in the case described in section 4 depends on our assumptions. The fact that, in the case now considered, the volume of consumers' goods is not decreased, suggests that the rise in prices would take place more slowly than in the former case. But it must be remembered that incomes will rise more quickly than before, since the increased production in the capital goods industries will be brought about more easily by the absorption of labour from among the unemployed than by a transfer from the consumers' goods industries.

The process may continue until all unemployed resources in the capital goods industries are fully utilized, after which equilibrium may result, as described in section 3 above.

(c) If we maintain our assumption that factors cannot be transferred between the two types of industry, but assume that unemployed resources are available both in *consumers' and in capital goods* industries, the resulting development will imply both an increase in incomes, accompanied by an increase in the demand for consumers' goods, and an increase in the production of these goods. Under certain assumptions the increased supply of consumers' goods may for some time be able to keep pace with the increased demand without a rise in their average price level. In any case a possible rise in this level will be more retarded than in case (b).

The development will change in character when the

* This is also true if the cost of providing for the unemployed is reduced when the latter find work. Even if the funds formerly devoted to this purpose should be wholly invested in securities, the total demand for consumers' goods will rise. For it seems plausible to assume that workers who have found employment will consume more than before, wages being assumed to be higher than doles.

178

unemployed resources are exhausted in one type of industry. If this occurs first in the capital goods industries, the same position is reached as in case (a) above; an equilibrium may thus be established. On the other hand, if the expansion is checked earlier in the consumers' goods industries, we shall have case (b), with continued expansion in the capital goods industries and a rising price level, until the point is reached when the capital goods industries are also fully employing their resources.

(d) Finally, we may introduce the assumption that a *transfer of factors* is possible from consumers' to capital goods industries, even if, as a result of friction, transfer can only take place to a limited extent in each period. The situation will then be such that the rise in prices must continue steadily. Even if the volume of consumers' goods increases in the manner already described, the transfer of productive forces to the capital producing industries will result in a still greater growth of the purchasing power of consumers, at least after a time.

If we first assume that there is unemployment only in the capital goods industries, the expansion of production following the lowered rate of interest is made possible in the first instance through absorption of the unemployed, and afterwards through the transfer of productive forces from the consumers' goods industries. As long as this absorption continues, the rise in prices will continue in the same way as in the corresponding case, when there was no transfer of factors (case b above). After all unemployed workers have been absorbed, the development will follow the same lines as those described in section 4.

If in addition there should be unemployment in the consumers' goods industries they will expand for a time as has already been stated, and the rise in prices will accordingly be somewhat retarded.

7. Is the Final Stage of the Process a New Equilibrium?

So far the result of our analysis has been that—except in special cases—the lower rate of interest sets up a dynamic process, characterized by the transference of factors from short to longer term investments together with a general price rise and, of course, with disturbances among relative prices as well. The problem is: how long will this process continue? Will a new stationary equilibrium gradually be established when capital resources have been so greatly increased that no more capital can be absorbed at existing interest rates?

The question has sometimes been put as follows: Has an alteration of the rate of interest a cumulative influence on the price level or not? This formulation seems to us unfortunate. As we have already shown, a lowering of the rate of interest has a cumulative effect on the price level so long as conditions on the capital market have not become adjusted to the lower rate. But the question here is whether the final result will be a new equilibrium, or whether the cumulative process will continue indefinitely.

We may distinguish two cases: (*a*) that individuals in each period expect existing prices to be maintained in the future; (*b*) that, seeing a price rise continue for a certain time, they think it most likely that prices will go on rising.

(*a*) Under the first assumption, which we have so far retained throughout, the transfer of factors to longer investments gradually comes to an end. The increase in longer investments diminishes their profitability, and the readjustment of production in every period will be carried only to the point where the return is equal to that to be obtained elsewhere. It should be noticed that the price rise, which, as we have shown above, is caused by the transfer of factors, does not in itself increase the profitability of long investments in relation to short term ones.

The effect is rather the opposite. This is partly because the rise in the prices of consumption goods is not uniform: the increase being relatively smaller for products requiring much capital in their production than for other goods. In addition, the decrease in real wage rates due to the time lag will be an influence increasing the profitability of short term investment. These two considerations which—unlike the general price rise—may be assumed to be partly foreseen by entrepreneurs in their profit calculations, will probably be of greater importance the longer the price rise continues. Even if the transfer of factors takes a long time on account of friction, it must gradually be completed. The investments made by entrepreneurs will tend to be confined to reinvestments corresponding to depreciation. Hence the output of consumption goods will after a certain time begin to increase once more, and as the new investments gradually mature, the total output of consumption goods will after a certain point be greater than in the original stationary equilibrium. This must act as a brake on the rise in prices and may by degrees bring it to an end. If other conditions permit the establishment of stationary conditions, that is, if there is no net saving (positive or negative), no alteration in population, in technique or in consumers' tastes, the economy will again become stationary with a larger amount of capital, a lower rate of interest and a higher price level.

Under these assumptions the question raised can be answered as follows: the price rise which is the effect of a lower rate of interest need not continue indefinitely, but comes to an end when the supply of capital has been increased until it corresponds to the new rate of interest. At the same time we may admit that a relatively long period will be required, even if the lowering of the rate and the volume of new capital investment caused thereby should not in themselves be very great. Sufficient time must elapse for the new investments to mature as consumption goods, before the supply of the latter will correspond to the monetary demand (unless the propensity to save has simultaneously increased).

(*b*) If we now assume alternatively that individuals, and especially entrepreneurs, expect the rising price movement to continue, the anticipation of higher prices will make longer investments, maturing at a later period when prices will be higher, appear still more profitable (even in consideration of the extra risk involved), than when only the change in interest rates was taken into account. This will accelerate the transfer of factors from the consumers' goods industries, with the result that the rise in prices of consumption goods will proceed at an ever increasing pace. Since this transfer of factors to longer processes will continue, the disproportion between incomes and the supply of consumption goods will not be removed and the rise in the price level of the latter will be cumulative, until the process is brought to an end by a crisis.*

If an increase in capital resources is regarded as desirable, it may be asked whether the lowering of the rate of interest by the banks is not an appropriate method of achieving this result. On the basis of the preceding analysis we may state that this method is theoretically quite feasible, but that, in the real world, it would present great difficulties. It must always be doubtful whether a new equilibrium will be reached and this will in any case take a long time during which prices are continually rising. It may then probably be necessary to arrest the movement before the amount of capital appropriate to

* The objection made by Cassel (*Theory of Social Economy*, p. 497) to Wicksell that a new equilibrium with a higher price level must always eventually be achieved when the rate of interest has been lowered, therefore holds good only under very special conditions, as shown above, but does not hold under more realistic assumptions.

the lower rate of interest has been accumulated. This will mean that a certain part of the capital newly invested will not give adequate returns (as it has been based on a lower interest calculation), and must be regarded as misdirected, with corresponding losses for the entrepreneurs. It must also be remembered that this investment has been made possible by the redistribution of incomes in favour of entrepreneurs and to the disadvantage of fixed income receivers and workers. From some points of view the disadvantage of this disturbance more than counter-balance the benefits of the increase in capital.

8. Analogous Effects of Raising the Rate of Interest

A raising of interest rates in a stationary economy has, broadly, results opposite to those which we have first indicated, and a briefer analysis will therefore suffice.

(1) The immediate results of a higher interest level is a decrease in all capital values which affects the longer investments most heavily. Total income (under the assumption of stationary conditions and a belief in unchanged prices) will be slightly higher. Its distribution, however, will be altered, the position of lenders being improved at the expense of borrowers. If no net saving arises as a result of these changes, the immediate effect on the price level would be a slight upward tendency.

(2) Assuming that productive organization is rigid and that it is not possible to transfer factors from the now less profitable longer investments, the prices for labour and other services in the capital goods industries must fall, if full employment is to be maintained. Entrepreneurs will thus be compensated for the higher rates of interest on loan capital by lower costs. So far, the effect of the higher rates is mainly a redistribution of the national dividend

183

in favour of capitalist lenders, at the expense of workers and other factor owners. The volume of saving will perhaps grow, and the price level will therefore probably have a falling tendency.

(3) We may now suppose that wages are completely flexible as before, but that a transfer of factors is possible. There will then be a reorientation of production to shorter investments. This implies first a decrease in stocks and consequently a temporary increase in the volume of consumption goods with a corresponding fall in their prices. The transfer of factors is, however, more difficult than in the movement from short to long term investments, as it takes a longer time for capital to be liberated from the longer investments and to become available for co-operation with other factors in shorter investments. If the quantity of stocks thrown on to the market is not large, the drop in prices will therefore not be very great to start with, especially if the community lives beyond its income. But the falling prices of consumption goods will occasion a decline in capital values which will cause fresh losses to entrepreneurs, who will be forced to reduce labour costs and other services still further. This reduction of consumers' income will cause a further downward pressure on consumption prices, and this will again react on capital values, and so on. Even in this case the prices of capital goods will fall more quickly than those of consumption goods. Since the output of consumption goods for each period is greater than it was to begin with, the capital of the community will by degrees be diminished. In this case the result is again brought about by the redistribution of income. Receivers of fixed incomes and workers, whose wages do not fall in the same degree as the cost of living, find their position improved. On the other hand entrepreneurs will be making losses, and must use up their capital resources for interest payments on

their loans and to keep up their standard of living. Thus, for the community as a whole, consumption will exceed total income in each period, and real capital resources will consequently diminish gradually, while prices will continue to fall.

(4) If, however, wages are assumed not to be flexible, the price fall will cause unemployment. This will be greatest in the capital producing industries, and the disproportion between total demand for and supply of consumption goods will therefore probably be intensified and the price fall will be accelerated.*

This drop in prices may also give rise to unemployment in the consumers' goods industries. Then the supply of consumption goods may decrease and may even sink below the level of the original output, without actually stopping, although it may retard, the downward course of prices.†

(5) Retaining the assumption that entrepreneurs in each period anticipate that ruling prices will be maintained, the decrease in capital production will not continue indefinitely. Even in this case there are two circumstances influencing the profitability of long investments in the direction opposite to the immediate effects of the changed rate of interest, namely the relative price rise of products that require more waiting, and rising real wages. It may thus occur that the nominal income of

* It is here assumed that the decrease in total wage payments will be proportionately greater than any reduction that may take place in the quantity of consumers' goods.

† In exceptional cases it may happen, that the price fall would be completely counteracted and give place to an unchanged price level: if factors cannot be transferred from capital industries to those producing consumers' goods, and if wages in the former industries were completely flexible, but in the latter rigid. The result will be considerable unemployment in the consumption goods industries, and a correspondingly restricted output, which may fall in the same degree as the monetary demand from all recipients of income.

185

the community gradually becomes adjusted to the supply of consumption goods. In this case the price fall will come to an end, and the community will become stationary, if other conditions do not prevent this. The supply of capital in the whole community will then have been reduced until it corresponds to the higher interest rates.

(6) If, as is most likely, entrepreneurs begin after a time to anticipate that prices will fall, their belief will tend to accelerate the movement. The expected fall will be an additional incentive to shorter investments and the results will be a greater dislocation of production and increased unemployment. In this case there will be no return to equilibrium and the situation becomes more and more intolerable until it is relieved through administrative or other measures.

We thus see that analogous reasoning may be applied to the analysis of the effects of both a lowering and a raising of interest rates. In both cases undesirable disturbances in production follow. But while lower rates cause an increase in production when unemployed resources make this possible, higher rates have the opposite effect, and the movement may continue indefinitely. Thus the effects of a price fall are more catastrophic than those of a price rise. Even those classes whose real income has become relatively greater may find their general economic position less favourable. This is especially the case with wage earners, since the increase in unemployment is not compensated by the higher real wages of individual workers who are still fully employed.

CHAPTER III

THE SIGNIFICANCE OF INTEREST RATE DIFFERENTIATION

1. DIFFERENTIATION BETWEEN SHORT AND LONG TERM RATES OF INTEREST

So far we have not considered the differences between different kinds of interest rates. We must now turn our attention to them, and to the complications to which they give rise. The main differences with which we shall be concerned relate to (1) short and long term loans; (2) deposit and loan rates; and (3) discrimination between customers according to the type of investment they wish to undertake.

The distinction between long and short loans has reference to their formal rather than to their real nature. A loan is short when it is taken for a few months, even if it is renewed again and again. A bond is a long loan even if it is withdrawn after a short time.

That the Central Bank under these conditions can regulate the interest on short term loans needs no demonstration. On the other hand, the influence of the Bank on the rates for long term loans, of which bonds of the type of consols form the most prominent example, may be questioned. For the bulk of long term credits may be supposed to be granted without the direct intervention of the Bank. How is the Bank then able to regulate interest rates on these loans?

In the first place, it should be noted that the long term rate—if we disregard exceptions due to the risk factor and other frictions*—is in principle governed by anticipated short term rates for future periods.† It is manifestly possible for the Monetary Authority to make an announcement concerning its future policy in respect of short term rates, that is, its discount policy, and by this means to influence the beliefs of the public concerning the future level of interest rates, and thereby also the bond rate. A rise in the discount rate believed to be temporary is of less importance for the long term rate than if it is expected to be permanent.

Secondly, it should be noted that the Central Bank can act as a buyer or seller in the bond market and exert a powerful influence on bond quotations through its operations. Theoretically, the bank can exert complete control over these quotations, if it is supported by the Government.

The Bank can *lower* the long term rate by purchasing bonds in the open market, and thereby raising their prices. Under our assumptions, these purchases may be extended as far as desired, since the amount credited to the previous owners of the bonds will be used in the repayment of loans, or will remain as interest-bearing deposits in the Bank. The power of entrepreneurs to issue new bonds has definite limits. It is conceivable of course, that speculatively-minded entrepreneurs, who do not agree with the Bank's opinion that future rates

* The importance of these factors in the actual determination of short and long term interest rates was discussed in detail by Karin Kock, *A Study of Interest Rates*, London, 1929.

† Under the above assumptions it must be irrelevant both for borrowers and for lenders, if a loan is taken at a fixed rate (R_t) for t periods of a given length (the interest is assumed to be payable at the end of each period), or if it is renewed for each separate period according to the short-term rates ($r_1, r_2; \ldots r_t$) that are anticipated for the respective periods. We can then write following equation:

$$(1 + R_t)^t = (1 + r_1)(1 + r_2) \ldots (1 + r_t).$$

will be low, may continue to issue bonds and utilize the proceeds for short term investment. If the short term rates of interest—for the present assumed to be the same for loans and deposits—are higher than the bond rate, this will evidently be profitable. But the entrepreneurs would evidently run the risk of corresponding losses, if the short rate subsequently falls. The Bank should have no difficulty in covering the temporary deficit by tax receipts, especially since a corresponding surplus may be expected later, if the policy is consistently followed.

Conversely if the Bank desires to *raise* the long term rate, its procedure will be to sell bonds as long as buyers are to be found, at the corresponding price. Especially if the short rate is kept lower than the long rate, it is conceivable that money will be borrowed on short term from the Bank for the purchase of bonds. In this case the Bank will also realize a deficit, which for the time being must be covered by taxation, but it will later be offset by a corresponding surplus, when the short term rates have risen—supposing that the Bank has judged the situation correctly. It is true that there may be times when the sale of the entire bond portfolio of the Bank is insufficient to press quotations down as far as is desired. In such cases, it would be necessary for the Bank to have the right to issue bonds itself, guaranteed by the Government.

We accordingly assume that the Central Bank, by means of public announcement and operations of this kind can keep long term rates of interest at a level different from the short term rates for the same period. The question then arises of how the price level will be affected by such a differentiation of interest rates.

2. The Effects of such Differentiation in a Typical Case

Our problem is to explain how a change in the relation between long and short term rates, deliberately brought about by the Bank, will influence the price level. The easiest method of approach is to start with simplified cases.

Let us start from a stationary situation in which the interest rates for different periods are the same, and suppose that the Central Bank at a certain point of time, t_0, announces that from that date until a certain future date t_1, the discount rate will be higher and after that lower than the initial rate (see curve A in the graph below). If the public has full confidence in the Bank, the result will be that rates for relatively short loans will rise while those for relatively long ones will fall—supposing that the date fixed for the lowering of the rate is not too far ahead. For loans that are repayable before the date named, t_1, the interest rate will rise as much as the discount rate. For loans falling due after the point in question the rate will fall gradually from the high level and at a certain point of time (t_2) it will be the same as the initial rate (see curve B). We may call loans that fall due before or at this critical date (t_2) short term, and beyond that long term. On this basis we shall try to make clear what are the effects of the differentiation between short and long rates.

The immediate result of the alteration in the rate relationship is that the value of short term investments, being discounted at a higher rate than before, will fall, while the value of long term investments, being discounted at a lower rate, will rise (see curve C). The fall of the former will be heaviest for loans falling due in the neighbourhood of time t_1 when the discount rate is lowered, and successively less for loans falling due before or after that moment. The increase in value of relatively long term investments will be greater the longer the period of the investment.

If it were as easy to transfer factors from short to long

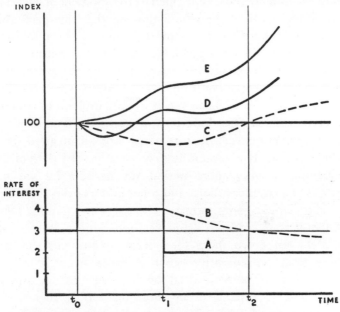

A. Discount rates for future periods as expected at t_0.
B. Interest rate at t_0 for loans of different length.
C. Relative change in value at t_0 of investments maturing at different future dates.
D. Price development of consumption goods when factors are not easily transferable from short to long investments.
E. Price development of consumption goods when factors are easily transferable from short to long investments.

DIAGRAM III

investments as to make adjustments within short term investments, the volume of all short term investments would fall (though not to the same extent), to the advantage of the now more profitable long term investments. The result would be a cumulative price rise of more or less the same character as that which we have seen to occur when rates as a whole fall. The most important difference from the former case would be, that not the very shortest, but the (slightly) less short, investments—namely those that ripen at the moment of lowering the interest rate (t_1)—would now be the least profitable and would therefore shrink most. Hence, at this minimum point there will be a particular scarcity of consumption goods, and therefore the rising curve of the price level would have a corresponding upward bump (see curve E).

In the real world, however, it is more difficult to transfer factors from short to long term investments than to make adjustments between factors which are all invested for a short period. It is especially easy to adjust the date of the ripening of very short period investments by varying stocks. To transfer labour and other factors from consumption to capital goods industries on the other hand is more difficult and requires a longer time. Hence it will pay best to cut down those short term investments that are now least remunerative—that is those which come to fruition at the moment when the short term rate is lowered (t^1)—and to expand other short term investments, the profitability of which has sunk relatively little, that is those that ripen at a relatively greater distance either before or after the point of change (t_1). Especially for the period after the starting-point (t_0), during which there will be a fall in stocks, the supply of consumption goods will be greater than before. This will lead to a price fall that, however, will subsequently give place to a price rise as the critical point (t_1) is approached. After that there will again be a tendency for a temporary weakening of price (see curve D). The price level will thus tend to follow an S-curve (first concave downwards and then convex), before the continuous price rise takes place. The most important causes of the rise are the investment of factors for longer periods, and, in the early stages, the increase of stocks after the lowering of the short term rate.*

This illustration enables us to get a clear idea of the effects of the differentiation between short and long term rates of interest.

The short term rate of interest works more quickly on the price level, but less permanently. Even if it could be assumed that a positive difference between short and long term rates could remain over a considerable period (since at every moment a decrease in the short term rate would be expected), the effects on the price level would not be cumulative. Under these conditions the raising of the short rate exerts a pressure on the price level only while stocks are being allowed to run down, and its effects are then exhausted. If the short rate subsequently returns to the old level, there will be a temporary price rise while stocks are being built up again.

The influence of the long term rate on the price level works more slowly, but is usually in the end of more importance. Even if the short term rate remains high for a considerable time, but the long term rate is low—since everyone believes that the short rate will fall soon—the long term rate will gradually come to dominate the price level.

The above reasoning can be applied analogously to all other possible cases when there is a difference between the rates, so that a further analysis under different

* The form of this S-curve will differ according as (t_1) the date for changing from high to low interest rates is more or less distant. If it lies far in the future, the downward bend will be much deeper and will be more or less of the same shape as described in chap. II, sec. 8. But if the high rate is held for rather a short time, the price fall caused by temporary decrease of stocks will not only be short-lived, but also relatively insignificant.

assumptions is hardly called for. If the short term rate sinks and the long term is high, events will be just the opposite of those described above: first a price rise and then a fall. If on the other hand both rates lie above the normal stationary position, but the short one is the higher of the two, there will of course be a price fall which will be especially strong for the first period, then somewhat retarded, and later accelerated again, on account of the influence of the long term rate. Events will be just the reverse of this when both rates fall, but the short term more than the long. There remain the cases when both rates follow the same direction but the short term lags behind the long. Here the price curve will not have an *S*-form, since the short rate will always pursue the same course as the long. Hence the curve of the price level will be smoother.

3. Differentiation between Deposit and Loan Rates of Interest

We must now turn our attention to the significance of the gap between loan and deposit rates. The margin between these rates is usually great enough for the banks to make a certain income from their credit transactions (which would not be the case if the margin only covered risks). This margin will differ according to the degree of monopoly that the banks can exercise, but there is no reason to suppose that the corresponding redistribution of income will exert an important influence on the price level, since those receiving the extra incomes are likely upon the whole to spend their incomes on similar lines to those from whom the banks are taking income by their loan charges.*

* If we drop our assumption that there are no cash holdings on account of the development of credit facilities, we must also notice that a low deposit rate will probably increase cash reserves. The

A wide margin between loan and deposit rates must stimulate the arranging of loans directly, without the mediation of the banks. In spite of the increased risk, there will be a somewhat higher net return on capital. This consideration, which, however, lies outside the field of our enquiry, seems to have no direct relevance for the problem of the height of the price level (see below). Of significance in this connection is the consideration that the bank deposit rate in certain circumstances determines the rate on which entrepreneurs will base their calculations. As a rule the deposit rate does not concern entrepreneurs who use borrowed capital, since they calculate merely with the rate of interest that they have to pay for borrowing. Even if they get their capital privately, the rate is often nearer the bank loan rate than the deposit rate. But entrepreneurs with relatively large capital resources of their own, who on account of the risk factor will not lend more than a limited amount directly to private persons, compare their profit rate on real investment (after necessary deductions for risk) with what they would get on deposit at the bank. Since it may be assumed that they distribute their capital in such a way that the net return is maximized, the height of the deposit rate determines the amount of capital they will retain in their own businesses. It is important to notice that in such circumstances the bank deposit rate is actually decisive in determining the period of investment for the capital in question.

desire to make deposits is less when the rate is low, since the loss of interest on cash holding is relatively less. This will have some significance for the distribution of income: the increased demand for notes will raise the income of the Central Bank while increased cash holdings will decrease the income of the former depositors. This quasi-levy in favour of the Monetary Authority or Treasury will of course influence the whole productive structure, but there seems to be no reason to suppose that it will cause the price level to move more in one direction than in another.

If we start from stationary conditions and assume that the deposit rate falls, while other rates remain unaltered, entrepreneurs with relatively large capital of their own will increase investment in their own businesses by reducing bank balances to the point where the anticipated return coincides with the lower deposit rate. And since this lower rate enters into profitability calculations, it is likely that they will choose longer periods of investment than formerly. The result will then be a dynamic process similar to that described above in the case where all rates are lowered together.

In estimating the full effect of the deposit rate on the price level, we must also take into account its influence on saving. If we may assume that *ceteris paribus* saving moves in the same direction as the rate of interest, and that a large part of what is saved will be deposited at the bank on account of risk factors, a low deposit rate will tend to diminish the total saving of the community.

It seems then that alterations in the deposit rate do influence the price level, but to a lesser extent than alterations in the loan rate. Since most entrepreneurs employ borrowed capital, and the rate demanded by private capitalists is likely to be similar to that set by the banks, the loan rate is of greater importance to entrepreneurs in calculating investment possibilities. Even if we assume that the rate of saving is determined more by the deposit than by the loan rate (which depends on the organization of the capital market), the argument above developed still holds true, since entrepreneurs' demand for capital is more elastic than the supply of saving coming forward.

4. Differentiation according to the Type of Investment

In practice, there is probably some discrimination of credit facilities between different borrowers; and so we ought to consider it as a means of influencing the price level. We shall content ourselves with some general reflections on this subject.

The average of the differentiated rates which keep a given price level constant may of course differ from the undifferentiated rate that would have the same effect. If the rates are kept relatively high for capital demands of high elasticity and low for demands of low elasticity, the total demand for loans may be met (within certain limits) at a considerably lower average rate of interest than if these rates were the same for all loans. With differentiation in the opposite direction, a higher average rate will be necessary.

From this it follows that a policy of discrimination may be used to strengthen the influences exerted by a higher or a lower level of rates. An important example of such a policy is discrimination between the rates for new and old investments. Outstanding credits are always more or less frozen, in the sense that capital only becomes free as capital goods give off their services. A raising of rates obviously tends to a shortening and a lowering of rates to a lengthening of the time before capital goods have fully matured. But on account of time lags this tendency can only exert a limited influence. The case of new investment representing either reinvestment or new capital is different. Here entrepreneurs are free to invest or not. Hence their demands for loans are relatively sensitive to changes in rates. Thus discrimination of this type is of great importance in influencing the total demand for loans, and hence the height of the price level.

Finally it may be mentioned that it may sometimes be

advisable to discriminate between new investments according to the average time which is expected to elapse before they become ripe. If at the beginning of a boom the Central Bank desires to counteract the transfer of factors to relatively long term investments, they may charge specially high rates for loans, required for particularly long investments, for example the building of factories. The opposite policy can be applied when there is a tendency towards depression. In this way the price level may be stabilized with much smaller movements of the average rate, than if the same rate were charged for all loans whatever their application.*

* If the policy of rate discrimination according to the period of investment is applied in the opposite manner to that described, the significance of changes in average rates will be weakened, both with regard to the effect of the height of the price level, and to the disturbances in production connected with the change therein. If for instance a lowering of rates, especially affects loans employed in relatively short term investments—which is not the same thing as a lowering of the rate for short term loans—then new investments in these lines will increase and factors of production will be transferred from other investments. The price rise that even in this case may occur will be counterbalanced because the new capital goods will be producing consumption goods within a short period, and thus increasing their supply.

THE RATE OF INTEREST AS AN INSTRUMENT FOR THE MAINTENANCE OF AN UNCHANGED PRICE LEVEL

1. INTRODUCTORY REMARKS

Our next task is to set out general rules whereby the methods of influencing the price level,* outlined in the last two chapters, can be used to carry into effect definite standard types of monetary policy.† For this purpose,

---

* The reasoning in the following two chapters is similar to that of D. H. Robertson in his outstanding little book, *Banking Policy and the Price Level*, where many of the same problems are discussed.

† The point of view governing the author's treatment of *the aims of monetary policy* in the earlier work, already referred to, was that *the risks and disturbances in economic activity following from imperfectly foreseen events should be reduced as far as possible.* The conclusion there reached was that the movement of the prices of consumers' goods in inverse proportion to productivity would be more effective in bringing about this result than an unchanged price level for these goods. The latter policy might on the whole imply a minimum of "price risks" for entrepreneurs. But if the former policy is followed, their *total* risks will be smaller, in spite of the actual price risk being greater. For the risk of falling prices is in this case, for all entrepreneurs taken together, associated with a chance of improved conditions and opportunities, and conversely, so that the expected changes in the monetary value of output will then be minimized.

In the present work, we shall not simply discuss the norm for monetary policy which we thus found most suitable. We shall instead investigate the means and possibilities of carrying into effect the alternative aims: an unchanged price level of consumers' goods, and its regulation in inverse proportion to productivity. For a final judgment on these two norms cannot be pronounced on the basis of the earlier discussion of their advantages and disadvantages. It is necessary also to investigate the comparative possibilities of applying them and the risks and disturbances that the monetary policy itself may give rise to.

we shall retain the simplifying assumptions formulated in chap. I, sec. 1.

In the first place it should be remembered that the effectiveness of a monetary programme is greatly increased if the objective is clearly set forth once for all, and if the policy to be followed in any given circumstance is explained as clearly as the situation permits. If the future were perfectly foreseen by all, the price level announced as the programme of the Central Bank, would automatically become effective, through the anticipations of the public. In controlling the price level by rational means, the first rule is therefore to influence general anticipations by published declarations of policy, so that the influence of public opinion on the price level will take the desired direction.

But the general problem is how other measures of monetary policy should be employed (under various conditions) in order to bring about the desired control of the price level. We shall attempt to resolve this question by discussing several "pure" cases in which certain primary changes that affect the price level are assumed to take place in isolation. For each of these typical instances we shall investigate the result of the application of an active monetary policy. As to the aim of policy we may make alternative assumptions. We shall thus enquire first how a constant price level of consumers' goods can be maintained, and secondly, in the case where productivity changes, how a movement of the price level in inverse proportion to productivity can be brought about. In so far as control of the price level according to one of these two norms is feasible, the further effects of the policy adopted must be compared. For our object is to determine which methods entail a minimum of risk and disturbance.

The most important tool at the disposal of the Central

Bank for the control of prices is of course the fixing of the short term loan rate of interest, i.e. the discount rate. But as the following exposition will show, in certain cases it is impossible to regulate prices by this means alone, and in certain other cases there are grave drawbacks associated with its use. Other available tools should therefore also find a place in a rational monetary policy. Among these, the control of the bond rate by open market operations is the most important and also the most difficult. In our treatment of various typical cases, we must therefore pay special attention to the relation which it is desirable to maintain between long and short term rates if the control of prices in the long run is to take place with a minimum of friction.

2. Changes in Consumers' Demand

If we set out from stationary conditions, in which, naturally, there is no problem of monetary policy, and introduce dynamic elements one by one, we may as a first step in our analysis assume that the consumers' demand for various goods alters from one period to another, but that the other primary factors affecting prices are unchanged. This means that changes in the supply of the factors of production are due only to changes in demand,* and that the general conditions affecting production, expressed as productivity functions, are unaltered. We accordingly also assume that the population remains the same, that there is no saving (positive or negative), and that technical knowledge and the psychological outlook of entrepreneurs towards the process of production are unchanged.

---

* In order to avoid unnecessary complications we assume that such changes take place only in so far as they are a necessary consequence of the assumptions as formulated in each particular case.

Since a change in demand does not in itself entail any change in general productivity, the programme of monetary policy from which we start out requires an unchanged average price level for consumers' goods. Our immediate problem is how this programme is to be carried into effect.

If the changes in demand were perfectly foreseen by all producers, the apparatus of production would evidently adjust itself well in advance to fluctuations in demand. Nor would there arise any violent modification in the volume of savings required during the transition. If a different rate of interest were called for because production required more or less capital than before, it would gradually be established while the readjustment in production was taking place.

Under real conditions, when producers can only foresee future demand with a higher or lower degree of probability, the productive apparatus will not be fully adjusted to the new position when a change takes place. The primary result will then be higher prices for those goods which are more urgently demanded, and *vice versa*. The extent of the resulting disturbances in production may vary.

If factors can be easily transferred, a new equilibrium at an unchanged price level will soon be reached,* without the necessity of monetary measures other than an adjustment of interest rates in accordance with any change that may have taken place in the demand for capital. But if such a transfer is more or less difficult, on account of frictions, then the change in consumers' demand will affect the general price level, above all through the

* The definition of the concept of an "unchanged price level of consumers' goods" presents considerable difficulty when the structure of consumers' demand is altered. However, this question, which has been touched upon in my book *Penningpolitikens Mål* (*The Aims of Monetary Policy*), pp. 15 ff., can be disregarded here.

necessity for new investment in the expanding industries. The capital producing industries receive a greater volume of orders during the transition, and will attract productive forces from other quarters. If monetary policy is passive, the result will be a rise in the total nominal income of the community and a temporary reduction in the supply of consumers' goods. Prices would therefore tend to rise while the reorientation of production was taking place.

If the Central Bank had foreseen this trend, it would have started at an earlier stage to adjust the rate of interest so that capital goods would mature as consumers' goods to a greater extent during the transitional period than otherwise. Thus, the balance between the demand and supply of these goods would be maintained without any considerable alterations in the interest rate during transition. In the absence of such foresight, the rate of interest must be shifted more violently, if prices are to be kept unaltered.

In the first place, the short term rate of interest must be raised during the transition. Stocks will then be reduced, and the supply of consumption goods will thus for the time being be increased, or at least will not be reduced to the same extent as production is restricted. The high level of short term rates will also diminish producers' demand for credit, and may tend to stimulate saving.

The general rule for the long term rate of interest is here that it should be kept lower than the short term rate. When the demand for new investment has become saturated, productive forces will become available for an increased production of consumers' goods. After the transition, short term rates should once more be reduced, and the long term rate should be adjusted to the new situation. Whether the rates corresponding to the new equilibrium will be higher or lower than those prevailing initially, will depend fundamentally on whether the expanding industries require more or less capital than those that are declining. Another important consideration is that the capital already invested in the declining industries is now less effectively employed. This means that the community as a whole is less adequately provided with capital than before, and this must in itself tend to raise the rate of interest. The final result in every actual case is vitally affected by such developments.

Summarizing, we may say that changes in consumers' demand call as a rule for increased investment, and thus lead to a tendency towards rising prices while the re-orientation of production is taking place. This tendency should be counteracted by raising the short term rate during the transition. The long term rate should correspond to the appropriate future level allowing for modification due to the higher rate during the transition. During this period it should, therefore, be kept below the short term rate.

3. Changes in Saving

We may next assume that *the quantitative relation between factors of production* is altered, but productivity functions remain unchanged, and demand functions are also unaltered save for adjustments necessitated by the quantitative changes.

The problem of keeping the price level for consumers' goods stable, can best be tackled by examining how short and long term rates can be so adjusted that the supply of consumers' goods in present and future periods will correspond to the total demand at an unchanged price level.

If the future were perfectly foreseen by all, only comparatively small variations in rates would be required to maintain equilibrium. Even a very great shift in the total demand for consumers' goods (whether brought about by fluctuations in saving or not) could then be counteracted by a comparatively small adjustment of the average time of fruition of all capital goods. The supply of consumers' goods would then fluctuate *pari passu* with the demand for them. And the necessary modifications of the time of fruition could be made at the time of investment, with only small changes in rates of interest. This would also to some extent be the case if the Central Bank alone can foresee developments, for it could then in each period encourage the correct development of the price level in future periods by its interest policy. When foresight is absent, and pressure can only be brought to bear after the time of investment, regulation in each period requires comparatively strong measures in order to affect the time of fruition of real capital and consequently the supply of consumers' goods.

(*a*) We may now assume that at a certain point of time the *propensity to save increases*, and that this new state of affairs is expected to be *permanent*.

If in this case interest rates were kept at their previous level, prices would fall. For the distribution of productive forces between the present and future is not directly determined by the quantity of saving (except in the case of saving *within* firms), but by money rates of interest, which are the decisive factor for entrepreneurial calculations. At unchanged interest rates, therefore, the supply of consumption goods will be the same as before. But since demand will fall off as a consequence of the saving, their average price level must decline in approximately the same proportion as the fall in total demand—if the producers and the traders believe that the lower price level will be permanent and have therefore no reason to alter the amount of goods held in stock.*

This drop in the prices of consumption goods which gradually leads also to a fall in capital values, brings with it a shift in the distribution of real income and property. As a result the original saving will be counteracted by reduced saving or capital consumption elsewhere. It will therefore not give rise to new real investment, but will be cancelled out by the decline in prices.

In order to facilitate analysis, we have subdivided this process into two stages, first the fall in prices in the transition from one period to the other, with the gains and losses arising in consequence, and then the transactions carried out within the periods, when demand and supply may be supposed to be determined by prevailing prices† (which remain unchanged during each period).

The process will be repeated, if the volume of saving does not alter and interest rates are kept at the same level. The further development will of course depend, both on the expectations of producers and traders as to future prices, and on the possibility of adjusting current costs to the lower price of output. If wage rates are rigid, unemployment and restriction of production are inevitable. Total income will decline and this will lead to a new fall in saving or rise in dissaving. The effect of the original saving will then be, not a formation of new capital, but a destruction of existing capital resources. Even when wages and other current costs are flexible,

* If they believe that the actual decline in demand is temporary, the process will be retarded. Prices will at first be unchanged but stocks will increase and thereby finally force down prices. If, on the contrary, they anticipate a continued downward trend of prices, the process will be accelerated.

† The gains accrue above all to lenders, whereas borrowers sustain losses. The contraction in saving in certain quarters is due above all to the necessity for entrepreneurs burdened with debts to live above their incomes.

the final result will thus, as already stated, be a changed distribution and a lower price level, without any resulting new investment.

In order to counteract the fall in prices, a reduction of interest rates is evidently called for, so that the period of fruition of real capital will be lengthened, and the consumers' goods maturing annually will be reduced to the extent required as a consequence of the saving. If the Central Bank had foreseen the larger volume of saving sufficiently early, it would then, as has already been pointed out, have brought about the desired lengthening of the period of fruition of real capital by a small reduction in the long term rate of interest in earlier periods. But if the management of the bank has regarded the increase in saving as improbable, and has not taken any preparatory measures, a more active monetary policy will be required to prevent the drop in prices. In the first place, the short term rates of interest must be reduced considerably in order to stimulate the holding of stocks, to expedite new investment, and to facilitate the lengthening of the period of fruition of older investments. The reduction in the long term rate, however, should not be so great.* For after the transition the short term rate of interest will gradually rise once more,† not to the previous level, but to the lower level determined by the increased volume of capital, and the height of the long term rate of interest must naturally adapt itself to this condition.

The contrary case, when there is a permanent *decline* in the propensity to save, can be treated by analogous

* If the long-term rate of interest were to be lowered as much as the short-term rate, the result would be a reduced supply of consumers' goods in certain future periods. This would give rise to higher rates of interest, with disturbances of various kinds.

† The rise must take place gradually, in order that no drop in prices shall be caused by reduced holding of stocks.

reasoning. There will then be a danger that prices will rise, and if the management of the Bank has not foreseen this situation, it will be necessary both to raise the short term rate of interest considerably and to see that the long term rate is also raised, but in a somewhat slighter degree.

(*b*) If we assume instead that the dynamic process is disturbed by an *increase* in saving of a more *temporary* nature, then the above analysis can still be applied, with certain modifications.

Since the short term rate of interest after the period of transition must be assumed to have returned almost to its old level before the new saving commenced, the long term rate cannot be reduced as much as in the case where the saving was expected to continue. The problem now is to adjust the apparatus of production, so that it can absorb more saving in a limited period of time than in earlier and later periods, and not so that it can in every period assimilate more saving than before. If the management of the bank had foreseen the temporary increase in saving sufficiently early, it would have adjusted the rates of interest relevant to this period in such a manner that the time of fruition of real capital would be lengthened throughout the critical period to a greater extent than it would otherwise have been. In this way, the volume of consumers' goods brought on the market would fall in the critical period, so that the supply would correspond to the contraction in demand. But when the saving comes unexpectedly, the short term rate of interest must be reduced considerably, as in our former case, but the long term rate should fall only to the extent determined by the lowering of the short term rate.

When saving *decreases* temporarily, the analogous problem arises of bringing forth an increased volume of consumers' goods, to meet the abnormal demand, by raising loan rates of interest. If the larger demand is unforeseen, a considerable upward adjustment of the short term rate is required to counteract the tendency for prices to rise. On the other hand, the upward adjustment of the long term rate should be comparatively slight.

In certain cases the maintenance of a constant price level will be a matter of considerable difficulty. Saving may for various reasons fall very considerably during a certain period, it may even become negative and take the form of capital consumption. An illustration of this would be if labour succeeded in putting through a considerable rise in wages, which at least temporarily increased its relative share in national output. Such a shift in the distribution of income in favour of those classes of the community which save comparatively little, will tend to cause a heavy increase in the total demand for consumers' goods. It may perhaps be possible to avoid the threatened rise in prices by raising the short term rate sharply. This would probably tend to increase unemployment and thereby reduce consumers' purchasing power, while at the same time it would increase the volume of consumers' goods in the manner already described. But since the discount rate cannot be raised too sharply without grave disturbance to entrepreneurs, the fiscal policy of the government might well be brought into play in such a situation. If tax revenues are maintained, but current public expenditure is reduced, or alternatively if income taxes are increased more than in proportion to the rise in expenditure, and greater amounts than before are devoted to repayment of the national debt, the net saving of the community will be increased, and the stability of the price level can be maintained even with a comparatively moderate rise in the rate of interest.

The most difficult situation arises when the financial policy of the Government, instead of smoothing out variations in saving, itself becomes a cause of such variations. It is true that in reality there is no great danger that the state may by an unexpected sharp reduction in expenditure with unchanged revenue initiate a tendency towards a fall in prices. But the contrary case is all the more important. In certain times of crisis as for instance in a war, the government's requirements of consumers' goods (including war materials) become so large that they cannot be compensated by reduction in demand caused by high taxation, high rates of interest and increased government borrowing. It is then impossible to avoid a rise in prices—with consequent changes in the distribution of income, through which a new equilibrium between the demand and supply of consumers' goods must be sought.

4. Changes in Productivity in the Capital-Producing Industries

We may pass on to deal with certain changes affecting the price level which may arise even where population is constant, where there is no saving, and where demand functions are unaltered. Such changes may be concerned with the material conditions of production, such as climate, etc., with public institutions and social conditions affecting the efficiency of production, or with the technical and administrative knowledge of entrepreneurs and their attitude towards production as a whole. All such changes may be said to influence the *productivity of a given quantity of factors of production.*

This distinction between the quantitative changes already discussed and such changes in the general conditions of production may perhaps not have any deep significance. For more profound analysis the dividing line between certain "quantitative" and certain "qualitative" changes tends to disappear. Here, however, we need the distinction in order to lay down a standard for the control of the price level which will minimize entrepreneurial risks. For we have found that these risks are diminished, if the price level is kept constant when a certain group of changes occur which on the whole are quantitative in nature, but is allowed to vary in a defined manner when certain other changes take place. Practical application of the standard should specially be kept in mind when attempting to draw the dividing line between these two types of situation. For this reason we have made the above-mentioned very simple distinction. Even if it had been possible to draw the boundary line in a manner more acceptable from the theoretical point of view, the value of the distinction as the foundation of the norm for the regulation of the price level would not in all probability be increased.*

First we shall enquire into the best methods of maintaining a constant price level when productivity is changing. After that we shall examine how the price level may with a minimum of friction be varied in inverse proportion to productivity.

Changes in productivity may occur either in the production of capital goods or in that of consumption goods. They may either last for a considerable time or

* The distinction made here agrees broadly with that in the author's work *Penningpolitikens Mål* (*The Aim of Monetary Policy*). There the norm was defined as follows: the monetary value of the output of production should grow in proportion to the growth of population and capital, while other changes should on the other hand give rise to a change in the general price level, so that the value of the output of production remained unchanged. How the distinction is drawn is not of great importance theoretically, and the above method seems to be simplest and most suitable from the practical point of view.

be purely temporary. From these two considerations we get four cases which call for separate analyses.

(a) The change in productivity takes place in some of the capital goods industries and is expected to be *permanent*.

If the change is of a purely psychological nature and has no material basis, it produces practically no complications from the point of view of monetary policy.* More interesting is the case when there is an alteration in physical productivity and consequently a change in the future output of consumption goods is to be expected.

Let us assume that on account of improvements in the technique or organization of the capital goods industries some *increase* of consumption goods is to be expected at a future point of time. It then depends on entrepreneurs' expectations of future prices whether the increase in physical productivity is expected to lead to an increase in value productivity. As we are assuming that the Monetary Authority aims at keeping the price level constant, it may be supposed that entrepreneurs do not anticipate falling prices in the future. In this case the improvement in productivity will immediately lead to an increase in the expected value of future output and therefore also in total nominal income. This will occur even if entrepreneurs in the lines where the improvements have taken place expect slightly lower prices, since they expect this movement to be compensated by higher prices elsewhere.

* We are thinking of the case where entrepreneurs are more optimistic about the future and more ready to take risks than before, or where the opposite is the case. An increase (or decrease) of profitability expectations occurs. If this situation is expected to continue, the rate of interest will rise or fall to such a degree that equilibrium between demand and supply of consumption goods will be maintained. The consequence of this will be some redistribution of income and some gains and losses, but no further disturbances.

If monetary policy is kept passive a disproportion will develop between total nominal income and the supply of consumption goods during the whole period between the application of the improvements and the increase in the output of consumption goods due to them. Since there is no reason to suppose that saving will expand sufficiently to absorb the whole of the additional income, there will be a tendency for a price rise. This tendency will be accelerated in the same degree as the increased profitability in the capital industries attracts factors from the production of consumption goods. The process will be of the same character as when in stationary conditions the rate of interest is lowered.

It will then be necessary to raise interest rates in order to keep the price level constant. But strictly speaking there should be a carefully adjusted differentiation between the rates for investments of different lengths.

To simplify the argument we shall assume first that the new productive methods require a certain period before they result in any increase in consumers' goods, but that when that time comes the whole of the greater product is available and that production is maintained at the same high level thereafter. From this point a permanent increase in the supply of consumption goods must be universally anticipated. (One example would be the case of a new fertilizer, applied to the whole of a particular crop. The increase in output will be realized at the future date when the crop is harvested, and it can be expected to continue during succeeding years.)

In this case it may be thought that for all loans taken before the point of time when the output of consumers' goods is expected to increase, and falling due for payment after it, an extra payment should be debited in proportion to the amount of the loan (inclusive of interest) and with a percentage corresponding to the increase in

output. This extra quota should fall due at the moment when the greater provision for current needs is available. The result will be that entrepreneurs are forced to keep wages and all other production costs at the prevailing lower level up to the time when the supply of consumption goods increases and the quota payment falls due. Such a policy would make it easier to keep the price level constant for this period, since total nominal income and the supply of consumers' goods would be the same as before.*
After the critical point entrepreneurs would no longer reckon with the extra quota, and wages and other current costs would rise in proportion to the increase in consumption goods, so that equilibrium would still be maintained.†

It is, however, also necessary that the ordinary rates of interest should undergo the appropriate adjustment. Immediately after the initial change of productivity the short term rate should be higher, partly because the need for saving has increased on account of the change in productive organization, partly because the supply of saving is likely to be diminished as a result of expectations of better provision in the future. After this period is over, the short term rate should sink again, not to the original level, but to a somewhat higher one, corresponding to the new productivity conditions. The long term

* From the point of view of entrepreneurs the effect of the increase in productivity would be for the most part neutralized by the extra quota payment. This is the case even when they have old loans which are assumed to be free from the quota payment, since the latter must nevertheless be included in their cost calculations. (Should they sell their capital goods and lend out the proceeds to the banks or private borrowers, the quota payment would be included in their returns.)

† It is here assumed that lenders do not count the quota as income but as an addition to capital value, so that its nominal amount, held by the lending class, would increase in proportion to the improvement in productivity.

rate, which for each period should correspond with anticipated future short term rates, should first rise somewhat under the influence of the temporary increase in the short term rate, and then gradually fall.

It is naturally possible to include the quota with the ordinary interest on capital. The total interest for a loan of a given length would then be increased to such a degree, that, at the point when the supply of consumption goods is augmented, the capitalized value of the differences would correspond to the quota calculated in the former manner. This implies that for all loans current at the critical point when the increase in output is expected to occur, a considerable increase of interest would be necessary, but greater for short than for long loans.

If we assume alternatively that the improvement in productivity in the capital industries produces a *gradual* increase in consumption goods—an assumption which seems nearer to reality—the adoption of the quota policy implies that during the period when these increases are taking place a surplus corresponding to the percentage increase in consumption goods should be added to the ordinary interest. For loans whose term extends beyond this period a correspondingly lower rate of interest should be applied.

In the real world we must naturally be content with a more summary procedure than that suggested above. The desideratum is in each case to keep the short term rate at such a level as to allow for the expected increase in consumption goods for the period. Hence the long term rate should be held at a (lower) level corresponding to the anticipated future level of short term rates.

If physical productivity has for one cause or another *declined* in the capital goods industries, and this lower scale of production is expected to continue, a reduction of the rate of interest is necessary to prevent a price fall. This reduction should be regulated in a manner exactly analogous to that required for raising the rate in the opposite case.

(*b*) If the changed productivity in the capital goods industries is *temporary*, the above reasoning must be modified in certain respects.

In so far as these changes are due only to altered expectations and valuations of risk on the part of entrepreneurs, and consequently have no material basis, they will not influence the supply of consumers' goods. The result will be merely a rise or fall in nominal incomes during the period of time occupied by the change. With a passive monetary policy, the larger or smaller total income of the community, if not neutralized by an opposite change in saving, would disturb the equilibrium between the demand and supply of consumers' goods, and thereby cause variations in the price level. This should be counteracted in the first place by raising or lowering the short term interest rate during the period in question. The long term rate determined principally by the future (unchanged) level of interest rates, should follow only in so far as this is necessary as a result of the shift in the short term rate. Excessive changes in rates, with their disturbing effect on productive activity, can in certain cases be avoided by supplementing discount policy by other monetary measures. For example, if incomes were higher as a result of a more optimistic attitude towards production on the part of a certain group of entrepreneurs, this would be neutralized with a minimum of disturbances if the interest rates for these particular entrepreneurs were raised (especially for new investment), but were maintained unchanged for others. Such a differentiation of interest rates or credit rationing naturally presupposes that the Central Bank is in a position to judge the situation accurately.

We shall now turn to the cases where physical productivity is temporarily altered in the capital goods industries, and consequently the future supply of consumers' goods will also change.

As a simple example we may assume that the cotton crop in a certain year is unusually large. A general belief in an unchanged price level of consumers' goods in the future will then raise nominal incomes, while the supply of consumers' goods under a passive monetary policy will for the time being remain the same. Since the larger income will probably not be neutralized through saving,* there must then be a tendency for prices to rise. In a later year, when the cotton goods are ready for consumption, and the total supply of consumers' goods will thus be increased, their price level will tend to fall. This tendency will be strengthened if incomes in the capital goods industries have fallen towards their old level.

In order to maintain an unchanged price level in this case, short term interest rates must be raised, from the year of harvest up to the time when the cotton goods are ready for consumption. The result will be that stock holdings will tend to be reduced in the year when the crop is harvested, thus increasing the supply of consumers' goods, and to regain their normal size in the year when the increased volume of cotton goods reaches fruition, thereby absorbing part of the current supply of consumers' goods.

Analogous reasoning can be applied in most cases when

* In accordance with the concept of income as interest on capital, generally employed in this work, the higher product values appear mainly as a capital gain, and the real increase in income will correspond only to the amount by which the interest on capital has risen in consequence of the larger volume of capital. However, this does not affect the validity of our reasoning, since the increase in the demand for consumption goods will probably be greater than the rise in income, in our sense of the term.

217

there is a temporary increase of productivity in the production of capital goods. If the larger volume of consumers' goods resulting from the greater productivity
reaches fruition more gradually in succeeding periods,
the only modification of our reasoning required is that
the lowering of the short term interest rate should also
take place more gradually during such periods.

In cases where the capital goods industries have been
working under temporarily unfavourable conditions,
and in consequence the supply of consumption goods will
probably be somewhat reduced in succeeding periods,
the analogy to the above reasoning is complete. An
illustration of great practical importance occurs when
the output of capital goods has declined as a result of
disputes between employers and workers (strikes or
lockouts, etc.). The consequent fall in the effective
demand for consumers' goods can be offset by larger
stock holdings induced by lowering the short term rate of
interest. When incomes have once more become normal,
but consumers' goods are scarce, the rate should be raised
so that stocks are reduced to their previous size.

5. Changes in Productivity in Consumers' Goods Industries

(a) When the change in productivity affect branches
of production directly engaged in the manufacture of
consumers' goods (or services), it may influence the
price level in various ways. We shall first discuss changes
which are expected to be *permanent*.

The cases where the change in productivity has appeared
probable for some time *before* it takes place, are very
similar to those described in section 4. Suppose that a
certain consumers' goods industry is expected to yield
greater returns after a certain date, and that entrepreneurs

anticipate unchanged prices in spite of the larger supply. Their demand for factors, based on their anticipation of a higher value for the product, will then cause a rise in income, not only for the factors directly employed in this industry, but also, and probably to a higher degree, for the industries manufacturing the capital goods used therein. In so far as the increased productivity depends on new methods of production or makes an expansion of operations profitable, it may actually—as has often been pointed out—give rise to a more than proportionate expansion in the capital goods industries. With a passive monetary policy, therefore, nominal incomes and consequently the demand for consumers' goods noticeably increase, even before the supply of the latter expands. Broadly, the same type of monetary policy is called for in order to counteract the rise in prices as that discussed in section 4.

It is also conceivable that an *unforeseen* improvement in productivity in the consumers' goods industries may be the *immediate* cause of large new orders in the capital goods industries. Even if the supply of consumers' goods then increases immediately the rise in incomes may take place still more quickly. In order to counteract the higher prices that tend to accompany this process, short term interest rates can be raised with advantage during the period when the adjustment of production is going on.

But if increased productivity in the manufacture of consumers' goods did not appear probable beforehand, and is not an immediate cause of larger orders in the capital goods industries, it may be expected that demand will not be increased as much as the supply of consumers' goods. Even if entrepreneurs in the consumers' goods industries expect an unchanged price level, there will be a number of elements of friction causing a time lag before incomes increase. In the first place, it may take some time before the earnings of the factors directly engaged in manufacturing consumers' goods are raised. A still longer time may elapse before the higher prices of the capital goods employed in these industries bring larger incomes to the factors producing these capital goods, and also before the higher prices of such goods employed in the capital goods industries themselves bring larger incomes to those producing them, and so forth. During this transition period, therefore, the public that is to absorb the increased volume of consumers' goods, will not have its incomes increased to such an extent that the goods can be disposed of at unchanged prices. If monetary policy is passive, there will accordingly be a tendency for prices to fall.

In these circumstances, therefore, monetary measures of the *opposite* kind to those just discussed are called for. A reduction of the short term rate during the period of transition is necessary in order to keep prices unchanged. This will stimulate the holding of stocks and accelerate the rise in prices and incomes in the capital goods industries, so that the larger supply of consumers' goods will be more or less synchronized with the increased demand for them. As soon as the apparatus of production manages to adjust itself to the situation that will be normal after the new technique has been adopted, the short term rate should once more be raised to an appropriate level—which may be higher or lower than before the change. The long term rate should as usual be adjusted to expected future short term rates.

If for some reason or other there is an unforeseen permanent *decline* in productivity in consumers' goods industries, short term rates should be raised temporarily in order to smooth out the transition to the new normal situation, which (if prices are unchanged) will be characterized by lower nominal incomes everywhere and less complete satisfaction of wants. The higher rate of interest will accelerate the adjustment of income, and will cause the reduction in the supply of consumers' goods to take place more gradually. The equilibrium between the demand and supply of consumers' goods will thus be maintained.

It is thus evident that the monetary policy to be used in order to maintain a constant price level when there are permanent changes in the productivity of consumers' goods industries, will depend on the circumstances of each given case.

(b) There remain to be discussed cases of *temporary* changes in productivity in the consumption goods industries.

If the yield of crops ready for consumption immediately or after a short process of manufacture is larger than usual in a certain year, there will be pressure on the prices of consumers' goods during the year. (There may indeed at first be a tendency for prices to rise where expectations of abnormal crops have caused a greater demand for consumers' goods before their supply has been increased through the harvest. Since the treatment of this case is analogous to that considered in section $4(b)$ above, we shall disregard it here.) To the greater supply there does not correspond any greater purchasing power on the part of consumers, if monetary policy is passive. If the income of farmers is higher in spite of the fall in the prices of their products (elasticity of demand > 1), this is offset by reduced incomes for the groups of producers whose goods are not purchased because of the desire to buy more farm products. In order to maintain a stable price level, the short term rate of interest must therefore be lowered to such an extent that the larger production of consumers' goods will in great part be neutralized by larger stocks. Evidently in this case the short term rate only should be altered and the long term rate remain on the whole unchanged.

A change in the supply of consumers' goods may of course also arise from causes other than climatic conditions. Of especial primary importance are the fluctuations due to the relations between workers and employers. If, as a result of trade disputes, there is reduction of output in some consumers' goods industries, there will be a smaller total supply of such goods during the year and no corresponding reduction in the nominal income of the community, since incomes in the capital goods industries may perhaps be reduced only slightly. With a passive monetary policy, there would then probably be a rise in the prices of consumers' goods. It is therefore also necessary in this case to raise the short term rate in order to restore equilibrium at an unchanged price level. This policy is also appropriate in other similar cases.

The examples which we have analysed have been "pure" in the sense that they have been characterized by isolated changes of a definite stated character. The events of the real world naturally do not conform to this simple pattern, but exhibit every possible combination of the assumptions which we have made. The monetary policy appropriate to any given concrete situation is not immediately apparent from our study. However, broadly it may be expected that the price level will remain constant in any particular complicated case, if the measures suggested for pure cases are suitably combined. To discuss all conceivable combinations here is obviously impossible.*

* Changes in the productivity of capital and consumers' goods industries can sometimes be combined in such a way that an unchanged price level is maintained in spite of a purely passive monetary policy. But such cases are exceptional. As a rule it is a very intricate problem of monetary policy to keep the price level unchanged in spite of changes in productivity.

THE RATE OF INTEREST AS AN INSTRUMENT FOR REGULATING THE PRICE LEVEL IN INVERSE PROPORTION TO PRODUCTIVITY

1. Changes in Productivity in the Capital-Producing Industries

If the aim of monetary policy is taken to be, not a constant price level, but a price level varying inversely with general productivity, then the reasoning advanced above requires considerable modification. In the first place the announcement of the adoption of this aim affects general expectations of future conditions and, consequently, the change in productive conditions will have different effects on the development of prices than in the cases already considered. Apart from the effects of the announcement, the carrying out of this aim calls for a somewhat different technique from that required to keep the price level constant.

We shall limit ourselves to examining the main differences in the situations created by these two forms of monetary policy in cases similar to those already examined.

(a) In the case of a *permanent* rise in productivity in some industries producing capital goods, the expected future increase in consumption goods is likely to generate expectations of a correspondingly lower price level for these goods. These two factors will to a great extent neutralize each other, so that the income level of the producers in the lines concerned may not be much affected. Thus a disproportion between the demand and the supply of consumption goods such as will occur if the price level is constant, during the period before the increased supply comes on the market, may not eventuate.

If all producers could correctly foresee the future prices which would result from this type of monetary policy, the total nominal income of the community would not be influenced at all by the change in productivity. The aim of such a monetary policy is thus just to keep total nominal income neutral and unaltered in respect of these two factors. But it does not necessarily follow that nominal income in each particular line will be unaltered. If for instance, owing to an increase in productivity in the capital goods industries, incomes there are increased (as a consequence of relatively elastic demand), incomes in other lines, whose products are relatively less demanded, will decline.

In the real world, however, it cannot be supposed that entrepreneurs fully foresee the course of those future prices with which they are specially concerned. It is possible that entrepreneurs in the lines where productivity has increased may underestimate the coming price fall for their products. Miscalculations of this sort are likely to take place, for this reason amongst others, that individual entrepreneurs are not usually in a position to survey the total output of the commodities which they are producing. It may also happen that mistakes are made by entrepreneurs in lines where productivity has not altered but where market conditions are changed as a result of productivity changes elsewhere. They may perhaps count on unchanged sales whereas in reality they may sell less, since purchasing power may be absorbed to a higher degree by those consumption goods directly affected by the change in productivity. (This will be the case if with increased productivity elasticity of demand is > 1 and with diminished productivity < 1). A rise or fall of total expected incomes may thus occur as a result of such miscalculations either in an optimistic or in a pessimistic direction. In so far as the change in income is not neutralized by a change in saving, there will be an increase (decrease) in the demand for consumption goods and hence a tendency for a rise (fall) in their prices. If this occurs it must be counteracted by suitable manipulation of interest rates during the period between the change in productivity and the increase in supply of consumption goods.

At this latter point the desired change in the price level in inverse proportion to productivity should come into effect quite automatically. Nominal incomes being in general on the same level, consumers' purchasing power will be much the same as formerly, hence the changed supply of consumption goods will occasion a change in prices. Interest policy at this point should regulate the extent of price change in appropriate relation to the change in scarcity. When a movement in prices occurs, there is always the danger that it may continue on account of the general expectation that it will continue. To prevent speculation of this type it may in certain cases be necessary temporarily to adjust the discount rate accordingly.

It was found that in order to keep the price level constant the rate of interest should be modified in order to include an extra increment or decrement corresponding to the alteration in the value of the product during the period in question, as a result of change in productivity. In the case now discussed this change in productivity is however compensated by a shift in the price level, so that the loan rate of interest can be adjusted without having to take this possibility into account. Such a monetary policy appears more "natural" in the sense that it is more easily realized and requires

225

comparatively small movements of interest rates and hence a minimum of disturbance to productive activity.*

(b) A *temporary* increase or decrease in productivity in some capital goods industry will also largely be neutralized by an expected future shift in prices in the opposite direction. During the period of transition, before the change in productivity has had time to affect the supply of consumers' goods, the ordinary relation between incomes and consumers' goods will be practically unchanged, and the price level will on the whole remain unaltered. Later, when the volume of consumers' goods increases (decreases), while nominal incomes are the same as before, the price level as a rule moves in the direction opposite to the supply of goods, so that the established norm for the value of money will broadly be realized.

It is conceivable therefore that this aim will be attained without the necessity for any active monetary policy. Since the changes in productivity are temporary, no question of the reorganization of production arises, such as might tend to raise or lower the demand for capital permanently and thus call for a general shift in the level of interest rates. Nevertheless, in certain cases it will probably be necessary to bring about the desired adjustment in the price level by varying short term rates of interest.

If, for instance, a labour dispute in the iron and steel industry has restricted production there during a certain period, the entrepreneurs (since we are dealing with a closed system) will probably receive a certain amount of compensation through higher prices of iron and steel. The workers, however, are not likely to receive any compensation. Their wages will therefore be reduced during

* Cf. D. Davidson, "Något om begreppet penningens värde" (Observations concerning the concept of the value of money), in *Ekonomisk Tidskrift*, 1906, p. 463.

this period, and consequently, their demand for consumers' goods will decline somewhat. There will therefore be a tendency towards falling prices, which will call for lower short term rates of interest.

But here again the difference in monetary objective will necessitate a different procedure in the later stage when the change in the supply of consumers goods has taken effect. Since the price level will then have a tendency to move in the opposite direction to productivity, a specific compensating monetary policy will be required (as has already been shown), if the price level is to be kept stable whereas its regulation in inverse proportion to productivity will come about more automatically.

2. Changes in Productivity in Consumers' Goods Industries

(a) In the case of a *lasting* change in productivity in industries directly producing *consumption* goods, the price level tends to move in the direction opposite to the change in the supply of commodities. As we have shown above, this will be likely to occur under certain circumstances even if a constant price level is announced as the aim of monetary policy, and people make their calculations on that basis. This tendency will be much stronger, if the movement is consistent with the declared aim of monetary policy.

But, in most cases, some positive monetary measures are necessary to make the price movement correspond with the programme.

It should be noted that the general level of interest rates may be shifted as a result of the change in productivity, since the new conditions may permanently increase or decrease the saving needed for real investment, by raising or lowering the marginal productivity of capital goods in relation to that of the original factors used in the manufacture of consumers' goods. Further, it is probable that during the transition period itself, while the readjustment of production is going on, there will be a temporary increase in the volume of capital required, thus calling for a certain rise in short term rates. Finally, it will frequently be necessary to modify these rates in order to prevent the movement of prices, once it has started, becoming more extensive than that which corresponds to the alteration in the satisfaction of wants. In practice, every price movement caused by a change in the supply of commodities, has a tendency to become larger than the corresponding change in this supply.

Two causes operate to produce this result. In the first place, it takes some time before the public has adjusted its habits of consumption to the changed situation. When commodities are scarce, the ordinary standard of consumption is maintained as long as possible, in spite of rising prices, and the volume of saving therefore decreases. When prices are falling, people may not increase their consumption in a corresponding degree, but are likely to save more instead. Such alterations in the volume of saving, arising from the rigidity of habits of consumption, evidently tend to aggravate price fluctuations.

In the second place, the public is easily led to believe that a price movement which has continued for some time will continue still further, and this very opinion has the effect of stimulating the movement. When prices are rising, dealers increase stocks and reduce the quantities offered for sale, while consumers accelerate their purchases, and *vice versa*. In order to combat these tendencies the short term rate of interest should in each given case be adjusted in such a way that the price level will vary exactly in inverse proportion to general productivity.

(*b*) Finally, if there are *temporary* changes in productivity in some consumers' goods industry, they will only have a slight effect on nominal incomes during the relevant period. The price level will therefore, as in our previous case, have a tendency to move in the contrary direction to the change in productivity. A more passive monetary policy will suffice here than in the former case. Since there will now be no readjustment of production and no permanent change in the demand for capital, long term interest rates may on the whole remain unchanged. Small changes in short term rates, however, may often be required to give the price movement the amplitude appropriate to the established monetary programme.

For there will sometimes be a danger that the scope of the movement may be larger than what would correspond to the change in productivity. The same causes are then operative as we encountered in discussing permanent changes in productivity, namely the disinclination of the public to alter its habits of consumption, and its belief that a price movement, when once under way, will continue. The first factor will in practice probably be more important when the change in the supply of commodities is temporary than when it is permanent. Thus if there is a temporary scarcity of commodities, the public will endeavour to keep up the usual level of consumption as far as possible, even if in consequence investment is curtailed. In the opposite case, when a temporary surplus has arisen, a very sharp drop in prices is sometimes required to bring about a corresponding expansion of consumption.

These tendencies, which intensify the price movement, are sometimes, however, counteracted by others. For in so far as producers realize that the change in supply and the associated shift in prices are temporary, they will adjust their stock holdings in such a way as to modify the price movement. During a temporary rise in prices they will reduce their stocks in order as far as possible to take advantage of the higher prices, and conversely.

If monetary policy is passive, the result of these counteracting tendencies will naturally vary in different cases. As a rule, however, as has just been stated, certain adjustments in short term rates are needed, if the course of prices is to be that desired, since they will particularly affect stock holdings and in consequence the volume of consumers' goods offered for sale.

There is no difficulty in extending the analysis of these particular "pure" cases, so as to include those of a more mixed nature such as occur in the real world.

3. COMPARISON BETWEEN THE TWO STANDARD TYPES OF PRICE CONTROL

When we compare the sorts of monetary measures which are needed to bring about our two standard objectives it becomes evident that the second objective (of prices varying inversely with productivity) is much easier to attain than the first (of a constant price level).

When changes in productivity immediately influence the supply of commodities, the price level has a natural tendency to move in the opposite direction to productivity. It is of course possible to keep prices unchanged in such circumstances, but as a rule practical difficulties are encountered which make great demands on the leadership of the Central Bank.

Again when changes in productivity are not expected to influence the supply of consumption goods until after some time has elapsed, it is more difficult to maintain a stable price level both before and after the change in the supply of such goods than to keep it stable until the volume of consumption goods changes, and then to regulate it in inverse proportion to productivity. In the former case, when the products maturing in the future represent greater or smaller values than before, the rate of interest must be raised or lowered during the transition period sufficiently to neutralize the alteration in these values. It is naturally easier to neutralize the change in productivity through a shift in the price level, without necessarily having any sharp fluctuations in the level of interest rates.

On the whole, therefore, it may be concluded that the maintenance of a constant price level presupposes relatively sharp movements in interest rates, adjusted on the basis of thorough knowledge of the character of the situation, whereas the regulation of the price level in inverse proportion to productivity can be carried out with a fairly moderate adjustment of interest rates. The disturbance to the business world will therefore be appreciably smaller under the second than under the first type of policy.

In my earlier investigation of the appropriateness of these "aims" of monetary policy, the question as to which was the easier to apply was disregarded. When preference was there given to a price level varying inversely with productivity, the question whether this result would require modification in view of difficulties attending the realization of this aim remained open. We may now conclude that the arguments in its favour, instead of being weakened, gain considerable strength, if the question of practicability is also taken into consideration. It may even be said that the advantages of the second type are so evident that in themselves they constitute a sufficient reason for deciding that it should be the true aim of monetary policy. If from other points of view the advantages were equal on both sides, or even if a certain preference had to be given to an unchanged price level,

231

the variation of prices in inverse proportion to productivity might still appear on the whole best to fulfil the requirements which in our opinion, should find expression in monetary policy.

4. Summary of Conclusions reached in the last two Chapters

We may summarize the results of the discussion of the application of the different means available to the Central Bank:

(1) The aim of monetary policy should be determined and announced, and in each case the reason for the measures taken should be explained. If the public is always fully aware of what the Monetary Authority is trying to effect by its measures, it will adjust its conduct accordingly and thus contribute to the realization of the programme.

(2) Short term rates should first be used to control the development of prices. In theory it is possible to control the price level by moving the discount rate alone in most cases. But this presupposes that the changes are both sudden and considerable. They will thus be likely to cause disturbance in the organization of production. One main point has been to show that the Central Bank should supplement discount policy by other means and thus allow of a less variable discount rate thus conducing to the stability of economic life.

(3) The Central Bank should follow movements in the bond rate and in certain cases influence them by open market policy.

If we abstract from elements of friction, which hinder full communication between the markets for long and short loans (and from elements of risk that may be greater for long term than for short term loans) then the general rule is that the bond rate should correspond with future short term rates.

Provided that the public can foresee, as fully as the Central Bank, the future development of interest rates required for carrying out the monetary programme, the interest on bonds will have a tendency to correspond to this level without the need for special measures on the part of the Central Bank. In some cases again it may happen that the public may differ in its reading of the situation from the Central Bank. If the Bank considers that the public is too optimistic or too pessimistic and that their speculations are reflected in an unduly high or low yield on bonds, it may influence the rate by selling or buying securities. By such an open market policy the Central Bank can exert a firmer grip on price movements and at the same time reduce fluctuations in the discount rate.

From the above discussion we see, however, that the regulation of the bond yield should not only be used to control present price movements but also to effect such an organization of production over time as will avoid future disturbance and consequent changes in interest rates. An appropriate control of the long term rate of interest will thus increase the stability of monetary policy.

(4) In certain cases it may be appropriate to apply differentiation of interest rates in other respects than between long and short term rates. Thus the margin between loan and deposit rates may sometimes be decreased or diminished to avoid such an alteration in the loan rate as would otherwise be required. The differentiation of the loan rate in accordance with the use to be made of the loan is however of much greater practical significance.

The aim is to vary rates only for marginal borrowers,

who are the determining factor in the direction of price movements. In this way the level of interest rates can be held steadier, and this must contribute to greater stability in production and stockholding. If differentiation of this type is to fulfil its purpose, it must be possible to make a clear distinction between marginal borrowers for whom a high or a low rate is desirable, and others. Since this is a matter of considerable difficulty, such differentiation is only suitable where considerable alteration in interest rates would otherwise be necessary to control the price level. Especially when it is desired to counteract a strong tendency towards a price rise, differentiation may be applied in the form of charging a higher rate on new investments than for outstanding loans. If the price rise has originated in over-optimism among entrepreneurs in certain lines, a further degree of differentiation may be applied so that rates are made especially high for these entrepreneurs. If pushed to its logical conclusion, credit differentiation becomes credit rationing.

(5) Public expenditure policy may be applied both where other monetary means are insufficiently effective, and where it is necessary to shift the price level in one direction or the other. If a depression is not removed by low rates of interest, or if the price level has to be raised with a minimum of friction, it is appropriate for the government to increase purchasing power directly. There is no difficulty in making the government increase its expenditure, and therefore this means of raising the price level is always available. When it is necessary to lower the price level, a change in purchasing power is more difficult to apply, since the government cannot easily decrease its expenditure in relation to income. But economy can be carried out if it is planned in ample time. Hence a deliberate reduction in prices during future periods can be brought about in this way.

5. Remarks on the Character of the Simplifying Assumptions in the Foregoing Analysis

Monetary problems have so far been treated under certain simplifying assumptions set out in chap. I, sec. I. We must now briefly indicate to what extent these assumptions limit the scope of the argument and to what extent they must be modified for the analysis to be applicable under more realistic conditions.*

(i) *Complications due to Cash Holding*

It should first be emphasized that our assumption regarding the absence of cash balances is not of essential importance. In a community where cash holding exists it is still true that the problem of price movements can be attacked by taking as the starting-point the factors determining the demand for and the supply of consumers' goods; and that the Central Bank by influencing these factors through its interest policy can influence price developments in a definite direction. The reason for our simplifying assumption has really only been our wish to emphasize that this approach to the price problem does not proceed by way of cash balances but takes up the supply and demand factors directly, and that the essential aspects of the pricing problem *can* be treated in complete abstraction from the special problems connected with the quantity of money. We have thus made a distinction between the theory of the movement of the general price level, i.e. the theory of changes in the value of money, and the theory of money in the more limited sense, which is concerned with the causes and effects of cash holding and changes in balances. In this study we have restricted ourselves to the first part of monetary theory as usually defined.

[* Considerations of space only permit of a few extracts from the Swedish original, in which these problems were treated in special chapters].

In a more complete treatment even of this theory, attention must also be paid to the complications arising from the holding of cash. Of subordinate importance are such influences as the circumstance that holders of cash assume *de facto* certain interest charges which in a system of paper money appear as income for the banks which create the means of payment. The modification in the distribution of income thus brought about does, it is true, modify the factors influencing the formation of prices in several ways,* but this fact presents no difficulties to theoretical analysis. Of somewhat greater importance is the fact that changes in cash holdings are sometimes associated with changes in the volume of saving. An increase in cash holding is generally financed by increasing debts, above all bank loans, by reducing loans or by changing other available assets into money. But an increase in cash holding can also be brought about by saving. If, for instance, consumers, as a result of higher incomes, find it advisable to hold larger cash balances, these are often secured by refraining from increasing expenditure as fast as incomes rise. This fact, which has been greatly stressed by some authors,† does not, however, complicate the analysis of price movements in any essential way. In the exposition of the cumulative process

* The importance of cash holding in these respects has been analysed more closely by the present author in a paper on "The Economic Importance of Short-term Credits," in *Ekonomisk Tidskrift*, 1925, pp. 223 ff. [Cf. J. R. Hicks, "A Suggestion for Simplifying the Theory of Money," *Economica*, 1935, pp. 1 ff., where the problem of cash balances, regarded by this author as the essence of monetary theory, is treated from the point of view that the holding of money is the most liquid form of investment of economic resources.]

† Cf. for instance, D. H. Robertson, *Banking Policy and the Price Level*, chap. v, where this form of saving was called "induced lacking." The theoretical system developed by Hawtrey in *Currency and Credit* and other works is also built on the fact that the difference between "consumers' income" and "consumers' outlay" causes fluctuations in "the unspent margin," i.e. total cash holdings.

already given it has been pointed out that a rise in incomes is generally associated with some increase in saving, and that in this way the tendency towards higher prices is to some degree counteracted. In so far as the larger incomes make larger cash holdings desirable, the result is an additional increase in saving, whereby the price-raising tendency is still further counteracted. With this small modification, therefore, the reasoning in foregoing sections may be retained.

The greatest difficulty for the general theory of price movements which is encountered when dealing with cash holdings is concerned with the very circumstance which may to a considerable extent be regarded as the cause of the existence of the cash holdings, namely the insufficient elasticity of the credit system and the associated factor of uncertainty. This factor gives rise to complications of various kinds which necessitate a more thorough treatment. It is necessary for instance to make a distinction between credits granted by banks and by private individuals. If the former are relatively elastic, it may be assumed that firms and individuals can at any given moment secure cash holdings as large as they believe to be necessary under prevailing conditions. In this way bank credits fill any gaps that may have arisen as a result of an unforeseen increase in turnover or of a reduction of private credits. When the insufficient elasticity of the private credit system is thus supplemented by greater flexibility in the granting of credits by the banks, variations in cash holdings do arise, but since they are secondary in relation to the development of prices, there is no difficulty in explaining the latter on the lines already set out. In reality, however, it is not always so easy for the banks to distinguish between variations in the demand for credits due solely to changes in cash holdings, and which therefore do not affect the price level, and variations that influence the relation between the demand for and the supply of consumers' goods, and which accordingly do influence the price level in a particular direction. The holding of cash, therefore, is not always of secondary importance in relation to price developments, but may modify the credit policy of the banks in different ways. Complications of the greatest practical importance may thus arise, as the history of crises shows.

In a more general treatment of the pricing problem, such as that given here, however, it seems legitimate to disregard these more special problems.

(ii) *Complications due to the Banking System*

Our next question is the extent to which the analysis must be modified when private banks are introduced into the system, and the Central Bank thus no longer represents the entire banking system. With this evidently a new group of problems concerned with the relation between the Central Bank and the private banks are added on. A more realistic treatment of the theory of prices must of course be based on definite assumptions on this point. If it is assumed that the private banks automatically adjust themselves to the interest rates determined by the Central Bank, our reasoning can broadly still be applied. But if this is not the case, the question of the relation between the activities of the Central Bank and price developments becomes more complicated than in our analysis.

In this connection we shall add only one or two remarks on the open market operations of the Central Bank. We have already shown in the foregoing that the regulation of interest rates for *long term* loans presupposes active intervention on the bond market by the Central Bank. When there are also private banks, this still holds true, but in this case the operations will *at the same time*—like operations with bills and other types of short term credit —influence the cash position of the private banks, and thus also their granting of credits, principally for *short* periods. The Central Bank, therefore, must find a suitable combination of operations with bonds and with bills in order to achieve the desired control of interest rates in any given case. If, for instance, the Central Bank wishes to lower both long and short term rates, it should buy bonds. If it wishes only to lower the bond rate but desires to keep the bill rate unaltered, it should, as in the former case, buy bonds but at the same time sell bills, so that the cash holdings of the private banks are not affected by the operations and their short term credits will therefore be unaltered in volume. If a rise in interest rates is desired, the opposite procedure should be followed.

(iii) *Complications due to a Gold Standard*

If we assume a gold standard, instead of the free currency presupposed in the preceding analysis, there naturally arise a number of complications, the character of which will depend on the organization of the monetary system and the supply and demand conditions for gold.

If we start from the comparatively simple case of a closed community with a fairly constant gold supply, in which gold does not circulate as a means of payment but, in so far as it does not find industrial uses, is held by the Central Bank, these complications are of minor importance. What is new in the situation is only that the Central Bank now also has the task of regulating the value of gold. But this takes place simply by letting the gold reserve absorb the gold that is not used in industry at the prevailing price level, without this necessarily having any special consequences for the quantity of means of payment in circulation, or for the factors determining the price level for consumers' goods.

The situation is different when the supply of gold can be increased by productive measures, for instance by mining operations. The productive forces employed in gold production will not bring any increase in the supply of consumption goods, either now or in the future. But nevertheless they will be drawing incomes which, if they are not saved, will increase the demand for consumers' goods. The result will thus be a tendency for prices to rise, in the first instance those of consumers' goods, but later also those of productive services and of capital goods. This price rise is associated with the larger note circulation; in contrast to the previous case, the net advances of the banks to the public are not diminished as fast as new notes are issued in return for gold. (The note circulation, however, does not necessarily increase by the same amount as the gold reserve, nor need there be complete proportionality between the increase in the quantity of notes and the rise in the price level.)

These tendencies may be counteracted in two ways: by raising interest rates or by means of income taxes.

As we have already explained, the primary effect of a *raised interest rate* is that the prices of capital goods will fall, and their production will thus be less profitable than before. There will therefore be a tendency to transfer factors to the industries producing consumers' goods. This tendency will be strengthened if the prices of consumers' goods are supported by an increased demand from gold producers, occasioned for example by the discovery of a new gold mine. To this extent the situation is similar to that which arises when an increase in productivity in some capital producing industries is met by raising interest rates (see above chap. IV, sec. 4). But there is this difference between the two cases, namely, that increased productivity in capital production normally increases the supply of consumers' goods in the future,

240

but this will not occur when the factors are producing gold.

In another respect also the situation differs from that already described. Higher interest rates, while depressing the prices of capital goods, cannot influence the price of gold. From the point of view of the producers the gold thus has the character of a consumption or final good, in the sense that its price is determined immediately in the present, without reference to any future prices (including interest rates). But further, in comparison with true consumers' goods, gold has a peculiar position in a gold standard system, since its monetary price is fixed, whereas the prices of other goods may rise or fall in consequence of a change in interest rates. The link here is that these higher rates exert pressure on the prices of the services of factors. In industries that do not require much capital, and where this reduction in costs is of greater importance than the higher interest charges, output will expand, with the result that prices will fall. On the other hand, output will contract in industries with more capitalistic methods of production, where these higher interest charges are more important than the lower prices of factors. In this case the prices of products will therefore rise. In both cases the price movements will counteract the original shift in profits. It is in this latter respect that the production of gold occupies a special position. In it profits are primarily affected in the same way as in the production of true consumption goods, but the shift in prices which in other cases is a counteracting factor is absent.

From this the interesting conclusion may be drawn that changes in interest rates have more accentuated effects on gold production than they have on that of consumption goods. If methods of production for gold were less capitalistic in nature—if, for example, gold was obtained by placer mining—a rise in the interest level would cause

241

a stronger tendency to expansion than in other similar cases, where the lower prices counteract the increase in profitability. For more realistic conditions, when the production of gold takes place principally by ordinary mining operations and therefore is markedly capitalistic in nature, it may in a similar way be expected that raising the interest rate will have a more contractionary effect on production than in analogous cases, when it is counteracted by the increase in the prices of the products.*

If alternatively an increase in the gold reserve is financed by *taxation*, either the tax burden will be increased or other public expenditure will be reduced. In either case the result will be a fall in consumption, although this will probably not be so great as the demand of the gold producers for consumers' goods. For higher taxes will probably to some extent reduce saving, and the reduction of public expenditure will probably not reduce total

* This last conclusion has practical consequences. But the former case, although not of current importance, is very interesting from the theoretical viewpoint. If one starts from a community with a gold standard, requiring comparatively little capital for producing gold, *higher interest rates* will mean that more factors than before will be absorbed in the production of gold. The result of this will be an increased demand for and a diminished supply of consumers' goods and this will give rise to a tendency towards *higher prices*. The limitation of consumption in other quarters required for financing the extraction of gold, can thus be greater at a higher than at a lower level of interest rates, while the need for saving for investment in true capital goods is always less when interest rates are higher. The consequence for the regulation of the price level will therefore be that the interest rate must be further increased, and to such an extent that the limitation of consumption in other quarters will be sufficient to counteract the greater consumption on the part of the producers of gold. This strange state of affairs is due to the circumstance mentioned above, that gold appears as a consumers' good from the standpoint of the producers, while monetary gold from the standpoint of society as a whole, and of the Central Bank, has rather the character of a capital investment, non-interest bearing but nevertheless necessary for regulating the price level under a gold standard.

consumption by the same amount. Hence in this case also some small increase in interest rates will probably be required in order to maintain the constancy of the price level.

This method differs from that previously discussed in that saving is increased by compulsory means, and consequently the formation of real capital does not have to be reduced to the same extent as the gold reserve is increased. Furthermore, the price level may be regulated as desired at a lower level of interest rates than in the former case. The first of these differences is of great importance from other points of view, but from the standpoint of the pure theory of money the latter is more important.

These appear to be the most important complications in price development in a closed community that arise with a gold standard.

(iv) *Complications due to International Relations*

The assumption of a closed community, on which the analysis is based, naturally entails a considerable limitation in its applicability to real conditions. Not only have the special international problems been completely neglected in this study, but further the national pricing problem appears in a somewhat different light when the more realistic assumption is made that the community has relations with other countries. Hence from this point of view also our analysis requires modification.

The problems now touched upon, however, are so involved that they would demand a special study, and considerations of space prohibit even a brief suggestion of its main lines here.* The foregoing analysis must therefore be regarded as a theoretical study preparatory to a

* [In the Swedish book this matter is treated at considerable length.]

more realistic treatment of the question of the importance of interest rates for price development. This limitation of its practical application is naturally a defect, which, however, it shares with a considerable portion of what is currently written on the subject of economic theory.

CHAPTER VI

WICKSELL'S CONCEPT OF A "NORMAL RATE OF INTEREST"

1. THE THREE CHARACTERISTICS OF THE "NORMAL RATE OF INTEREST ON LOANS"

The foregoing analysis is in the main based on Knut Wicksell's* pioneer work. Wicksell's theory of the relation between the rate of interest and the price level starts from the position that changes not only of relative prices but of the price level as a whole, can be explained in terms of the relationship between the demand for and the supply of goods.† A similar point of view can be traced in many modern theories, even where the writers have not come directly under the influence of Wicksell.

There is, however, a formal difference between the approach given here and that of Wicksell, in that we do not employ the concept of "the normal rate of interest on loans" which plays such an important part in Wicksellian theory. This calls for explanation. If the concept could be considered to have a clear and precise content, it would undoubtedly be an instrument of great service

---

* *Interest and Prices* (first published in German, 1898, under the title *Geldzins und Güterpreise*) and *Lectures on Political Economy*, vol. ii (first Swedish edition 1906).

† "Every rise or fall in the price of a particular commodity presupposes a disturbance of the equilibrium between the supply of and the demand for that commodity, whether the disturbance has actually taken place or is merely prospective. What is true in this respect of each commodity separately must doubtless be true of all commodities collectively. A general rise in prices is therefore only conceivable on the supposition that the general demand has for some reason become, or is expected to become, greater than the supply." *Lectures*, vol. ii, p. 159.

in the analysis of changes in the price level. In the following we shall therefore start from Wicksell's own definition, in order to analyse more exactly whether the concept "normal rate of interest" can be defined so that it becomes of scientific value.

According to Wicksell, the "normal" rate has three characteristics: (1) it corresponds to the *natural* or—as it was later called—the *real rate of interest*; (2) it establishes *equilibrium between the demand for and the supply of saving*; and (3) it is *neutral in relation to the price level*—whereas a rate of interest above or below "normal" will influence the price level in a downward or upward direction.*

We shall try to maintain that the two first characteristics have under realistic assumptions broadly the same content as the third, and that the normal rate of interest may thus simply be defined as that which is neutral in relation to the price level. We shall then add a few reflections on the significance of the concept.†

* "There is a certain rate of interest on loans which is neutral in respect to commodity prices, and tends neither to raise nor to lower them. This is necessarily the same as the rate of interest which would be determined by supply and demand if no use were made of money and all lending were effected in the form of real capital goods. It comes to much the same thing to describe it as the current value of the *natural rate of interest on capital*." *Interest and Prices*, p. 102.

"At any moment and in every economic situation there is a certain level of the average rate of interest on loans which is such that the general level of prices has no tendency to move either upwards or downwards. This we call the *normal* rate of interest. Its magnitude is determined by the current level of the natural rate of interest on capital, and rises and falls with it." *Interest and Prices*, p. 120.

"That loan rate, which is a direct expression of the real rate, we call the normal rate. . . . The rate of interest at which *the demand for loan capital and the supply of savings* exactly agree, and which more or less corresponds to the expected yield on the newly created capital, will then be the normal rate." *Lectures*, vol. ii, pp. 192–3.

† [The contents of this and the following sections have been allowed to stand as originally written in 1929, although the views of the author have since been modified in certain respects, concerning which the reader is referred to the additional note at the end of the chapter.]

2. The Natural or Real Rate of Interest

In general the real rate of interest cannot be determined independently, but only as the rate which preserves equilibrium between the demand for and the supply of saving.

Only under very special assumptions is it possible to conceive of a natural or real rate of interest determined purely by technical considerations, and thus independent of the price system. For this to be true it must be supposed that the productive process consists only in investing units of goods or services of the same type as the final product, the latter increasing with the passage of time alone without the co-operation of other scarce factors.* In these circumstances the real rate of interest on capital can be expressed as the relation between the quantity of matured units of product and the quantity previously invested, this relation being reckoned for the same time unit as the rate of interest itself. This holds true, even if the percentage increase in value per unit of time varies with the length of the investment period. In these circumstances the most profitable investment period will always be adopted.† With free competition the loan rate of interest must always correspond to this real rate of interest, based on technical conditions.‡ If we abstract

* A possible illustration would be a scarce agricultural product, sown on free land with help of free labour. The cost of production would then consist only in the seed and in the interest thereon.

† Even if saving changes in different periods, the technically most profitable process would generally be applied, though some disturbances may arise in the process of adapting the supply of consumption goods to the demand in each period.

‡ It is here assumed, that this maximum rate is obtained in all lines, even if investment periods differ. If this condition is satisfied, the production of goods of different types will not alter the reasoning. If, however, the situation is such that the real rate of interest in one branch of production is greater than in another, a stationary equilibrium is not conceivable. It must then be supposed,

from the risk element implicit in both lending and real investment, and suppose that all loans are given and paid for in kind, the loan rate cannot be higher than the real rate, since this would check all real investment. Nor can it be below it, since than no lending would take place.

Under more realistic assumptions it is not possible to measure the investment and the product in the same real unit. To compare services invested and the resulting products, they must be expressed in a common unit which presupposes that the price relation is given. Then the real rate of interest does not depend only on technical conditions, but also on the price situation, and cannot be regarded as existing independently of the loan rate of interest.

On the contrary, the actual loan rate of interest is of direct importance for the price relations that are relevant to the real rate of interest on capital. The real interest factor in a certain period can be expressed as the relation between anticipated future product values (with appropriate reductions for risk) and the values invested during the period. The prices of invested services are, however, influenced by the demands of entrepreneurs, and these in turn are influenced by the loan rate of interest itself. When this rate is low, the demand for services to be invested in the production of real capital rises, and their price therefore rises to the point where the invested values may be supposed to bear interest at the current loan rate. Conversely, a high loan rate of interest brings with it a pressure on the prices of all services invested during the period, so that the actual remunerativeness will also, under the circumstances, correspond to the

that the price of the former commodity gradually declines in relation to that of the latter until the real return in both lines of investment becomes equal. But we can then no longer speak of a real rate of interest, determined by purely technical conditions.

rate of interest on loans. We accordingly find that the real rate of interest on capital, as here defined, has a tendency to adjust itself to the actual loan rate of interest in every period. Agreement between the real rate and the loan rate in a certain period, therefore provides no foundation for characterizing the latter as "normal."

When it has been attempted, in capital theory analysis, to show the manner in which the rate of interest on real capital is determined by certain factors, this rate has in fact been identified with the rate of interest on loans, and has had reference to that interest situation which under the existing conditions, secures equilibrium of the price system. The concept of the real rate of interest has then been taken in a meaning different from that iust defined, namely as the rate of interest on loans which emerges as a result of the pricing process, when equilibrium between the different factors, above all between the demand for and the supply of saving, has been attained. We have therefore reached the second definition of the concept "normal rate of interest," given by Wicksell. Our next task will be to analyse its meaning.

3. The Equilibrium Rate of Interest for Saving and Investment

When a "normal rate of interest" is said to bring about equilibrium between demand and supply with respect to saving, it is implied that it does not set in motion any tendency towards a shift in the price level.

The net demand for saving from producers during a certain period can be measured by that part of total net output which consists of an increase in capital equipment. Again, the net supply of saving in a certain period is the amount by which the incomes of consumers exceed their consumption.* Our problem is whether a particular rate of interest is necessary to bring about equilibrium between these two factors. Equilibrium between the demand for and the supply of saving evidently implies equilibrium in respect to the demand and supply of consumption goods during the period.

In a community where the future was perfectly foreseen by all, a certain loan rate of interest in each period must be demanded under given conditions in other respects, if the system is to be consistent. If a change in this rate is imagined, the simultaneous equations by which the equilibrium in the system can be expressed will no longer be applicable, and equilibrium must therefore be destroyed. Under the assumption of perfect foresight, therefore, no objection can be made from the logical point of view against the definition of the normal rate of interest as the rate which secures equilibrium between the demand for and the supply of saving. Since this rate must also be neutral in relation to the price level, Wicksell's definition is thus valid in this connection.

The same will be true even if the future is imperfectly foreseen, if there is complete mobility in the community. If for the moment we neglect the complications arising from the various types of interest rate differentiation, it follows from this atomistic premiss that, other circumstances remaining unchanged, the rate of interest must have a particular level if equilibrium is to be maintained.

[* It should be observed that in both cases it is a question of the amounts *planned* by producers and consumers. The "unintentional" part of saving and investment that brings about equality in a retrospective calculation should thus not be included. Using the newer and more precise terminology of Part I, we may substitute "net investment *ex ante*" for "net demand for saving" and "net saving *ex ante*" for "net supply of saving." Although it is not explicitly stated, all terms of this type used in the present study refer to prospective magnitudes].

If this level is disturbed, the process of production will instantly assume a different orientation, and the discrepancy between the demand and supply of consumption goods thus brought about would be accompanied by such an avalanche of price level movements that no equilibrium could be established between the factors determining prices, even for very short periods.*

The matter is quite different under the frictional conditions of the real world. The interest level in any period may then vary within certain limits without immediately disturbing the equilibrium of the price system. The price level may, it is true, have a tendency to move in one direction or the other, but owing to frictions it does not find expression in the period under observation. It should further be noted that when the tendency towards a shift in the price level comes into effect, the shift takes place only gradually and in such a manner that the supply of saving in each period adjusts itself to the needs of production at the interest level in question.† In reality, therefore, a loan rate of interest that gives rise to a shift in the price level, will literally fulfil Wicksell's requirement for a "normal" rate of interest, namely that of securing equilibrium between the demand and supply of saving, if a short period is taken into consideration. What is intended by the definition in question is naturally that the equilibrium will be attained without the necessity for any shift in the price level such as would alter the distribution of incomes, and thence the supply of saving, and even without any tendency towards such a shift arising from the interest level itself. But fundamentally this is equivalent to the statement that the rate of interest is neutral in respect of the price level.

* Cf. above chap. II, sec. 4.   † Cf. above chap. II, sec. 5.

4. The Neutral Rate of Interest

A *neutral* rate of interest does not necessarily imply an unchanged price level, but rather such a development of prices as is in accordance with the expectations of the public, so far as this is possible.

In a community with perfect foresight, the height of the loan rate of interest depends on the anticipated course of prices. As we have already demonstrated, the price level may vary in any manner (complications arising through cash holding being neglected), if only the rate of interest for each period is adjusted so as fully to compensate for changes in the value of money. No other rate of interest can maintain the system in equilibrium and cannot, therefore, be defined as "normal" in the Wicksellian sense.

Even under real conditions, when the community is dependent on guesses as to future conditions, the normal rate of interest must be calculated with due regard to the course of prices which is believed to be most probable. For example a 5 per cent rate of interest may be normal if the community expects an unaltered price level in the future, but a 7 per cent would in that case be normal, if the price level were expected to rise at the rate of 2 per cent per year. In such circumstances a 5 per cent rate would be subnormal since it would occasion a sharper price rise than the community expected. A rate of interest that is normal in relation to a certain foreseen course of prices would thus be abnormal in relation to other anticipated developments, even if in other respects the conditions in which it influenced the demand for and the supply of saving were unaltered.

This definition of the concept "normal rate of interest" presents certain difficulties. Under actual conditions, expectations regarding future conditions do not everywhere coincide. It is therefore impossible to speak of a generally anticipated future course of prices. The price development to which the loan rate is to be related must thus be conceived as a sort of average of different individual expectations of future prices.

Since a certain amount of arbitrariness can hardly be avoided in a construction of this kind, the concept "normal rate of interest" has some corresponding arbitrariness. This brings to light a certain imperfection in the concept. But it can hardly be eliminated by any other interpretation of its meaning.

If for instance the notion "normal rate of interest" is defined as the loan rate which is accompanied by an unchanged price level, whatever the character of the expectations of the public—the usually accepted meaning of the term—it may be objected that this definition is not an adequate formulation of the basic train of thought. This is most clearly apparent from the fact that it is impossible to retain this definition if it is assumed that the future is perfectly foreseen by all. For, as has just been said, no other rate of interest is then *conceivable* than that which has been modified in accordance with the anticipations of the public regarding price developments. Under more realistic assumptions it may naturally be conceived that even if the public believes in a shift in the price level, the result of a certain interest rate level will be unchanged prices. But in that case the rate of interest has exercised *pressure* on the price level in the opposite direction from that in which it has been affected by the anticipations of the public.* The effects of such an interest policy are in important respects similar in nature to cases where a high or low rate of interest has resulted in a divergence between anticipated and actual developments : at the same time as

* It is assumed here that interest rate policy does not cause any change in the opinion of the public as to the future price level. If the public first believes that the price level will change, but afterwards, as a result of the interest policy of the monetary authority, realizes that the price level will remain unchanged, then the rate of interest in question will be "normal," whichever interpretation of the concept is used.

the orientation of production and its requirements of saving are changed, the distribution of income is modified, so that the supply of saving corresponds to the demand and the equilibrium of the capital market is maintained. It can scarcely be said of such a rate of interest that it is "neutral" in relation to the price level.

A more acceptable method of making the concept "normal rate of interest" independent of the anticipations of the public would be to define it as the interest rate, not on loans in an ordinary currency, but on loans in an unchanged money value. We should then have to deal with a loan rate of interest, which gives no compensation for anticipated changes in the value of money, and which, therefore, would appear to be "normal," *if* the public counted on a stable currency in the future, or *if* the repayment of loans were to take place according to a certain index of changes in the value of money. But even this definition is not quite unimpeachable. In the first place it depends upon the concept "unchanged value of money," concerning the meaning of which opinions differ; the meaning of the concept "normal loan rate of interest" will vary with these opinions. Further, the problem still remains, how, starting from this imagined normal level it will be possible to arrive at the loan rate of interest that will be "normal" under the conditions actually prevailing. If this problem is given up as insoluble, there is practically no place for the concept "normal loan rate of interest" in the treatment of problems of monetary policy. For here it is necessary, at least in the last stages of analysis, to start from assumptions which correspond to real conditions.

We find, therefore, that our definition of the term "normal loan rate of interest" though it is no doubt imperfect, but is nevertheless the best attainable, if the notion is to be used at all in the analysis of the theory of money. Starting with this definition, we shall therefore take up for discussion one or two questions, the disputed nature of which has in all probability been due to vagueness about what is meant by a "normal loan rate of interest."

The first question is concerned with the nature of the development of prices when productivity changes, but the interest rate on loans is kept at the "normal" level. The answer is, of course, that it will depend on the anticipations of the public. If the price level is expected to remain constant, in spite of altered productivity, and the public acts in accordance with this view, the rate of interest on loans which leaves the price level unchanged must be characterized as "normal" according to the definition given here. Again, if it is generally believed that the price level will vary in some other way, for instance in inverse proportion to productivity, then this development of prices will take place at a different interest level, which under the conditions must be regarded as "normal."

The same answer must be given to the other question, whether a "normal loan rate of interest" prevents a rise in prices, if government expenditures are partly covered by the issue of new notes, or, with a gold standard, if the production of gold rises in a higher degree than the requirements of the circulation. The tendency towards a rise in prices in these cases is due to the fact that the total demand for saving is increased in relation to the supply. If the loan rate of interest is raised to meet these conditions, the equilibrium of the capital market can be maintained without the necessity for any change in the price level that has not previously appeared probable. Such an interest level must therefore be called "normal" in the sense used here. The retention of the loan rate of interest at the level that would be "normal," if there were no extra demands for saving, would bring with it a rise in prices of the same general character, as occurs when a reduction in saving has come about for some other reason.*

* Starting from another definition of the "normal rate of interest" than that put forth above, a rise in prices of the type referred to here, which is a direct result of the increase in the quantity of money, has

255

Finally, it should be noted that in carrying out a certain monetary policy the requirement that the rate of interest shall always be "normal" in the sense defined here cannot always be fulfilled. In certain cases the aim is best attained by making use of a rate of interest above

sometimes been called "direct inflation," as contrasted with a rise in prices caused by a "subnormal" interest rate, called "indirect inflation." Common to these types of inflation would be the fact that their causes were to be sought on the "monetary side," in contrast to other price rises, the causes of which are to be found on the "commodity side." By analogy, "direct deflation" would occur when a fall in prices is brought about by fiscal policy, and "indirect deflation" when it has been caused by a rate of interest above "normal." On the other hand, a fall in prices due to increased supplies of commodities would not be deflationary in character at all.—If the definition of the concept "normal loan rate of interest" given in the text is accepted, it will no longer be possible to maintain these distinctions, at least not in the same way. For then what have been called "direct inflation" and "direct deflation" must also be regarded as determined by the deviation of the loan rate from its normal level. We have thus no clear dividing-line between the "direct" and the "indirect" types of inflation and deflation. (A similar view was maintained by B. Ohlin and G. Åkerman in papers in the *Ekonomisk Tidskrift* in 1921. Cf. the discussions in the same journal in 1921 and 1922 arising out of Åkerman's paper.)—Nor can the boundary between "inflation" and "deflation" on the one hand, and other changes in the price level on the other, be drawn in the manner suggested. For in reality every price movement depends on a change in factors lying both on the demand and on the supply side, accordingly both on the monetary and on the commodity side. If, for example, the primary reason for the shift in the price level is a reduction of the interest rate, this will cause both an increased demand for and a smaller supply of consumers' goods. And if the primary event is a reduction in productivity, this will bring with it not only a reduced supply of goods but probably also some modification in consumers' demand. Hence it would seem to be hopeless to attempt to give precision to the notions of "inflation" and "deflation" by starting from the actual *causes* of price movements, the clarification of which as a rule entails considerable difficulty. (From this starting point, if the views expressed above in the text are applied, a distinction would appear between changes in the price level that are in accordance with the expectations of individuals, and others determined by the deviation of the interest rate from its

256

or below normal. The proof of this statement will be regarded as having been given in our exposition of the adoption of varying monetary policies under different assumptions. From this investigation it appears that if the expectations of the public do not conform to the objective of monetary policy, its realization generally requires interest levels that are not neutral in relation to the price level. But if the objective has been accepted by the public with full confidence, the rate of interest should broadly be maintained at the "normal" level. It should, however, be observed that this statement is not a complete characterization of a rational monetary policy. This would also entail a detailed differentiation of the loan rate of interest, and sometimes additional supplementary measures, for instance the use of fiscal policy to secure a direct control of saving.

5. Differentiation of Interest Rates

The "normal rate of interest," as we have defined the concept, should not be regarded as a uniform rate but as a combination of different rates for different types of loans. Its composition may vary with regard to the duration of loans and in other respects. Hence the concept is not uniquely determined.

normal level. But this distinction is not directly relevant to the concepts "inflation" and "deflation.")—The definition of these concepts becomes less questionable if it is founded on a comparison between the actual price movements and some ideal standard. For example, every divergence, upwards or downwards, of the actual course of prices from the development that would have taken place if the price level were regulated in inverse proportion to productivity, might be called "inflation" or "deflation." But such a definition would manifestly have a purely conventional meaning, and its applicability is therefore questionable from many points of view. To avoid unnecessary misunderstandings and fruitless controversy we have taken care not to use the terms in this book.

In a stationary economy, rates for long and short term loans must coincide, if we disregard possible deviation due to differences in risk and in cost of administration. But in other respects, especially with regard to loan and deposit rates, and rates for various types of loans, there may be many alternative possibilities of differentiation, which will not entail any disturbance in a stationary economy. Under given conditions, therefore, many different combinations of rates may be conceived, with various average heights, all of them "normal" in the sense that they keep the system in equilibrium.

Under dynamic conditions there may be a differentiation in rates with respect to the duration of loans. If the future were perfectly foreseen, only one single combination for short and long rates in each period would maintain equilibrium. That is to say, the long term rate of interest must be adapted to the expected short term rates in such a manner that the total cost of a long term loan would be the same as that of a series of short term loans at varying rates of interest, for the same period.

In reality the public cannot completely foresee future short term rates, and the Central Bank has therefore within certain limits the power of controlling the long term rate for each period. It is thus possible to imagine *a number of combinations of long and short term rates which will all be neutral* in respect of the price level, during a certain period. A rise in the short term rate of interest may for instance be compensated by a lower long term rate and *vice versa*.

The height of the long term rate in one period may, it is true, influence the orientation of production for the future, and in consequence also the need for saving during coming periods. If the long term rates in a certain period have been too high or too low, it becomes difficult to maintain equilibrium during future periods. Of the

258

many possible combinations of short and long rates which in a certain period have no immediate effects on the price level, the one that makes it possible to maintain a stable price level, with the smallest possible variation in interest rates during future periods, has some claims to be regarded as most "normal." A further ground for calling this rate normal *par excellence* would be that it ought to lead to the greatest possible agreement between the long term rate for one period and a corresponding succession of short term rates (it is only with perfect foresight that complete agreement is possible).

This interpretation of the concept, however, suffers from the weakness that it is only possible to judge whether the rate for a certain period was normal or not after a considerable lapse of time. Strictly speaking it would be necessary to analyse economic conditions over a considerable stretch in order to be able to state how long and short term rates should be combined in each period in order to maintain equilibrium with rates as stable as possible. Obviously the concept "normal rate" has here been given a more specific interpretation than in Wicksell's definition. If we retain the latter, it must be remembered, that under actual conditions the concept is indeterminate within certain limits, since it will not solve the important problem of rate differentiation.

6. CONCLUDING REMARKS

Our present analysis will probably be found to be a satisfactory account of the reasons why we have avoided the use of the term "normal rate of interest" in our exposition. We have as a matter of fact shown that the common interpretation of the term is somewhat confused, since the completion of the train of thought that has led to this concept entails consequences that are not in agreement with the ordinary sense in which the concept is used. It has also been made clear that the content of the concept is rather vague, since it may include varying combinations of interest rates. And finally, the suitability of the term itself may be called in question, since it is open to a rational monetary policy to apply rates of interest other than those that are "normal" in our present sense.

In an explanation of the causal determination of prices and of the rational means for attaining a given monetary aim, we may confine ourselves to showing that different interest levels, determined in respect of their *average height* and their *differentiation,* lead to different developments of the price level, when other conditions remain unaltered. For this analysis it is not necessary to denote any of these interest levels by the term "normal."

7. ADDITIONAL NOTE (1939)

The foregoing study was devoted to the question whether it is possible in every particular case to determine some definite loan rate of interest, or some definite combination of loan rates of interest, which would be regarded as being "normal" in any definite sense. We were led to conclude that considerable difficulties are encountered as soon as we drop the assumption of simple stationary conditions on which the older theory was based. I am still inclined to uphold this conclusion, and I also believe that the arguments adduced above in its support are broadly correct when judged from the methodological standpoint maintained throughout the study (see sec. 8 of chap. I above). But now, after ten years, I am inclined to think that this method led to a certain limitation of the scope of the argument. I still believe that to regard a dynamic process as consisting of a series of successive positions of equilibrium is a method that can frequently be defended as a suitable approximation, and that it can lead to interesting results even when it is applied to a study of the more complicated processes met with in real life. But the alternative method, by which economic processes are regarded as series of successive disequilibria, must undoubtedly be held to be more generally applicable, for reasons set forth in the first part of this book. The distinction made by this method between estimates *ex ante* and *ex post* opens up the possibility of a more detailed treatment of some of the concepts associated with the problem of the normal loan rate of interest. For this reason I now wish to modify somewhat the exposition given above in order to attain greater generality of treatment. A few words may also be added to clarify one or two other points.

(i) With regard to the *natural or real rate of interest*, the question still remains how this concept is to be applied with the least risk of misunderstanding. Wicksell's own view and his use of the term seem gradually to have changed somewhat, as is apparent from a comparison between his earlier and later works. In *Interest and Prices* he speaks of the natural rate as that which would prevail if loan transactions were made in kind, but in his *Lectures* he abandoned this somewhat doubtful* construction. Instead he connects the real rate of interest with the profits of capitalists, received in the form of money. The real rate thus becomes the same as the profit rate, and is broadly parallel to Professor Irving Fisher's "rate of return over cost" and Mr. Keynes' "marginal efficiency of capital." These later expressions seem to be an improvement on Wicksell's, since the expression "real rate" is sometimes used with an entirely different meaning—as the rate that would apply if the value of money were unchanged. The terms money rate and real rate are then analogous in use to the expressions money wages and real wages.

The real rate of interest in the sense of the prospective profit rate will vary in practice not only from firm to firm but also for different investments within the same firm.

* For a critical appraisal, see G. Myrdal, "Der Gleichgewichts-begriff," etc., in *Beiträge zur Geldtheorie*, ed. by Hayek, pp. 391 ff. Cf. also P. N. Rosenstein-Rodan, "The Co-ordination of the General Theories of Money and Price," *Economica*, 1936, pp. 257 ff., where an acute analysis is given of the notions of "barter economy," "monetary economy" and "neutral money."

This complex of rates, which can be visualized by means of an investment schedule having reference either to the gross or to the net amounts, will indeed have been influenced in various ways by the loan rate in preceding periods, but it can nevertheless be regarded as independent of the loan rate during the current period. The exposition given above should be modified accordingly. However, the conclusion remains that it is impossible on the basis of this investment schedule alone to single out any definite real rate as having a decisive influence on the loan rate.* What can be inferred is only how great the *demand* in the capital market will be at different interest levels. But if the *supply* side is not known, nothing can be said about what rate of interest is normal. The only reasonable meaning of the demand that the loan rate should agree with the real rate of interest on capital, therefore, is that it should bring about equilibrium between demand and supply on the capital market. Now these factors can be determined in different ways, but if the net amounts are considered in both cases, the equilibrium should have reference to the planned net investment and the planned net saving.

(ii) There seems to be no doubt that Wicksell's later conception of the *equilibrium rate* as one which equalizes *saving and investment ex ante* is fundamental for his entire conception of the normal loan rate.† That Wicksell him-

* From this point of view Myrdal's exposition in the work just cited is open to criticism. Myrdal treats the profit rate (*Ertragsquote des Kapitals*) as an independent factor determining the normal loan rate of interest, and even attempts to prove that agreement between the profit rate and the loan rate in certain circumstances means that saving and investment are equal. (An examination of the argument reveals that the latter equality arises through the assumptions introduced, and is thus independent of the former one.)

† The following passage concerning this point may be cited from a paper by Dr. Dag Hammarskjöld in the *Ekonomisk Tidskrift*, 1932, pp. 172–3: "To Wicksell, the normal rate must have appeared as being among other things an ordinary equilibrium price, which could be determined graphically as the point of intersection between the curves for the supply and demand for loan capital at a given moment of price formation. The demand curve, judging from Wicksell's general theoretical starting-point, would have been conceived by him

self was thinking of the amounts planned, and not of those calculated after the event (the latter, on the ordinary definitions, being always necessarily equal in a closed community), is also evident from some of his own statements.*

If an attempt is made to make this concept more precise, certain difficulties are encountered. Numerous combinations of interest rates of various kinds may be conceived in a given situation, all of which bring about equality between investment and saving *ex ante* for a fairly short period ahead. This is of great importance in dealing with different combinations of short term and long term rates. The latter are based on assumptions regarding the short rates in future periods, and a definite combination of this kind can therefore be regarded also as a programme for future interest policy. The question then arises what relations this interest programme will bring about between saving and investment in future periods. One then arrives at the distinction between those combinations of interest rates which bring about equilibrium only for a relatively short time, and those which result in equilibrium for a fairly long period. With regard to the latter a new distinction must be applied, as suggested in the last sentence. In judging how the interest level in the long run will

more or less as a line, with every interest rate on the price axis corresponding to a point on the quantity axis at which the *marginal* investment had a degree of remunerativeness equal to the interest rate in question. When looked at in this way, the question of the relation between the interest rate that brings equilibrium on the capital market and the remunerativeness of investment disappears; the latter factor is not on the same level as the former as a determining factor for the normal rate, and still less can the capital market condition be deduced from the condition of remunerativeness. The importance of the latter for the determination of the rate of interest is limited to deciding the form of the demand curve. Typically enough the condition of remunerativeness, seen marginally, is fulfilled wherever the point of intersection between the two curves may lie, i.e. whatever rate of interest may be normal from the point of view of the capital market."

* Cf. the following passage in the *Lectures*, vol. ii, p. 192: "The accumulation of capital consists in the *decision* of savers to abstain from the consumption of a part of their income in the immediate future."

adjust itself to the plans for saving and investment, so that equality is established between them, one may either start from the plans *existing* at the time in question, although they are not final but may be modified because of later events, or else one may attempt to form an opinion how the plans will be *altered* before they are applied, and what development of interest rates therefore will actually make saving and investment *ex ante* equal for a long period ahead. If we may use the terms "uncorrected" and "corrected" for these two types of equilibrium rates, we can thus, for every given short period of time, distinguish between the following three kinds of equilibrium between saving and investment *ex ante*: (*a*) short term, (*b*) uncorrected long term, and (*c*) corrected long term equilibrium.

(iii) Finally, the concept of the *neutral rate of interest* may also be regarded as an equilibrium rate, although in this case we are mainly dealing with relations other than that holding between saving and investment. In determining the meaning of this concept, it is easy to dispose of the interest levels that are not neutral in important respects, namely those that give rise to cumulative processes as described above. The positive delimitation of the concept is more difficult, and the difficulties vary with the character of the positions taken as starting-points. We shall now consider a few of the more important typical cases.

(1) In a stationary economy with full employment, certain definite combinations of interest rates (which, however, do not admit of variation with regard to long and short rates) are as a rule required if stationary conditions are to be maintained. It is of course legitimate to call such combinations neutral.

It is an interesting question whether such a neutral rate is identical with the equilibrium rate for saving and investment which we have just been describing. In my opinion, this is not necessarily so. As has already been shown in the present work,* divergence between saving and investment *ex ante*, disregarding international complications, only means that the sum total of sales for all entrepreneurs will be larger or smaller than they have

* See above, p. 127.

264

anticipated. Now it is naturally possible to assume, even in stationary conditions, that the future is not perfectly foreseen, but that the entrepreneurs, even though the situation has remained the same for some time, either hope that it will be improved or are apprehensive that it will deteriorate. These optimistic or pessimistic expectations will themselves be the basis for the actions giving rise to the stationary state.* This can only mean that with the prevailing neutral interest rate saving and investment *ex ante* will *not* be equal.

Such a divergence between these two interest rates, which is thus possible even under stationary conditions, when there is an optimistic or pessimistic bias in the expectations of entrepreneurs, can naturally make itself felt still more under dynamic conditions. On the one hand, for the reasons mentioned it is not necessary for equality between saving and investment *ex ante* to be brought about by a neutral state of equilibrium. Nor, on the other hand, is equality between these two prospective magnitudes sufficient to enable us to characterize the interest situation as neutral. Equality between saving and investment *ex ante* only means that the total value of the actual transactions corresponds to the total value of the expectations of all sellers. But even if that is the case, there may be differences, positive on one side and negative on the other, between realized and expected selling values, differences that may be characterized as disturbances incompatible with the concept of a neutral rate of interest.

(2) Again, if we have a stationary economy with unemployed resources, the level of interest rates that conserves this state can in a sense be called neutral. If we conceive a series of such economies, all of them similar except that the volume of unemployment differs, we thus obtain a series of such neutral interest rates, which in general fall as unemployment decreases. We owe it to Mr. Keynes that these problems, which are of such great practical importance at the present time, have come to the forefront in current economic literature.†

* Cf. below, p. 287 note.

† Cf. *The General Theory of Employment, Interest and Money*, p. 242, where Mr. Keynes states that previously he had "overlooked the fact

If one starts from such a society it seems appropriate to make a certain distinction with regard to the interest rates that do not meet the requirement of strict neutrality. It may be conceived that a moderate reduction of loan rates below the neutral position might lead to a cumulative expansion with increased employment, but that the higher prices for consumers' goods would be counteracted by the simultaneous increase in the quantity of such goods.* On the other hand, a higher level of interest rates may lead to a movement of contraction at a more or less unchanged price level for consumers' goods. Such interest levels are not completely neutral, but they are fairly neutral in one respect, namely in relation to the price level of consumers' goods. They can therefore be distinguished from the more extreme interest levels which also influence the price level in one direction or the other.†

(3) Finally, if we start from completely dynamic con-

that in any given society there is, on this definition, a *different* natural rate of interest for each hypothetical level of employment. And, similarly, for every rate of interest there is a level of employment for which that rate is the 'natural' rate, in the sense that the system will be in equilibrium with that rate of interest and that level of employment." ("Natural" rate has here the same sense as "neutral" rate in our exposition above. Keynes uses the term "neutral" rate in a more special sense, namely as equivalent to that "optimum" rate which is consistent with *full* employment.)

* Cf. above ch. II, sec. 6.

† In this connection it should be observed that if in certain given conditions such a semi-neutral rate causes a productive expansion and a reduction of unemployment with a relatively unchanged price level for consumers' goods, this interest rate is not necessarily the same as that which would be completely neutral when unemployment has completely disappeared. In certain cases it may be assumed that the latter rate is higher than the former—in other words, that it will be necessary to stop the cumulative movement by raising interest rates when the unemployed resources have been completely absorbed. In other cases, however, it is possible that a reduction of the interest level will be required, when the retarding of the rate of expansion makes it impossible for the entrepreneurs to look forward to further increases of profits. The question must therefore be decided on the basis of the special circumstances present in each concrete case.

266

ditions, the complex of problems already discussed concerning the relation between long and short rates of interest becomes of great importance. In dealing with the concept of a neutral rate of interest we must also distinguish between short term and long term equilibria, and with regard to the latter we must in addition apply the distinction between those positions that are in harmony with the attitudes prevailing at the time in question and those of which it can be said afterwards that they would have been neutral in relation to the price level, or in other respects. With regard to the conditions in relation to which the interest level is to be neutral, we may apply the three terms (*a*) short term equilibrium, (*b*) uncorrected long term equilibrium, and (*c*) corrected long term equilibrium, just as we did when dealing with the relation between saving and investment.

The concept of the neutral rate, however, can be differentiated in a still higher degree, since the neutrality may have reference to different conditions: it can refer both to the price level and to the volume of production, or to one of them only, or to some other stated factor. With regard to rates that are not neutral, it is also possible to distinguish between cases when the movements arising in consequence of the level of interest rates are non-cumulative or cumulative, and in the latter instance between expanding and contracting cumulative movements. In the complex conditions of reality there is thus a very wide group of problems associated with the concept of the neutral rate of interest, and the mere introduction of the concept does not take us very far.

The practical conclusions from this argument are accordingly no different from those given previously, namely that the concept of the normal rate of interest under dynamic conditions is not unambiguous, and therefore should not be used without further explanation. The most important difference between the earlier and the present analysis is that we have now attempted to uphold a distinction between the equilibrium rate for saving and investment *ex ante* and the neutral rate as two independent concepts. Whether the notion of the normal loan rate should refer to the former or the latter is a terminological question of no great fundamental importance. However, considerations of expediency seem to point to the conclusion that, if the concept of the normal rate of interest is to be used at all, it should be associated with some definite interpretation of the concept of the neutral rate.

THE PLACE OF CAPITAL
IN THE THEORY OF PRICE

THE TRADITIONAL SETTING OF THE PRICING PROBLEM

1. INTRODUCTION

The purpose of the theory of price is to investigate the relation between prices and other economic factors under the complicated and varying assumptions that correspond to real conditions. The following exposition is intended as a contribution to the solution of the problem of price formation from a particular point of view. It takes into account some of the complications due to the existence of a *time factor* in production, i.e. to the complex of problems where the theory of capital and interest and the general theory of price meet. It is true that this important aspect of the pricing problem has been investigated in some detail during recent years, but a further analysis still appears necessary in order to bring the theory of price into closer contact with reality.

An analysis of the practical aspect of this difficult problem must naturally for the most part fall outside the scope of the present paper. Our aim is the more modest one of discussing first the method of approach to the problem and secondly certain methodological questions relevant to its solution.

2. THE SITUATION WHEN COMPLICATIONS DUE TO THE TIME FACTOR ARE DISREGARDED

The starting-point for our discussion will be a community where the time factor is assumed to be of no importance, where accordingly neither capital nor interest exists. The study of price formation under these simplified conditions provides a convenient background for an analysis of the complications to which the time factor gives rise.

Since the implications of this assumption are seldom made clear, a few words may first be said on this point.

The assumption of the non-importance of time can hardly be said to mean that production does not require time. For production implies the utilization of productive services for the attainment of certain ends, and since these services, in Irving Fisher's words, are a flow in time, it follows that time must enter as a dimension in the concept of production. "Timeless production" is thus, strictly speaking, impossible. The assumption should therefore be formulated by saying that everything has a time dimension, but that this time factor has no economic relevance.

The content of the assumption is not exhausted by the statement that technical conditions only permit of production for immediate use. Even if the total consumption of a community during a certain period cannot be increased or diminished at the expense of, or in favour of, total consumption during a future period—for this is implicit in our assumption—the relation between the present and the future is of importance, since individuals can themselves exchange present and future income and thus modify their income-streams. The problem of interest on capital accordingly still exists, although in a very simplified form.* We shall return to this case later. If the future

* The statement of the problem will scarcely be improved by combining the assumption in question with the supposition that the price of the time factor, i.e. the rate of interest, is equal to zero. For this zero rate of interest is then a result of certain assumptions as to the factors controlling individual estimates of present and future values: i.e. the relation between the size of present and expected future incomes in comparison to wants (possible under- or over-

has no influence on the economic actions of individuals, these cannot influence the future satisfaction of wants either via production or via exchange. This may be expressed differently by saying that individuals have no ideas as to the future and so only think of satisfying the desires of the moment. This limited outlook should naturally not be stressed too strongly : a certain minimum of thought for the future must necessarily be assumed, if productive co-operation is to be possible. But individual economic plans must be regarded as so short sighted that the relation between the present and the future remains obscure, and there is therefore no process by which the price of the time factor is determined.

Not all the complications due to time can in this way be eliminated. Since the determination of prices involves time, the individual actions that give rise to a certain price level must be assumed to take place before prices are settled. If individuals cannot foresee correctly what price level will be the result of their combined activities, they must base their actions on ideas which are more or less uncertain. Here, evidently, a risk factor enters, giving a dynamic stamp to the pricing problem, even though the economic plans of individuals are assumed to cover only very short periods of time. In order to eliminate such dynamic aspects of the problem due to the time factor, it must therefore *in addition* be assumed that individuals in every concrete instance have such a knowledge of the conditions determining prices that they can let their sales and their demand be governed by the prices that are the result of these conditions. Then all prices within a certain

estimates as to the satisfaction of future wants compared with present ones), and, finally, the complications arising from uncertainty concerning the future. All of these factors are variable, and only in some of the possible combinations will interest disappear. Such a formulation of the problem represents therefore a very special case, and scarcely advances the treatment of the problem.

period will be determined jointly and simultaneously, and the time factor will give rise to no complications. The formation of prices in each period is an independent process, and there is no connection between the prices prevailing during successive periods.

3. Other Simplifying Assumptions

Besides this basic abstraction from the time factor itself we shall make the following simplifying assumptions, which will serve to facilitate our reasoning without modifying the general usefulness of the conclusions in any further degree:

(1) All individuals have full knowledge of all relevant prices during the period in question.*

(2) All entrepreneurs seek to secure the greatest possible surplus of income above expenditure. No entrepreneur, therefore, pays higher wages to his workers or sells his products at lower prices than the market calls for. Consumers are also assumed to aim at securing goods as cheaply as possible.†

(3) Factors of production and products are both completely mobile, i.e. they can immediately and costlessly be transported anywhere within the community. As Myrdal has shown, this premiss, carried to its logical conclusion, also implies complete divisibility, since divisibility can be regarded as mobility between parts of a compound factor of production.‡ Together with the two

* According to our previous assumption, the knowledge of individuals was as great at the beginning of the period as at the end. Here, however, the extent of knowledge is specified. The two assumptions are therefore not identical.

† This assumption eliminates the complications arising from actions due to special motives on the part of particular public or private enterprises, or to preferences on the part of the public for certain producers, to whatever cause they are due.

‡ Gunnar Myrdal, *Prisbildningsproblemet och föränderligheten* (*The Pricing Problem and Change*), Uppsala, 1927, p. 12, note 1.

previous assumptions this "atomistic" premiss implies that at every moment of time there is a uniform price for productive services and goods of any specified type. The community in question, which must naturally be conceived either to be an isolated one or else to embrace the world as a whole, will thus constitute a uniform market.*

(4) Large and small scale production is equally remunerative. This assumption is made in order to facilitate the description of the technical conditions of production. If the prices of factors are given, a certain definite proportion between them will be found by all firms producing the same kind of goods to be the most advantageous. And this will be true whatever the size of firms, since variations of size do not affect returns. The assumption just made is not identical with the premiss of mobility formulated above. It is true that the comparative immobility of factors is an important cause of the greater remunerativeness of large enterprises in comparison with small ones, up to a certain point at least. But even if there is complete mobility, in the sense that both complete productive units and the parts of such a unit can be moved at will and without cost, a particular size of firm may still be the optimum on account of certain technical considerations (which we can disregard at present). When this is the case, it will still be true that all units of a product are produced with the same combination of factors, if all firms are of the optimum size. In most cases, however, there will also be room for a few firms which are not of the optimum size,† for which a different combination of

* We shall therefore neglect the problems generally discussed in the theory of international trade.

† Cf. Bagge, *Arbetslönens reglering genom sammanslutningar* (*The Regulation of Wage Rates through Collective Bargaining*), Stockholm 1917, p. 52, where it is pointed out that when the most advantageous size is large in relation to the scale of production, enterprises that are either too large or too small may continue to exist alongside of the most advantageous units.

factors from that used by the firms of optimum size may be the most economical.* This complication is in many cases unimportant, but nevertheless it makes an exact formulation of the problem more difficult. We have attempted to avoid it by introducing the assumption of constant returns to scale alongside of the atomistic premiss.†

(5) No limitation of supply or demand takes place in order to raise or lower prices. Certain instances of price determination by monopolies, associated with the greater remunerativeness of large enterprises as compared with small ones, have already been ruled out through the assumption of constant returns to scale. Our present assumptions also enables us to neglect other monopolistic manifestations arising from associations or institutional factors.

4. THE EQUATIONS OF WALRAS, CASSEL AND BOWLEY

The process by which the determination of prices takes place under the simplified assumptions just made may

* If the atomistic premiss is dropped, the situation becomes even more complicated. Then the validity of the assertion that a certain combination of factors of production is best for all firms manufacturing a certain product becomes still more questionable. When a certain degree of immobility exists, the various firms are as a rule so differently situated with regard to the substitution of factors, that it would be exceptional for the same minimum unit costs to be attained by firms employing factors in exactly the same proportions. It also follows that the best size is not the same for all firms in a particular line. The contrary would hold unconditionally only if substitution were the same for all firms. When this is not the case, a certain size may be found to be the most economical in any given case. If the types of firms of optimum-size are then compared, it will probably be found that a number of different sizes (usually associated with different combinations of factors) are equally remunerative, owing to the variation in conditions.

† The complication in question might also be avoided through the assumption that the extent of the market for each firm is so great that all enterprises can reach the most advantageous size.

best be elucidated algebraically by a system of simultaneous equations. This is really the problem, more or less simplified in the manner outlined above, which is discussed in most mathematical analyses of the general nature of price determination. In particular, the complications due to the time factor have been neglected in these analyses, and they therefore start from the same fundamental abstraction, which we have endeavoured to make explicit. There is thus no place for the time factor either in Cassel's* or Bowley's† systems of equations—to take two of the best known analyses. A comparison between the two is, as it happens, instructive in showing that Cassel, as easily appears, strictly speaking needs all the simplifying assumptions made above, whereas Bowley, who operates with individual functions and also discusses the determination of monopolistic prices, only needs the first three. The advantage of Bowley's system therefore lies in its greater generality. Cassel's system, on the other hand, gains greatly in simplicity at the expense of its general validity. As the starting-point for our own analysis, which only aims at throwing light on that aspect of the pricing problem which is of interest from the standpoint of the

* *Theory of Social Economy*, pp. 134 ff. Cassel's simplification of the problem is conscious. Particularly in his earlier exposition, he expressly emphasizes the fact that the problem is discussed under the assumption that the factors of production (= raw materials, "Rohstoffe") that are used up in the process of production, are regenerated in the same way as the services of nature (from which it follows that they are not real capital in the narrower sense), and also that production, practically speaking, takes no time,—this in addition to the general stationary presupposition. Cf. "Grundriss einer elementaren Preislehre" in the *Zeitschrift fur die gesammte Staatswissenschaft*, 1899, p. 442.

† Although Bowley disregards the time factor in his equations, he seems to assume that saving takes place in the society. See *The Mathemical Groundwork of Economics*, Oxford 1924, p. 51. This inconsistency was pointed out by Wicksell in *Ekonomisk Tidskrift*, 1925, p. 111.

theory of capital, we may take the simpler system used by Cassel, and which, as is well known, was originally set forth by Walras in his 20th Leçon.* In our description of this system, however, we have found it advisable to use the more elegant terms introduced by Bowley.†

Walras' and Cassel's equations for the determination of prices are expressions of the basic position that if certain conditions are given, (*a*) the supply of services of the various factors of production, (*b*) the demand functions of individuals in respect of the different products, and (*c*) the technical and economic conditions under which the productive services co-operate in the manufacture of the products, then it is possible to determine *inter alia* the prices of all products and productive services. The solution of the problem depends on the following equations: (1) the price of each article is equal to the sum of the prices of the productive services used in its production (the so-called cost principle); and (2) the total supply of productive services is equal to the total quantities used in the production of the goods demanded. The first of these states that the prices of productive services and of products are connected in a certain definite manner. At each of these price combinations there is on the one hand a certain supply of productive services and on the other a certain demand for goods, and thereby indirectly a certain demand for productive services. The second equation states that of these price combinations that one will be realized at which supply and demand will be brought into equilibrium.

* *Elements d'économie politique pure,* 4 éd., Lausanne et Paris, 1900, pp. 208 ff. In the later part of his exposition Walras also takes into account the importance of capital for production. In his 24th Leçon he accordingly sets up a new system of equations into which the interest on capital enters. We shall return to this in the following.

† [As mentioned in the Preface, the Walrasian notation was used in the Swedish original.]

5. Algebraic Discussion

Since we shall refer to these equations in the following analysis, a short account of the Walras-Cassel system may be useful here. With a few modifications we shall follow Walras' own exposition but as already mentioned translate it into the terms used by Bowley.

The problem is to determine the values of the following terms:

$X^1 \ldots X^r \ldots X^m$: total demand for various finished goods and services, m in number;

$P^1 \ldots P^r \ldots P^m$: prices of these goods and services, m in number;

$Y^1 \ldots Y^s \ldots Y^n$: total supply of different productive services, n in number;

$\Pi^1 \ldots \Pi^s \ldots \Pi^n$: prices of these productive services, n in number;

$Y^{sr} \ldots$ that is, the whole quantity of (Y^s) used in the manufacture of (X^r); since s varies from 1 to n and r from 1 to m, there are mn such terms; if Y^{sr} is divided by X^r, we get the quantity of (Y^s) necessary for the production of one unit of (X^r), the so called "technical coefficients."

In solving the problem we have to utilize the data through equations for the supply of services, the demand for goods, the technical coefficients, the costs of production and the amounts of the factors used.

The total supply of the various productive services depends to a certain extent on the general price situation. For each single factor of production the price of its own services is naturally the most important factor. But this price is also influenced by the other productive services which the owners of the factor may have in their possession, and in addition by the prices of finished goods, since the latter prices determine how much of each article demanded, the owners of the factor can in the last resort obtain in compensation for a certain supply. We accordingly obtain the following (n) functions for the *supply of services*:

$$Y^s = F^s \left(\Pi^1, \Pi^2 \ldots \Pi^n; P^1, P^2 \ldots P^m \right) \text{ for } s = 1, 2 \ldots n \quad (1)$$

279

The data for the layout of individual demands can be expressed by functions exhibiting the connection between the total demand for every article and the prices of the various goods *for every given income position.* The income positions are functions both of the various individuals' offers of productive services, and of the prices of these services. The individual offers of productive services, as has been said, are themselves functions of the general price situation. In this manner the total demand for every article can be determined as a function of the general price situation. If the total demand for all articles but *one* is known, then the total demand for this article can also be determined, since it must correspond to the residue of the incomes of individuals after they have satisfied other wants. Since this equality can be derived from the following systems of equations* (see below), it is not included here, and we therefore obtain only $(m - 1)$ functions for the *demand for goods and services,* which may be written in the following manner:

$$X^r = F^r \left(\Pi^1, \Pi^2 \ldots \Pi^n; P^1, P^2 \ldots P^m \right)$$
$$\text{for } r = 2, 3 \ldots m \quad . \quad (2)$$

In order to characterize the technical conditions of production, Walras introduces the term "coefficients de fabrication." The technical coefficients for a certain article are the quantities of the services of the various factors of production required for the manufacture of a unit of the article. The functions determining the sizes of the coefficients for various prices of the factors are regarded as known. The number of these functions for *technical coefficients* is mn and they are written

$$\frac{Y^{sr}}{X^r} = F^{sr} \left(\Pi^1, \Pi^2 \ldots \Pi^n \right) \quad \text{for } \begin{array}{l} s = 1, 2 \ldots n \\ r = 1, 2 \ldots m \end{array} \quad . \quad (3)$$

They may evidently be derived from the functions expres-

* This circumstance, expressly pointed out by Walras, is not sufficiently taken into account by Cassel, and his exposition is therefore formally not quite correct. See Wicksell, "Zur Verteidigung der Grenznutzenlehre" in *Zeitschrift für die gesammte Staatswissenschaft,* 1900, pp. 588–9. The same objection may be raised against other more recent theoretical constructions founded on Cassel.

sing the relation between the quantities produced and the quantities of co-operating factors. From these productivity functions, which therefore represent the primary data for the technical conditions of production, it is possible to determine the marginal productivity of each factor for every given combination of factors. As entrepreneurs endeavour to manufacture the articles as cheaply as possible, they will combine factors in such a manner that the marginal productivity of each factor will stand in a certain ratio to its price. Under the assumption made above, that production is equally remunerative* whatever the scale of production, the technical coefficients are then unambiguously determined.†

* This premiss implies that the productivity function is homogeneous and linear. Every increase of a factor of production that co-operates with a certain quantity of other factors, therefore results in a proportionately smaller increase in the quantity of the product. If in a given case the quantity of each factor of production is multiplied by its marginal productivity and these quantities are added together, the total will always be equal to the total quantity of the product. Cf. Wicksell, *Lectures on Political Economy*, vol. i, pp. 126 ff.

† The productivity function for the article (X^r) may be written

$$x = f(y^1 \ldots y^s \ldots y^n)$$

where x denotes the quantity of the product that results from the co-operation between the quantities $y^1 \ldots y^s \ldots y^n$ of productive services. If the prices of the services are denoted by $\Pi^1 \ldots \Pi^s \ldots \Pi^n$, the cost of production of x is

$$\sum_{s=1}^{n} \Pi^s y^s$$

We shall now determine the minimum for this expression under the assumption that the relation expressed in the productivity function is valid. The result is:

$$\frac{1}{\Pi^1} \frac{\partial f}{\partial y^1} = \cdots = \frac{1}{\Pi^s} \frac{\partial f}{\partial y^s} = \cdots = \frac{1}{\Pi^n} \frac{\partial f}{\partial y^n}$$

From these equations, together with the productivity function (n equations in all) we can for every value of x determine $y^1 \ldots y^s \ldots y^n$ expressed in $\Pi^1 \ldots \Pi^s \ldots \Pi^n$. And since

$$\frac{Y^{sr}}{X^r} = \frac{y^s}{x}$$

the general relation between the functions of the technical co-

Having obtained the functions which express the data in the system, we have next to set up two more systems of equations for the solution of the problem of price determination. The first states that the prices of the goods demanded should correspond to their *costs of production* (*m* equations):

$$P^r X^r = \sum_{s=1}^{n} \varPi^s Y^{sr} \quad \text{for } r = 1, 2 \ldots m \quad . \quad (4)$$

The second system states that the quantity of services of each factor offered is equal to the total quantity of services utilized in the production of the goods demanded. Since the number of productive services is *n*, we obtain *n* equations for the *amounts of factors used*:

$$Y^s = \sum_{r=1}^{m} Y^{sr} \quad \text{for } s = 1, 2 \ldots n \quad . \quad . \quad (5)$$

The equation not included in system (2), through which the demand for the *m*th article can be determined if the other demand functions are known, can be derived from systems (4) and (5). If the two sides of the equations of system (5) are multiplied respectively by $\varPi^1 \ldots \varPi^s \ldots \varPi^n$, and the equations in each system are then added, two equations are obtained, the right-hand sides of which are identical, which gives us between the two other sides the equality

$$\sum_{s=1}^{n} \varPi^s Y^s = \sum_{r=1}^{m} P^r X^r$$

Through this equation,* which states that the total incomes of the individuals are equal to their total expenditures, it is evidently possible to determine the total demand for the article, which was not already determined by system (2).

In all we have $(2m + 2n + mn - 1)$ independent equations for the determination of $(2m + 2n + mn)$ un-

efficients and the productivity function are shown in this way. If the productivity function is homogeneous and linear, the functions of the technical coefficients will be the same for all values of x.

* Cf. Walras, op. cit., p. 214.

known. If all prices are expressed in a certain commodity, e.g. (X^1), and thus $P^1 = 1$, the number of unknowns is reduced by 1, and the problem is fully determined. If the prices, however, are expressed in an arbitrary monetary unit, the problem is determined except for a certain "multiplicative factor"* which enters into all money prices and determines the absolute height of the general price level and the value of money.

* Cf. Cassel, *Theory of Social Economy*, p. 151.

CHAPTER II

PERFECT FORESIGHT AND STATIONARY CONDITIONS

1. THE SIGNIFICANCE OF THE ASSUMPTIONS

We now proceed to study the alterations in the setting of the problem arising from the introduction of the time factor. These complications occur *partly* because individuals consider not only the needs of the moment but also those of the future in their economic actions, *partly* because future conditions are variable and not a mere repetition of the present situation, and *partly* because individuals' ideas concerning future changes have the character of probability judgments, so that a risk factor enters into all economic planning. The significance of these complications can be most easily elucidated if they are introduced one at a time. Both in this and in the next chapter we shall therefore neglect the considerable analytical difficulties due to the inability of individuals to foresee the future completely. If we assume that their expectations are fulfilled we shall further enjoy the advantage of being able to continue the mathematical treatment of the problem in approximately the same manner as hitherto. In this chapter we shall simplify the problem still further by assuming stationary conditions. And moreover we shall attack the stationary problem by degrees, proceeding from the simpler to the more complicated cases. For the whole analysis the simplifying assumptions already made in chap. I, sec. 3 will be retained.

To begin with, a few words on the basic assumptions of this chapter, are necessary—the assumptions namely that the future is completely foreseen and that the community is in a stationary condition.

The assumption of Perfect Foresight implies that individuals have full knowledge of all future data which they take into consideration in their economic planning. (In the real world of course they have to be satisfied with more or less uncertain guesses.) They therefore know not only future prices but also the manner in which they themselves, as owners of factors, as consumers, or as entrepreneurs, will react to these prices in the future. A person with foreknowledge of the future prices of the productive services that he can offer and of the consumption goods that he intends to purchase, would, however, manifestly not avoid speculative errors, unless he also knew his own productive power and the size of his wants during the relevant future periods. In the case of the productivity functions, the assumption must be interpreted as implying that individuals know when a technical change takes place, and what consequences it will have for production. They can therefore take steps to secure that the apparatus of production will at the time in question be completely adjusted to the new technique. (Their knowledge should, however, not include the *nature* of a technical invention, for in that case the invention would be introduced immediately.) Although individuals must therefore be supposed to be aware both of future prices and of the forms of functions that determine the dependence of supply, demand and the technical co-efficients on these prices, economic developments must nevertheless be regarded not as determined beforehand, but as the result of the actions of individuals. The real import of the assumption in question is, therefore, that individuals' ideas concerning the future are such that their actions bring about exactly the conditions which they anticipated. The theoretical treatment of the problem

285

seeks to clarify how prices will be determined so as to satisfy this condition, if the relevant functions are regarded as given.

The characteristic feature of stationary conditions is the absence of change. This invariably applies primarily to the factors determining prices, i.e. to the functions governing the offers of productive services, the demand for consumption goods and the technical coefficients of production. As a consequence of this assumption unvarying prices are secured.* The functions in question can naturally not be assumed to be unvarying under all conditions.† Even in cases when the mental attitudes on which the functions are based can be regarded as unchanged, a development may take place in a certain

---

* Unvarying prices can also be attained under a less narrow assumption, namely if only such changes in the factors determining prices are conceived as will cancel out. If the term "static" is taken to mean unchanging prices, then not only the stationary type of society but also a society progressing at a uniform rate, of which Marshall and Cassel speak, would be static, and also numerous other conceivable societies, within which the changes although not uniform compensate each other's effect on prices. This becomes important when we drop the assumption that the future is fully foreseen; for if the primary changes are of this kind, they do not run contrary to the cost principle, whether they are foreseen or not (See Myrdal, op. cit., pp. 67–8, where this circumstance is expressly pointed out.) This definition of the term "static" seems to come nearest to Marshall's and Cassel's use of the concept.

† Cf. Myrdal, op. cit., p. 5, note: "If the fact is noted that the quantities of certain factors of production are not primarily given but are in turn functionally determined by their prices, i.e. depend *inter alia* on relative valuations by different people, it is then found that underlying the static theories there is an assumption of a *certain definite* valuation—and not only of *any* unvarying one—on the part of the individuals of the society. This valuation is that which under given conditions will keep the quantities of the factors of production unchanged, or, in the other case, proportionally increasing. The valuations of the various individuals in this respect may differ and possibly also vary, but the resultant for society must have this definite size."

direction, such a development that may, but does not necessarily, give rise to conditions producing a stationary state. If, for instance, we like to assume that a certain wage rate would be necessary to maintain the population unchanged, then population and other factors determining prices must have time to develop in such a way that this wage rate comes into existence, before unvarying functions and stationary conditions can be assumed. The stationary premiss must therefore be used with care: by assuming that certain functions are unvarying under certain given conditions, assumptions regarding the concrete meaning of these functions are in reality introduced.

As we have here combined the assumption that the future is correctly foreseen with the stationary premiss, it should be noticed that the latter does not include the former. The fact that everything actually remains unchanged in a community does not prevent its members from continually fearing or hoping that certain changes will take place. If this is the case, even in a stationary state some elements of the complex of problems concerned with risk and profits are also relevant.* These dynamic factors determining prices are only eliminated by assuming that the ideas of individuals regarding the future agree with what actually happens. This premiss thus implies a greater simplification of the pricing problem than the stationary assumption in itself, and we have therefore taken the former as the main premiss in our exposition. By combining both premisses in this chapter we obtain the pure "static" problem of price determination.

* As an example, we take a stationary society living by agriculture and fishing. Although these pursuits give the same returns each year, better returns from the fisheries are continually hoped for. Expenditure in excess of income is therefore repeatedly made in the fishery business. The result is a recurring loss which may be conceived to be covered by income from agriculture. In this case the cost principle is *not* valid, in spite of the stationary assumption.

2. Interest in the Absence of Capitalistic Production

The simplest case is represented by a community in which there are no time-consuming processes of production, but the time factor nevertheless has economic relevance, since individuals can exchange present for future income among themselves.* As a result of the competition between those offering present income, i.e. savers, and those demanding present income, there arises a premium or discount on present incomes in relation to those of the future. In this manner the time factor itself is given a price—if present incomes are at a discount in relation to future incomes, the price may be negative—and a rate of interest exists in the community.† The level of the rate of interest, like other prices, will determine individual offers of productive services and demands for consumption goods. (Under the assumptions made, however, it will be of no importance for the determination of the technical coefficients.) Here lies the real difference in comparison with the price problem

* See above, p. 272.
† In his work, *The Rate of Interest*, New York, 1907, Irving Fisher discusses the problem of interest through a series of successive approximations. His first approximation, namely, that the income streams of individuals are determined and certain to start with, but can be modified by exchanges between the individuals, has in view the same problem as that outlined here. Fisher's conclusions are also applicable to our case. Cf. p. 131 : "Thus, the rate of interest is the common market rate of preference for present over future income, as determined by the supply and demand of present and future income. Those who, having a high rate of preference, strive to aquire more present income at the cost of future income, tend to raise the rate of interest. These are the borrowers, the spenders, the sellers of property yielding remote income, such as bonds and stocks. On the other hand, those who, having a low rate of preference, strive to acquire more future income at the cost of present income, tend to lower the rate of interest. These are the lenders, the savers, the investors."

already discussed. We have a new unknown in the problem, the rate of interest, and a corresponding new equation, namely that the demand for and the supply of loans, as functions of the rate of interest and other prices, are equal. Since we assume stationary conditions and full knowledge of the future, the system of equations will otherwise be the same as before.

This case is instructive. It shows with all desirable clarity that the influence of the time factor in increasing productivity is not a necessary prerequisite for the creation of a rate of interest.* Even in a society where real capital in the sense of produced factors of production does not exist, the time factor is given a price, which determines the value of all future income. Even in this case it is possible to speak of "capital values" in the sense of future incomes capitalized at the current rate of interest, of "real capital" as the concrete foundation of these incomes (people and land), and of the "interest" on capital in the sense of the increase of value accruing to capital on account of the passage of time. The justification for extending the application of the concept of capital beyond produced factors of production is thus made clear.

This does not prevent us from making certain useful analytical distinctions within this wider concept of capital: in the first place between people on the one hand and material capital goods on the other, and further within the latter group between original and produced and also between permanent and non-permanent capital goods. The two latter grounds of distinction coincide under stationary conditions, when real capital is either produced and non-permanent (i.e. "circulating"), or original and permanent (i.e. "fixed"); but they do not coincide under dynamic conditions, so that it is necessary to distinguish

* Cf. the criticisms of Böhm-Bawerk's "third main ground" by Irving Fisher and others.

between these two bases of classification. The importance of these distinctions will appear in the course of our investigation.

In connection with what has just been said regarding the concept of capital a short digression on the much-discussed question of *Böhm-Bawerk's three main grounds* for the existence of interest on capital may be in order.

In the case just mentioned the rate of interest was caused and its size determined by the *second* ground alone, that is by the foreshortened view and underestimation of future values in relation to present ones. A case may also be constructed in which the *first* ground alone, i.e. the greater provision of goods in the future compared with the present, gives rise to an interest rate and determines its size. This would occur in a community which although it had taken no measures for the satisfaction of future wants, had better times in store (for instance, on account of climatic conditions), and in which consequently the satisfaction of marginal future wants in general was less highly valued than the satisfaction of marginal present wants, although no underestimation of future in relation to present wants (occupying the same place in the preference scale) existed. But the *third* ground, the productive influence of time, cannot in itself alone determine the rate of interest. Here Böhm-Bawerk's critics are manifestly right.

The matter can be most easily explained as follows. The rate of interest is a price which under the simplifying assumptions made here, is determined by the relation between the supply and the demand for present goods against those of the future.* While the two first grounds are operative on *both* the demand and supply sides and therefore each alone can cause and determine this price, the third ground affects only the demand side. For this reason no interest rate can arise, unless one of the other two grounds is operative at the same time and thus provides the necessary determinant of the value of the supply of present goods against those of the future. (Obviously

* Cf. Cassel's treatment of the problem in *The Nature and Necessity of Interest*, London, 1903.

the third ground is intimately connected with the first since the productivity of the time factor tends to increase the future provision of goods. But this influence can in certain cases be conceived of as neutralized by other factors.)

Although the third ground is therefore not a necessary condition for the existence of a rate of interest on capital, it is actually of the most decisive importance for the concrete level of the interest rate, as a determining factor on the demand side. Owing to the importance of saving for production, the demand for saving is elastic to a considerable degree, whereas the supply, which is determined by the two other grounds (the effects of which are cumulative) is relatively inelastic. A shift in the demand curve therefore influences the level of thè rate of interest to a much greater degree than a corresponding change in the supply curve. The third ground therefore predominates in the problem of the rate of interest,* and in the following analysis we shall in the main be dealing with the complications in the process of price determination arising from this source.

3. Durable Capital Goods with Instantaneous Processes of Production

For the next more complicated case we assume that the relation between the satisfaction of wants in present and future periods can be influenced by using productive services in the current period to make capital goods, lasting for a larger or smaller number of succeeding periods, and meanwhile furnishing an unvarying quantity of productive services per period. The costs of these capital goods are assumed not to include any interest

* This problem can most suitably be determined by referring all effects of the first two grounds to the supply side. Then the total supply of saving will be diminished by the demand for consumption loans in the strict sense. The demand will in this way be determined by the third ground alone, by the need of new saving for the purposes of production.

charges, but correspond only to the value of the productive services that have been employed in production.*

Owing to the fact that production may thus absorb savings, the stationary assumption, which is still to be regarded as valid, becomes more complicated than in the preceding case. Only if certain special conditions prevail can both the supply and the demand for net savings for productive purposes be assumed to be $= 0$. These conditions may be conceived to be obtained in the following manner. The value of the capital goods is evidently equal to the sum of the present values of their future services, discounted at the prevailing rate of interest. At a given rate of interest and under given conditions in other respects the production of new capital goods will be remunerative only up to the point at which the prices of the productive services used in the manufacture of these goods have so risen, and the prices of the services of the latter have so fallen, that costs of production correspond to capital values. At a given rate of interest, therefore, the demand for net savings to be used in production ceases when the circulating real capital has attained a certain volume in relation to the other factors of production; the production of capital will henceforward only correspond to the renewal of the old capital goods. If in this situation offers of net savings are still made, the rate of interest will fall. Through this the value of the capital goods will be raised, and, it should be noted, in a higher proportion for the more permanent equipment. It therefore becomes re- munerative to continue the production of capital, and if at a certain cost level a choice is possible between capital assets with a relatively short lifetime, but which

* This assumption may most simply be conceived to be realized by assuming that the productive services receive their compensation at the end of every period of time. (For the production of the capital goods only one period is required.) The first assumption becomes the more plausible the shorter the periods.

are relatively valuable, and more durable capital goods with less valuable services per period, the tendency will be to choose the latter. In this manner the absorption of savings into production is increased. Just at the point when production is saturated with capital and therefore does not demand more net savings, the supply of the latter is *also* assumed to give out. If other factors too are unchanged, the community will then be in a stationary state.

If we compare this stationary condition with that discussed in the previous section, we can note the following differences. The sources of the supply of productive services are partly "original" factors of production and partly manufactured capital goods with a limited lifetime. We shall consider that to the former group belong all capital goods of unlimited durability, and also those produced before the community reached stationary conditions. (After that there will obviously be no production of such goods.) For after the capital goods have once been created, the question of their origin is irrelevant. Since they have the same attributes as the really original factors of production, they should in consequence be classed with them. The stationary assumption makes this division into the two groups clear-cut. All available services of these two groups of factors are used up in the production of the consumption goods which are demanded, and of the capital goods that are to replace those worn out during the period in question. The total demand for consumption goods will therefore be equal to the total value of the productive services minus "gross savings," i.e. the amounts set aside by the owners of the capital goods for their replacement. In both branches of production the cost principle applies. In the case of the capital goods this means that costs correspond to the capitalized value of their output at the prevailing rate of interest.

With these modifications the system of equations given above can also be applied to the present case.

This is the case discussed by Walras, when he introduces the time factor into the pricing problem. His exposition is, it is true, not quite satisfactory in one or two respects,* but the system of equations set up by him provides on the whole a solution of the problem of including capital and interest in a mathematical analysis of the determination of prices under certain simplifying assumptions. Walras' achievement in this respect lies particularly in the fact that he links the problem of capital with the general

* Walras first shows (correctly) that the amount by which the total value of the productive services (i.e. gross income) exceeds the total demand for products (i.e. consumption) corresponds to the demand for new capital goods, but adds afterwards, that if the latter demand is positive, then the society is *progressive*. See op. cit., p. 252: "Puisque nous avons cru devoir placer les offres supposées positives de services dans le premier membre et les demandes supposées positives de produits dans le second membre de l'équation d'échange, nous placerons à la suite de ces dernières la demande de capitaux neufs *toujours supposée positive*. En faisant cette supposition, nous nous bornons a l'étude de la production des capitaux neufs dans une société progressive et nous négligeons celle de la consommation des capitaux existants dans une société retrograde." This is naturally a mistake. The society is progressive, only in so far as net savings are positive, and, as Walras himself has noted, positive net savings do not exist unless the demand for new capital goods is larger than the amortization and insurance on the old capital goods. "L'épargne est la différence positive entre l'excédent du revenu sur la consommation et le montant de l'amortissement et de l'assurance des capitaux proprement dits." (Op. cit., p. 250.) The society discussed by Walras is accordingly not necessarily progressive. As Wicksell pointed out in *Ekonomisk Tidskrift*, 1919, p. 201, note, his formulae can be better applied to a stationary society. Our comments, therefore, do not imply any criticism of the system of equations itself. Concerning the latter, the objection may be raised, that offers of services of capital goods should not have been regarded as a function of the general price level only. They should rather have been connected with the number of existing capital goods, which in a stationary community is equal to the quantity of new capital goods produced in each period, multiplied by their lifetime.

pricing problem. Unlike the Böhm-Bawerkian school, he does not separate the two by assuming in the theoretical analysis of capital only one commodity, one kind of original productive service (labour), one category of capital goods, etc. On the other hand, Walras' treatment of capital is less penetrating than that of the Böhm-Bawerkians. By regarding the replacement ratio for the capital goods and therefore their duration as a datum he excludes the possibility of a study of the important connection between the length of time of investment and the rate of interest. This problem has been analysed in detail by Gustaf Åkerman,* though only under rather simplified conditions.† A task still remaining for economic theory would be to combine these two analyses, i.e. to generalize Åkerman's so as to make it valid under assumptions as general as those on which Walras bases his system.

A discussion of this problem would undoubtedly lead to a number of valuable results, but would take us too far afield. In what follows we shall seek instead to make Walras' analysis applicable under more general assumptions. For the importance of the time factor in production does not lie solely in the possibility of producing durable capital goods, but also in the opportunities for varying the quantity of time used in the process of production itself. This latter circumstance is relevant in all production, and should therefore be taken into considera-

* Gustaf Åkerman, *Realkapital und Kapitalzins*, vol. i–ii, Stockholm, 1923–24.

† A more general mathematical treatment of the problem was given by Wicksell in *Ekonomisk Tidskrift*, 1923, pp. 157 ff., in his review of Åkerman's work. (This review has been translated into English and printed as an appendix to *Lectures*, vol. i.) Myrdal has also made an important contribution to the solution of the problem along more general lines, by introducing in a symmetrical manner the function of the size of enterprise in his exposition of the static problem of productivity (op. cit., pp. 192 ff.).

tion in the case of durable capital goods also. But it was completely overlooked by Walras who therefore greatly diminished the generality of his analysis. In a general treatment of the pricing problem the time factor must evidently be taken into account in both these ways. We shall proceed to state the problem accordingly.

4. ROUNDABOUT PROCESSES OF PRODUCTION

We therefore make our final assumption that production takes time, and that a process of production requiring more time often brings larger results than one that needs less time, owing to the productive influence of the time factor itself.

This means usually that productive services from various periods of time are used up in the manufacture of a particular article, and that the results of productive activities increase at a diminishing rate with the average space of time between the input of factors and the resulting output of finished goods or services, i.e. with the average period of investment.* When the rate of interest is positive, however, interest costs increase with the length of the period of investment, and therefore it does not pay to lengthen it further than to the point where the increment in the value of output exactly counterbalances the increase in interest charges. The technical coefficients, which must be specified in respect not only to the nature of the factors, but also to the periods of time at which they enter the productive process, therefore become functions not only of the prices of the services of factors, but also of the rate of interest: at a lower rate there is usually a shift in favour of earlier periods.

In a stationary community, the quantity of services invested for future needs in each period must be equal to

* This notion will be defined more exactly below.

the quantity of previously invested services that have "matured" during the same period through the appearance of the output on the market. Otherwise the capital equipment which these invested services represent will not remain the same. The total quantity of services of varying ages required for the output in a given period will therefore equal the total demand for original services belonging to this period. The difference in value between the services from earlier periods "maturing" in the said period and those invested for their replacement, represents the interest on the circulating capital in this period.

Durable capital equipment of limited durability can be inserted into the system in *two* different ways. (Permanent capital goods, which do not require amortisation, should, as has already been stated, be regarded as "original" factors of production, even if they were in fact produced.)

One alternative is to take special account of the services of such equipment (and to denote them by special signs) when estimating the total supply of services in each period, as is done by Walras. The services belonging to a certain period will therefore be derived partly from the non-permanent durable capital and partly from the original factors of production. Corresponding to this supply we have the total quantities used up: partly in the production of new durable equipment to replace that worn out during the period, partly for investment in other circulating capital corresponding to previously invested services used up during the period, and partly in the direct production of consumers' goods.

According to the second alternative, the services rendered by a durable capital instrument are expressed *in terms of the original services invested* in it at the time of its production. The original services are regarded as "maturing" as the instrument renders services of its own. Since in this case we really have indivisible costs of production for a series of outputs—how the former services are accounted for among the latter is more or less a conventional matter. But the theoretical treatment of the problem is greatly facilitated by imagining that "the cost principle," which under stationary conditions must apply to the capital asset as a whole, also applies to the special services successively received from it. Thus in the first period during which the instrument is in use, so much of the original services are supposed to "mature" as corresponds to the value of the services rendered, discounted at the current rate of interest to the time of investment. For the next period another part can be calculated in the same manner, and so on. Thus the total quantity of the original services is distributed over the different periods of use. Each portion can then be treated as a separate investment bearing interest in the same way as other independent investments in circulating capital. The capital instrument as a whole can thus be regarded as a *bundle* of such investments, successively "maturing" over the different periods of its lifetime.

This method is easy to apply in the case, where only original services from one short period of time are needed for the production of the capital asset that will furnish services of its own in later periods. When the production of the good is completed, the value of the services invested is, under our assumption, equal to the sum of the discounted values of the services rendered by the asset during the succeeding periods. Each period will thus require so much of the original services as corresponds to this discounted value of the services rendered.*

* A simple example may serve to clarify the problem. In the production of a durable asset 31·7 labour units are used up in one period of time. The asset subsequently furnishes services in four succeeding periods, having a value of 10 labour units in each period. If the value of these services is discounted at 10 per cent at the end of the production period (when the wages are supposed to be paid), we get the following figures for the four periods: (1) 9·1, (2) 8·3,

The same principle can be applied if the original services used up in the production of the capital asset have their origin in different periods. The services invested in each period can then be distributed among the periods during which the asset is in use in proportion to the dis-

(3) 7·5, (4) 6·8, the sum of which is 31·7. The whole investment can thus be dissolved into four investments, in the manner just indicated, each of them bearing interest at 10 per cent: the first comprises 9·1 labour units and matures after one year with a value of 10 units, the second comprises 8·3 units and matures after two years with a value of 10 units, etc.

In this connection it should be pointed out that this scheme for the maturing of the units invested should not be employed as a scheme for the *amortization* of the capital value. For in principle the amortization of a capital asset should correspond to the actual depreciation during each period. And if we calculate the depreciation of the asset in our example (by comparing its value at the beginning and at the end of each period) we get the following series for the four periods: (1) 6·8, (2) 7·5, (3) 8·3, (4) 9·1. (Thus the figures are the same as before, but they now come *in the reverse order*.) If we retain our concept of the capital good as a bundle of separate investments with different terms of maturity, this apparent contradiction can be explained as follows. During the first period when the maturing investment is to be replaced by 9·1 units, the other investments contained in the asset have through accrued interest gained in value an amount corresponding to 2·3 units. This amount should be deducted from the former in the amortization of the whole capital, and we then get 6·8 units in accordance with the second scheme.

Now the maintenance of stationary conditions presupposes *both* that in each period so many units are reinvested as have matured during period *and* that the value invested corresponds to the actual reduction in value of the good. Otherwise the total amount of invested units and the total value of the capital equipment will not be the same as before. Our example shows clearly that these two prerequisites cannot be fulfilled at the same time in the case of a single capital instrument. But they can be fulfilled with respect to capital equipment as a whole, when production is co-ordinated (*gestaffelt*) with a series of capital instruments of all ages. If in our example a new capital instrument is produced in each period to replace the wear and tear on four others originating in four consecutive periods of time, then both the total of invested units (according to the first scheme) and the total of invested values (according to the second) will remain constant. Thus the assumption of co-ordinated production is essential for a stationary society.

299

counted value of the services then rendered. Other combinations, however, which fulfil the requirement of the same rate of remuneration on all investments are also conceivable.

Finally, if a durable capital asset is produced with the aid of the services of another capital instrument, these services must similarly be regarded as derived from those used up in the production of the latter. If these services have in turn also partly been obtained from a durable capital instrument it is necessary to go back to the services used up in the production of this third instrument, and so on. Thus the origin of a diminishing proportion of the services of the first capital asset may be looked for step by step, farther and farther back in time.

In stationary conditions—which may last for any length of time—the very beginning, when nothing but original services exists can usually not be reached. For as a rule the production of durable real capital must be assumed to take place with some assistance from the services of a durable capital which has been made at an earlier date. As a rule, therefore, the services of a given durable capital asset are dissolved in an infinitely long series of original services "saved up" from earlier periods of time, a series that is convergent and the terms of which therefore become smaller and smaller and finally infinitely small. The fact that this view is extremely abstract does not prevent it from being valuable in a theoretical exposition.*

Of these two methods of treating durable capital goods the first has the advantage of being a better approximation to conditions in the real world. It therefore makes a

* The difficulties which we have found in the concept of the services of a durable capital asset as original services saved up from earlier periods are also present, though to a smaller extent, with regard to other kinds of capital goods. Even if there were no durable capital assets in the community, and each rendered its services in one single period only, it would sometimes be necessary to go far back in time in order to find the original productive services, when the services of earlier capital goods have been used in the production of a capital asset, and still older capital in the production of the former, etc.

foundation for a more penetrating analysis of the complications arising from the diversified nature of capital equipment. In each case it is possible to manage with a relatively small number of technical coefficients and they have a relatively concrete meaning. Thus the analysis of special problems is facilitated. The second method has on the contrary the advantage that it is unnecessary to introduce special terms for durable capital or for the technical coefficients concerned in its production. Since the services of the durable goods are assumed to be dissolved in the original services invested in them, they may be treated according to the same principles as other capital goods. This method therefore allows of the uniform treatment of all capital investments, and hence the equations become much simpler than in the former case.

In a more detailed analysis of the problem of capital the first method would naturally be preferable. But since our present object is only to clarify the general relations affecting the determination of prices, taking account of the phenomenon of capital, we are free to adopt the second and simpler method.

5. ALGEBRAIC DISCUSSION

In the mathematical analysis of price determination under the above assumptions we may take as our starting-point the system of equations set up in the preceding chapter on the model of Walras, Cassel and Bowley. We may therefore refer to our previous exposition, and concentrate here on the modifications necessary when the time factor is introduced.

To begin with it should be pointed out that the setting of the problem itself has been shifted. While in the former case the equilibrium position could be determined if the functions for supply and demand, and the technical coefficients were given, and the individuals were assumed to have foreknowledge of these equilibrium prices, in the present case in addition the *conditions for stationariness must be regarded as given.* The problem is therefore not to determine the stationary position that can be expected to arise in the long run under certain assumptions regarding supply, demand and the technical coefficients. This problem belongs to dynamics and must be treated according to methods other than those indicated above. The present problem may rather be stated as follows: *if* a certain state of stationary equilibrium is supposed to have been established, and *if* then *both* the size of the circulating capital, *and* the functions that under just these stationary conditions determine the quantities of original productive services offered are known, besides the demand for consumption goods and the technical coefficients for their production—what are then the prevailing prices and the rate of interest, how much of each commodity is produced, etc.?

Now the introduction of circulating capital has certain important consequences for the character of the stationary equilibrium. These are more easily explained, if the capital goods are resolved into the "original services" of land and labour from different periods that have been used up in production. These saved-up services can be conceived as "maturing" during the period when the capital goods are rendering services of their own. Retaining the symbol previously used (Y^s) for original services referring to the present period, we may use the symbol Y^s_τ for services saved-up from earlier periods, the suffix τ having reference to the period during which the services were invested, thus denoting the *age* of the services. (Since past periods are denoted by negative signs, τ will have the following values: $-1, -2, \ldots - \mu$, where μ is assumed to be the maximum age, reckoned in whole periods, of services invested in capital goods. The periods, here taken as time units, are assumed to be so short that it is of no importance either from the standpoint of efficiency or of costs how the services are distributed *within* a certain period.)

Between these various services "stored-up" in the capital goods, certain definite relations must be established, for a stationary equilibrium to be possible. Their nature is elucidated in the diagram below, employed by Wicksell in his discussion of the capital problem.* The lowest row of rectangles represents the quantity of services of a certain type (Y^s) that will be used up during the present period in the production of a certain good (X^r). They are here arranged according to their age, the oldest to the left and the current ones to the right. The next row contains the quantity of stored up services that will mature during the next period, and so on. Stationary equilibrium pre-supposes that for each combination of productive services (Y^s) on the one hand and of consumption goods (X^r) on the other, the time structure of the capital is of the character shown in the diagram, and that there is no incentive for entrepreneurs to alter this structure or to transfer capital from one category of these alternative lines of investment to another.

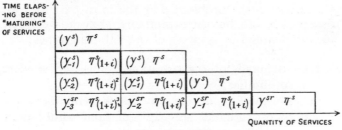

DIAGRAM IV

Thus the following two conditions must be fulfilled: (1) The different ages of the services used up in a certain period should in every branch of investment be represented in such proportions that their marginal productivities will increase for higher ages in a degree that corresponds to the prevailing rate of interest (here denoted by the sign i). Since the prices of previously invested services must include the interest charges accruing between the period of investment and the period of maturity, the marginal productivity must be increased in the same way, if no alteration of the investments is to be profitable. (2) For each quantity of services used up in the present period, there must exist the same quantities of stored-up services

* See for example *Lectures*, vol. i., p. 152.

of more recent periods that will mature in the same way during subsequent periods. Otherwise the productive process could not be continued on the same lines.

The static premiss thus implies a rather definite time-structure of circulating capital. As has already been said, in the theoretical treatment of the static problem the realization of this time-structure must be assumed, as well as the circumstance that the circulating capital has the form required for stationary conditions. But only the total amount of the circulating capital can be regarded as known, determined in one way or other as a sum of saved-up services. The distribution of this capital among different types of services and among services of various ages belongs to the unknown factors of the problem, like the rate of interest. Otherwise the problem would be overdetermined.

After these preliminary remarks we may give a list of the *unknowns* in the problem. For the most part they are the same as before, but the capital terms have to be added. They are denoted by symbols of the following types:

X^r: total demand for consumption goods and services, m in number;

P^r: prices of these goods and services, m in number;

Y^s: supply of "original services" of land and labour, n in number;

Π^s: prices of these services, n in number;

Y^s_τ: supply of circulating capital goods, that is, of "saved-up" services of (n) different categories and (μ) different "ages," $n\mu$ in number;

Y^{sr}: whole quantity of (Y^s) used in the manufacture of (X^r), mn in number;

Y^{sr}_τ: whole quantity of (Y^s_τ) used in the manufacture of (X^r), $mn\mu$ in number;

i: the rate of interest, 1 in number.

For the determination of these factors we can set up the following equations.

The functions for the supply of "original" productive services presuppose that the factors have adjusted themselves to prevailing price conditions. This applies both to the size of the population, the distribution of labour among different occupations and the supply of produced capital goods of infinite durability which are here placed in the same category as land. (During the time when this adaptation is taking place, other supply functions are evidently valid.) It is further assumed that the owners of these factors possess the circulating capital, the quantity of which is given, in accordance with the conditions proper to the stationary state. Under these assumptions the total supply of every category of productive services is evidently a definite function of the prices of these services, and of the rate of interest that determines the income from capital, and of commodity prices. We are accordingly in a position to express the *supply of the original productive services* in the following n equations:

$$Y^s = F^s(\Pi^1, \Pi^2 \ldots \Pi^n; P^1, P^2 \ldots P^m; i)$$
$$\text{for } s = 1, 2 \ldots n \quad . \quad . \quad (1)$$

The total demand for each consumption good is, in given income situations, a function of commodity prices and of the rate of interest. The income positions, again, are functions of the general price level, since the quantities of circulating capital possessed by individuals are assumed to be given. In this way the total demand for each good becomes a function of the general price situation. We therefore obtain as before $(m - 1)$ equations for the total *demand for various consumers' goods and services:*

$$X^r = F^r(\Pi^1, \Pi^2 \ldots \Pi^n; P^1, P^2 \ldots P^m; i)$$
$$\text{for } r = 2, 3 \ldots m \quad . \quad . \quad (2)$$

The technical coefficients, denoting the quantities of different productive services used up in the manufacture of a unit of each commodity ready for consumption, must in this case be specified with reference both to the nature and the age of the services. For every commodity we get n technical coefficients for the current services of land and labour and $n\mu$ technical coefficients for the services of capital goods which, as has been explained above, can be resolved into the original services used up in the production of these goods. (In view of the fact that, especially with regard to durable capital goods, the period of circulation for certain saved-up services can be infinitely long, μ can be conceived to be any large number. The greater number of these coefficients must, however, be $= 0$.) These coefficients are evidently functions of the prices of the original productive services (which in a stationary community are the same in all periods of time) and of the rate of interest, which determines the size of the interest charges to be added for the services saved-up from earlier periods.)* The *technical coefficients* for all consumers' goods and services are accordingly determined through the following mn equations for original services belonging to the present period and $mn\mu$ equations for previously invested services, thus in all $mn(\mu + 1)$ equations:

$$\frac{Y^{sr}}{X^r} = F^{sr}\left(\Pi^1, \Pi^2 \ldots \Pi^n; i\right) \quad \text{for} \begin{array}{l} s = 1, 2 \ldots n \\ r = 1, 2 \ldots m \end{array}$$

$$\frac{Y^{sr}_\tau}{X^r} = F^{sr}_\tau\left(\Pi^1, \Pi^2 \ldots \Pi^n; i\right) \quad \text{for} \begin{array}{l} s = 1, 2 \ldots n \\ r = 1, 2 \ldots m \\ \tau = -1, -2 \ldots -\mu \end{array} \tag{3}$$

As before, we may then set up a system of equations stating that the prices of the goods demanded are equal to their *costs of production*, i.e. the costs of all services used up in the manufacture of the goods plus accrued interest during the period of investment. The value of the goods is calculated at the end of the period, and we also assume that the remuneration of the productive services and the interest on capital† are payable at the end of each period.

* The relation between these functions and the productivity functions can be described in the same manner as in the previous case (see note 2 on p. 28), except for the modification that the interest factor $(1 + i)$ enters into the prices of the saved-up services.

† If the interest on capital is payable at shorter intervals—or, the most suitable assumption in certain cases, is payable continuously—it can of course also be counted for the same period as before, all amounts of interest paid during the period being added together. Equal amounts of interest, however, will then be obtained at a rate of interest somewhat lower than in the former case. Cf. Irving Fisher, *The Nature of Capital and Income*, pp. 191 ff.

The equations will therefore be the following (m in number):

$$P^r X^r = \sum_{s=1}^{n} \Pi^s \left[Y^{sr} + Y^{sr}_{-1} (1 + i) + Y^{sr}_{-2} (1 + i)^2 + \ldots \\ + Y^{sr}_{-\mu} (1 + i)^\mu \right] \\ \text{for } r = 1, 2 \ldots m \quad (4)$$

Furthermore, we obtain a system of equations stating that in every period the total quantity of current services used up is equal to the supply. With regard to each category of productive services of land and labour (Y^s) the total quantity utilized in one period can be calculated by adding together the quantities of this category of *all ages* used in the manufacture of the different consumption goods during the period in question. For in a stationary society the utilization of all saved-up services must be replaced by an equally large new investment of current services during the same period. (See the diagram on p. 303.) We accordingly obtain the following n equations for the *entire use of original factors*:

$$Y^s = \sum_{r=1}^{m} (Y^{sr} + Y^{sr}_{-1} + Y^{sr}_{-2} + \ldots + Y^{sr}_{-\mu}) \\ \text{for } s = 1, 2 \ldots n . \quad (5)$$

Analogously we can set up a similar system of equations for the use of the services saved-up in the capital goods. With regard to each category of services (Y^s), the total supply of saved-up services of any given age must be equal to the amount of services utilized during the period, both of this age and of all *greater* ages. (See the diagram.) We thus get the following $n\mu$ equations for the *whole use of capital*:

$$Y^s_{-1} = \sum_{r=1}^{m} (Y^{sr}_{-1} + Y^{sr}_{-2} + \ldots + Y^{sr}_{-\mu})$$

$$Y^s_{-2} = \sum_{r=1}^{m} (Y^{sr}_{-2} + Y^{sr}_{-3} + \ldots + Y^{sr}_{-\mu}) \quad \text{for } s = 1, 2 \ldots n \quad (6)$$

$$\cdot \quad \cdot \quad \cdot \quad \cdot \quad \cdot \quad \cdot \quad \cdot \quad \cdot \quad \cdot \quad \cdot$$

$$Y^s_{-\mu} = \sum_{r=1}^{m} Y^{sr}_{-\mu}$$

Finally we may set up an equation in which we use what may be regarded as given in respect of the size of the circulating real capital. Wicksell who has treated the problem on lines similar to those followed here assumes in some cases that the average time of investment is known* and in other cases that the size of capital is given as an amount of exchange value.† For reasons to be explained later, we let the given factor here be the *weighted average time of investment* of *all* original services used up in a given period, including the services consumed during the period for which the time of investment is zero. We let T stand for this average time of investment and define T as the number of periods, during which the total value of all original services supplied in a given period with compound interest at the given rate, becomes equal to the total value of all services maturing and consumed during the same period.‡ We thus get the following equation for *the total income,* earned in a given period:§

$$\sum_{s=1}^{n} \Pi^s Y^s (1+i)^T = \sum_{s=1}^{n} \Pi^s \sum_{r=1}^{m} [Y^{sr} + Y^{sr}_{-1}(1+i)$$
$$+ Y^{sr}_{-2}(1+i)^2 + \ldots + Y^{sr}_{-\mu}(1+i)^\mu] \quad . \quad (7)$$

If the two sides of the equations of system (4) are added

* Cf. *Lectures*, vol. i, p. 179.   † Cf. op. cit., p. 204.
‡ [T is thus a function of i. Since i is unknown, what is given is the form of the function, not the value of T. Cf. J. R. Hicks, *Value and Capital*, pp. 217 ff.]
§ If we subtract from the two sides of this equation the remuneration of the original services, that is, the income of land and labour,

$$\sum_{s=1}^{n} \Pi^s Y^s$$

the equation will refer instead to the total interest on the circulating capital. If we further capitalize this amount by dividing it by the rate of interest, i, we get, by aid of system (6), the following expression for the *value of the circulating capital* at the beginning of a given period:

$$\sum_{s=1}^{n} \Pi^s Y^s \frac{(1+i)^T - 1}{i}$$
$$= \sum_{s=1}^{n} \Pi^s [Y^s_{-1} + Y^s_{-2}(1+i) + \ldots + Y^s_{-\mu}(1+i)^{\mu-1}]$$

together, an equation is found whose right side is identical with that of equation (7), and from the two left sides the following equation can therefore be formed:

$$\sum_{s=1}^{n} \Pi^s Y^s (1+i)^T = \sum_{r=1}^{m} P^r X^r$$

Through this equation, which states that consumption and income for the community as a whole correspond to each other, it is manifestly possible to determine the total demand for the mth article, which was not determined by the equations of system (2).

The number of unknowns is, as can be seen from the list above $(2m + 2n + mn(\mu + 1) + n\mu + 1)$. For the determination of them we have now set up $(2m + 2n + mn(\mu + 1) + n\mu)$ equations. As in the previous case only one equation is missing—for the determination of the absolute height of the monetary prices. The problem is thus fully determined except for the "multiplicative factor."

6. Difficulties Inherent in the Assumption of Stationary Conditions

The general relationships in the determination of prices under stationary conditions have now been sketched. An extension of the analysis should among other things be directed to a study of the functions for the technical coefficients. For since we have specified the latter with reference to saved-up services, they can be combined into groups representing the services of concrete capital goods. It is evident that in each group, the functions are intimately connected. Furthermore, there is the task of determining these and other given functions in a more definite form and of elaborating new functions on the basis so provided. We can, for example, try to determine the rate of interest as a function of the size of capital,*

* To each magnitude of circulating capital there corresponds a certain time-structure, that satisfies the equilibrium conditions

keeping the basic thesis of the modern theory of capital in view, namely that with an increased amount of capital and a falling rate of interest longer investments are on the whole increased in a greater degree than the short ones.* This important and extensive task cannot, however, be attempted here. We shall only add a few remarks concerning the setting of the problem itself.

In a study of the pricing problem under stationary conditions it is presumed, as has already been stated, that a condition of equilibrium already exists, and the investigation proceeds to show how the prices, the rate of interest, the time-structure of capital, etc., then prevailing are determined by certain given factors. This relation may be expressed by saying that the values in question are a necessary condition for the continuation

indicated in the previous section, and for each time-structure a certain rate of interest must be assumed. The rate of interest can therefore, other conditions being given, be determined as a function of the size of the circulating capital. In traditional capital theory, this function has generally been studied with abstraction from the complications arising through the occurrence of many different categories of productive services and of products. (Cf. for example the works of Böhm-Bawerk and Gustaf Åkerman.) In the present paper we have tried to indicate, how this capital theory can be related to the general theory of price.

* This fundamental thesis is not clearly explicit in Böhm-Bawerk, who only takes into account an average period of production for the community as a whole and ignores the question of how this average time is compounded of investments of various lengths. As a consequence he can only say that an increase in capital entails a lengthening of the average period of production, which lies in the nature of the case, and elucidate how a lengthening of the investment becomes remunerative from the private point of view also. The credit for having clearly formulated the thesis that different existing capital investments are then not increased proportionally but that *relatively long investments predominate*, and that through this the increase in wages and the prices of other original services due to the increase of capital is counteracted, seems in reality to be due to Wicksell (cf. e.g. *Lectures*, vol. i, p. 162). It may perhaps be said to constitute his foremost achievement in the field of capital theory.

of the stationary state, but not that they are a necessary consequence of certain given functions concerning supply, demand, etc. For if other prices were conceived to be introduced into the system, a dynamic process would set in, concerning which nothing definite can be said without more precise assumptions as to anticipations and planning, etc. A stationary state may possibly arise in the course of time, but it may differ more or less from the original state on account of what has happened in the meantime. In elucidating the way in which the nature of the given factors in the system influences the price equilibrium it is impossible to proceed by the method of letting a change take place in the factors determining prices in a particular stationary situation. For even if the changes were regarded as so extensive that conditions necessary for a new stationary situation would arise immediately in the forms of the given functions, the result would, as has been said, be a dynamic process the result of which would be uncertain.

The analysis must instead be linked with a *comparison* between independent stationary communities which are conceived to exist in isolation and which, in respect of the factors determining prices, show both resemblances to and differences from each other. Such a comparison is however also beset with methodological difficulties.

If it is to be fruitful, the difference between the types of community compared must be confined to one or a few of the factors determining prices, while the others are regarded as unchanged.* At the same time it must be presumed that the necessary conditions for a state of stationary equilibrium exists in both cases, i.e. that all

* Owing to the manner in which the demand functions have been written in the above, they are directly connected with the other functions. They can, however, be made independent, if they are regarded as the functions applying to the demands of individuals at different levels of income and of commodity prices.

factors determining prices are to the requisite degree adapted to stationary conditions. This combination of assumptions must impose a certain degree of constraint in the treatment of the problem. For it is founded on the assumption that the unvarying factors determining prices are quite as well adjusted to one stationary state as to another. This assumption may undoubtedly be said to be remote from reality. The functions in question for supply, demand and productivity are in practice not independent of one another, and may perhaps all be found to depend on certain basic common factors. (If for instance the supply function for labour and also the demand propensities of the workers were to change simultaneously, some change in the general mentality of the labouring class should be looked for.) It therefore appears extremely probable that if in a stationary situation some important factor were changed all the functions would have to be modified to a greater or less degree, before new stationary conditions could arise.

Another objection to the static formulation of the problem which is connected with what has just been said, envisages the difficulty of determining the factors affecting prices in such a way that an exact comparison can be made between different stationary situations.*

* In this connection an observation may be made regarding the meaning of the functions applying to the supply of productive services and to productivity. They may be written in different ways, depending upon whether one regards knowledge of technique and organization and certain external conditions ("wind and weather," etc.) that influence the result of production as qualifications of the factors of production themselves, or as conditions for their co-operation. According to the former view a change in technical knowledge would mean that the factors of production (especially those that take an active part in its organization) are changed, whereas the productivity function remains unchanged. According to the latter view, the factors would be regarded as the same as before and the change in the result of production would accordingly be attributed to a

If one of the factors determining prices has been changed, what is then meant by saying that the others are unchanged, and can the degree of change in the varying factor be measured? Such questions, which continually crop up in the treatment of static problems, are sometimes not so easy to answer. Here we can only add a few reflections on the most important point in dispute, namely the method by which the *quantity of capital* should be measured under stationary conditions.

7. A Digression on the Measurement of Capital

In the analysis of the theory of capital two principal methods have been employed to reach an estimate of the quantity of circulating capital:

(1) The size of the capital has been expressed as the sum of the original values of the services used up in the production of existing capital goods. In stationary conditions this will be equal to the total return from existing capital to be used in the future for purchasing services for reinvestment. If the services invested are a certain kind of labour, the question accordingly is how large an amount of wages has been paid in advance by the capital, how large a *wage fund* it represents. The awkward thing about this method is that the invested values are added together without account being taken of the interest that has

change in the productivity function. The same points of view may be applied if the results of production have been altered on account of climatic conditions. This case can also be conceived either by altering the factors of production or the productivity function. Which of these methods best serves the purposes of the analysis and is thus preferable should no doubt be decided in view of the setting of the problem in each case. Under the simplifying assumptions on which we have founded our treatment of the pricing problem, it seems most suitable to regard all "free factors of production," and thus all knowledge of technique and organization that is a *commune bonum* and also all external productive conditions not under the sway of man, as elements determining the productivity function. On the other hand, technical knowledge possessed for instance only by certain individuals and which is therefore a source of additional income to them, should be regarded as an attribute of their labour.

accrued from the time of investment. The "wage fund" will in this way vary in proportion to the average time of investment, computed as an *unweighted arithmetical mean* of the lengths of time elapsing before all original services delivered in a given period mature in consumption goods. An estimate of the quantity of capital according to this method underlies Böhm-Bawerk's well-known calculations concerning the relation between the height of wages and the average length of the period of production, and Wicksell, in his earlier writings, followed Böhm-Bawerk's example in this respect. This concept of capital was also of fundamental importance in the investigations of Gustaf Åkerman.

(2) The capital can evidently also be measured by the sum of values which it represents. Under stationary conditions this sum of values will be equal to the values of the invested services *plus* accrued interest. The concept of an average time of investment can be utilized also when estimating the capital as a sum of values, but it must then, as has already been indicated, be determined differently, namely as a *weighted average* of the investment periods of all original services, including those whose time of investment is zero. The weights will be the interest costs relevant to each period of investment, calculated at *compound interest.** (If simple interest is used, this will evidently lead to the same result as in the previous case.) This mode of measuring capital, which is the usual one, is the one we have adopted.

When it is a question of establishing the manner in

---

* While the "wage fund" varies in direct proportion to the average time of investment, calculated as an unweighted arithmetical mean, the relation between capital as a sum of values and the average time of investment, weighted with respect to interest costs is more complicated. Using the same symbols as before, we have the following equations:

$$\bar{K} = \bar{T} \sum_{s=1}^{n} \Pi^s Y^s \quad \text{and} \quad K = \frac{(1 + i)^T - 1}{i} \sum_{s=1}^{n} \Pi^s Y^s$$

where $\bar{K}$ denotes the wage fund and K the capital value, $\bar{T}$ the unweighted and T the weighted average time of investment, determined in the manner indicated above.

which a *change* in circulating capital influences the formation of prices when the other factors determining them are unchanged, the first of these two methods of measuring capital can be used only in so far as the "wage fund" varies in the same direction as the capital expressed as a sum of values. This does not always happen. It is possible to conceive instances when an increase in this capital (due to saving) will be associated with a reduction of the wage fund, and also instances when an unchanged capital may be invested in different ways, so that the wage fund will vary greatly, although the result will be the same as far as the interest received from the capital and the remuneration of other factors of production are concerned.* From

* In order to make this clear, we may take the following simple schematic example. In a certain community, agriculture and forestry are equally remunerative occupations (within a rather wide margin). The conditions of production are assumed to be such that the capital (expressed as a sum of values) in agriculture is divided in equal proportions between one-year and ten-year investments (raw materials and tools), whereas in forestry all capital has a period of investment of forty years. It is further assumed that the original factors of production, calculated in labour units for the sake of simplicity, will under prevailing price conditions be distributed between the two branches of production in the same proportion as the capital. The labour units not invested in capital goods are supposed to be occupied in the production of final goods in co-operation with the capital goods (e.g. in felling and floating timber, etc., in forestry). We assume that in this community a stationary state first prevails, that a capital equal to the value of 100 labour units is then gradually transferred from agriculture to forestry (together with a corresponding quantity of original labour), and that a new stationary equilibrium is eventually reached with the same wages and interest on capital, (which may also be assumed to be unchanged during the transition period). In comparing these two stationary situations one can clearly speak of an unchanged quantity of capital : for there has been no saving associated with the transition from one state to the other. The total capital value is also unchanged, but if we look at the wage fund, we find—supposing the rate of interest to be 6 per cent—that in agriculture a wage fund of 88 labour units corresponded to the capital value of 100 labour units transferred therefrom to forestry, whereas the new wage fund in forestry has only 26 units. The total wage fund is therefore reduced by a value corresponding to 62 labour units.

this it appears that it is not possible to rely on the wage fund when the concept of an *unchanged volume of capital* is to be determined. For it is implicit in this concept that in a transition from one stationary situation to another no saving is necessary. In some cases this criterion is valid, *in spite of* the variation in the wage fund. The estimate of capital on the wage fund method can perhaps in certain instances be defended as a simplification of the problem when one confines oneself to calculating with simple interest;* but beyond this it would hardly seem to have any scientific value.†

By this I do not mean that the problem when the volume of capital can be regarded as unchanged is solved through the ordinary concept of capital as a sum of values. In some cases, it is true it is possible to manage with this concept or the closely related "weighted average time of

---

* That such considerations and not theoretical speculations led Böhm-Bawerk to treat capital as a wage fund in the sense indicated is plainly evident from his work. Cf. *Positive Theorie des Kapitales*, 3rd ed., Innsbruck, 1909–11, p. 604, note 1, where the author admits that the tables are not quite correct, since he has omitted to use compound interest.—Gustaf Åkerman, on the other hand, has for reasons of principle used the estimate of capital as a wage fund. Cf. my review of his work in *Statsvetenskaplig Tidskrift*, 1923, pp. 349 ff., and 1925, pp. 80 ff.

† What has been said contains no adverse judgment on the so-called *wage-fund theory*, the true import of which is that wages (together with other kinds of remuneration of original factors), are advanced by the capitalists, and that the volume of wages therefore depends on the size of the fund available for this purpose. This theory, which is naturally quite correct as far as it goes, and which has been shown to be especially fruitful in the formulation given by Böhm-Bawerk, does not pre-suppose that a special "wage fund" is set apart from other capital values. For it is possible, and strictly speaking is more correct, to regard all capital as a fund out of which wages, etc., are advanced. That this fund includes not only wages themselves (including the remuneration of other original services), but also interest payable before the results of labour, etc., mature, is manifestly no impediment to the application of this point of view. Böhm-Bawerk's basic idea was probably this last one. He often speaks of the "Subsistenzfonds" as being represented by the entire wealth of the community.

investment."* But sometimes it seems impossible in the nature of the case to determine any fixed points for a comparison between different stationary situations.What is for instance meant by saying that two separate communities with different populations, on different cultural levels and with different technique and consequently quite different price relations, have the same quantity of capital? To regard this as being the case if the circulating capital has the same value (estimated in some common money term) or if the weighted average investment period is equal in the two communities is evidently a purely conventional idea. For this reason the possibilities of an analysis of the pricing problem on these lines are somewhat limited.

The difficulties here mentioned are associated with the stationary setting of the problem. On account of its artificial and very special assumptions the static problem has little or no connection with the phenomena determining prices in the real world. Therefore the attempt must be made to build up on this foundation an improved analysis which will have more general validity.

* [Both these methods of measuring capital have the advantage that, when perfect foresight is assumed, all changes in capital can be ascribed to positive or negative saving. On the other hand, both have the disadvantage, that the measure of capital is made dependent on the prices of the services invested and on the rate of interest—which belong to the unknown factors of the problem. When unexpected events occur that bring about a change in these factors, the size of capital will usually also be changed, if it is measured by one of these two methods, that is, as an amount of exchange value or as a certain length of the average investment period of all original factors. Since no better method seems to be available, we must, however, choose one of these two measures of capital. And in the algebraic treatment of the problem given above, we have preferred to use the second, which seems on the whole to be less influenced by unexpected changes in prices or in the rate of interest (since such changes only affect the weights applied in the calculation of the average investment period).]

CHAPTER III

PERFECT FORESIGHT AND DYNAMIC CONDITIONS

1. The Setting of the Problem

In our first statement of the dynamic pricing problem we shall retain the basic assumption that individuals fully foresee the future, which we used in the previous chapter and of which the import was there explained. We also still retain the general simplifying assumptions formulated in chap. I, sec. 3.

Under these assumptions the dynamic problem differs from that just discussed principally through the occurrence of changes in the factors determining prices.* In contrast to the stationary case, which is in fact a series of repetitions of one and the same state, we now obtain a series of states differing more or less from one another with regard both to the factors determining prices and to the prices themselves. This dynamic process is in reality continuous, but its analysis will be facilitated if it is subdivided into relatively short periods of time during which prices are assumed to remain unaltered. The changes are accordingly assumed to take place at the points of *transition*

---

* This divergence is least when the community is progressing or retrogressing *uniformly*, in the sense that the supply of all factors and the demand for consumption goods show a *proportional* growth or diminution, while the technical coefficients remain unchanged. In these cases, prices will also evidently be unchanged, and the problem can be treated in the same manner as before. The system of equations in chapter II can still be applied, if for each period all functions determining (Y^s) and (X^r) are multiplied by the factor which expresses the size of the change, reckoned from the initial period.

318

between the different periods, and in each period the average state is assumed to last during the entire period.

As in the stationary case, the price situation in each period is regarded as the result of the demand for consumption goods, of the supply of productive services, and the measures taken by entrepreneurs in the use of these services for the production of consumption and of capital goods. As before, we have as conditions of equilibrium that prices and costs of production shall coincide, and that all productive resources shall be fully employed. The factors affecting prices are in both cases functions not only of the prices ruling during the period in question but also of those ruling in later periods, of which individuals take account in their economic activity.

But while in the stationary case the prices in succeeding periods are equal to the prices in the present period and thus do not introduce any new unknowns into the problem, in the dynamic case they will differ more or less from the prices in the first period. For this reason the dynamic problem becomes very much more complicated than the stationary one. In discussing the price situation in a certain period, the different price situations in succeeding periods must be examined simultaneously, and this presupposes a knowledge of the factors affecting prices in these periods also. The problem may thus be stated as follows: if the factors which take an active part in the formation of prices in all periods entering into the dynamic process are known, what will be the price situations in these various periods?

A further dissimilarity in the nature of the problem in the two cases is due to the difference in the initial assumption as to the nature of the capital equipment. In the stationary state it was possible to divide all capital goods into two groups such that the one consisted of original and permanent capital goods ("land") and the other of those representing saved-up services, which are at the same time non-permanent ("circulating capital"). In the dynamic case the two grounds of distinction used in this division cannot be supposed to coincide, as has already been pointed out above (pp. 289 ff.). On the one hand it is to a certain extent possible to acquire equipment of practically unlimited durability through the productive process. By emptying lakes or blasting away rock, for instance, it is possible to produce land that is in no way different from the original land. On the other hand, not all original productive resources are permanent. Above all, mines and similar natural resources must to a certain extent be classed with the group of non-permanent real capital.* The division of capital goods into original and produced resources will therefore be independent of the distinction between permanent and non-permanent capital. Both classifications must be used but for different purposes.

In the analysis of the dynamic problem, as it has been formulated here—i.e. under the assumption that the future is completely foreseen—the first distinction becomes useful in the following way. During the initial period in the dynamic process under observation, all existing capital equipment in the community can be regarded as original, including any that has actually resulted from the production of earlier periods not covered by the analysis. For since at the starting-point a knowledge of the nature of all capital equipment must be presumed, the question of its actual origin is irrelevant. Produced capital goods have the same significance for price formation as true

* In a stationary community no permanent capital goods are produced, nor is the supply of original factors reduced. Should this take place, the conditions are not stationary. That certain permanent capital goods may have been produced *before* the stationary state was reached is, as has been pointed out above, of no relevance to our problem.

original sources of similar kinds. For the same reason capital goods belonging to subsequent periods can also be regarded as original, so long as they have not been produced in the periods included in the analysis. In so far as they have been, they must evidently belong to the produced group, which will thus represent services invested in capital goods during the periods under observation. The latter must be treated as a special group, since they cannot, like other capital goods, be included among the given factors. Their production is, on the contrary, one of the quantities that, together with prices, are determined by the given factors.

In a more detailed analysis of the problem the other basis of classification can also be applied. Both the "original" and the "produced" group can thus be subdivided into permanent and non-permanent capital goods. This point of view is especially relevant in the following respect. Non-permanent capital goods, which can in time be replaced by other investments, are in their nature a variable part of the capital of the community, whereas those of unlimited durability, when once produced, must be assumed to have practically unchanged properties in the different periods.

Making use of these concepts, we shall now attempt to extend our system of equations so that it will be valid in dynamic conditions also, under the assumption that the future is fully foreseen by every one.

2. ALGEBRAIC DISCUSSION

Accordingly we have the following problem: If the supply of productive services, the demand for consumption goods and the technical coefficients relevant to the production of these goods are given for all periods—starting from a given point of departure—as functions of the prices and of the rates of interest that will actually be realized during these periods, what are these prices and rates of interest, and which goods will be produced and consumed in all these periods, etc.?

In the treatment of the problem we require special symbols for the different periods that go to make up the dynamic process. They are numbered 1, 2, 3 . . .ν, which figures are as before written as suffixes. We regard the period ν as so far distant that conditions in the periods following it are of no importance for the price situation in the periods that are chosen for investigation. The situation in these earlier periods of the dynamic process would accordingly not be changed, if the community reached stationary conditions in period ν. In order to simplify the analysis we *imagine* this to be the case.

In the initial period (1) all productive factors are regarded as "original," independently of whether they have been produced or not during earlier periods not entering into the time-space under observation. In the subsequent periods (2, 3, 4 . . .) only such factors are regarded as "original" as have not been produced during earlier periods (1, 2, 3 . . .) of the observed time space. The other factors are, as in the stationary case discussed above, conceived as services saved up from the previous periods. For these saved-up services we need two time suffixes, one denoting the period when the services are invested and the other the period when they mature. The first of these (τ) can of course not have a higher value than the latter (t). The sign $Y_{\tau t}^{s\prime}$ thus denotes the quantity of the factor (Y^s) that is invested in the period τ and matures in the period t in the production of the consumption good (X^r).

It must be admitted that the distinction between "original" and "saved-up" services is not so unambiguous in this case as in the stationary one. In the initial period there exist, according to our assumptions, only "original" factors, but it is naturally questionable how much of the services of these factors should be referred to the initial period or to those following. If it is possible to utilize a given factor either now or later, this factor can be referred either to the present or to the later period. (For instance in the case of growing forests, which may be felled in their entirety in the initial period but are

322

actually in great measure saved for later periods, two different points of view are possible. The entire value of the forest in the initial period may be regarded as original services available for this period. In so far as the forest is then allowed to grow until later periods, these services are saved-up and the forest becomes "produced" real capital. *Or* else the actual felling in the later period can be regarded as "original" services of the forest, attributable to this period, and then the forest will remain an "original" factor of production throughout its entire lifetime.) A theoretical treatment of the problem can be based on either of these ways of viewing the case. But the functions for the supply of the factor manifestly presuppose that the question is solved in a definite manner. If the first alternative is adopted and the supply of the factor in question is thus referred to the initial period, the saved-up services must bear interest at the prevailing rate until they mature in consumption. An application of the second alternative presupposes, on the other hand, that the supply functions for the later periods are made dependent, not only on the prices, but also on the technical coefficients. In order to avoid over-complication in our formulae, we have adopted the first alternative, although, from a purely theoretical point of view, it is probably less satisfactory.

It should further be noted that under dynamic conditions positive or negative net saving may exist in each period, and thus the stock of capital goods may be increased or diminished. The functions determining this net saving have, however, not been included explicitly among the known factors in the treatment of the problem given below. We have preferred to regard all functions referring to the demand for consumption goods as given; we thus have m such functions for each period, whereas their number in the stationary case was only $(m - 1)$. Since saving is defined as the difference between income and consumption during each period, factors which are determined in our solution of the problem, the saving in each period can evidently be calculated as a remainder. We shall return to this question at the end of this section.

We may now turn to the mathematical problem. The *unknowns* are denoted by terms such as:

323

X_t^r : total demand for consumption goods and services in each of the ν periods, $m\nu$ in number;

P_t^r : prices of these goods and services, $m\nu$ in number;

Y_t^s : supply of "original" productive services in each of the ν periods, $n\nu$ in number;

Π_t^s : prices of these services, $n\nu$ in number;

$Y_{\tau t}^{sr}$: whole quantity of (Y^s) invested in period τ and "maturing" in period t in the production of (X^r); when $\tau = t$, the services are consumed in the same period as they are delivered; since τ cannot be higher than t, the total number of these terms is: $\frac{1}{2}mn\nu(1 + \nu)$;*

i_t : the rate of interest prevailing in each of the ν periods and applicable to loans running to the next period, ν in number.

These unknowns are determined by the following equations:

The total *supply of "original" productive services* during the initial period is determined by the prices and the rates of interest prevailing in this and succeeding periods. In any later period the total supply of such services depends not only on the price situation then and in succeeding periods, but in the earlier ones also, all the way back to and including the initial period. This follows as a consequence of the assumption that the future is fully foreseen. For on this assumption people may be supposed at the very beginning to make economic plans for all the periods, based on their knowledge of the situation during these periods, and these plans later govern their future acts.†

* In the initial period the total number of terms such as (Y^{sr}) is mn, in the next period $2mn$, in the following one $3\,mn$, and in the νth period νmn. For every new period the number is thus increased by mn, since saved-up services are used for one period more. If we add up this arithmetic series, we get the sum indicated above.

† The supply of productive services is a function not only of the prices of these services but also of the prices of consumption goods and of interest rates. It should especially be noted that the latter determine the volume of individual savings in the different periods and thus also the incomes from produced capital goods, incomes which to a certain degree, influence the supply of "original" services.

The supply of productive services can therefore be expressed in the following (nv) equations:

$$Y_t^s = F_t^s(\Pi_1^1, \Pi_1^2 \ldots \Pi_1^n; P_1^1, P_1^2 \ldots P_1^m; i_1; \Pi_2^1, \Pi_2^2 \ldots \Pi_2^n;$$
$$P_2^1, P_2^2 \ldots P_2^m; i_2; \ldots \Pi_v^1, \Pi_v^2 \ldots \Pi_v^n; P_v^1, P_v^2 \ldots P_v^m; i_v)$$

$$\text{for} \quad \begin{matrix} s = 1, 2 \ldots n \\ t = 1, 2 \ldots v \end{matrix} \quad . \quad (1)$$

According to the same principles, we can state the *total demand for each consumption good* in every period as a function of prices and interest rates in all periods. Both income and saving are thus functions of the said variables; the distribution of total consumption between various goods in a given period is, on the other hand, a function of the prices of these goods. The equations, mv in number, are therefore written as follows:

$$X_t^\gamma = F_t^\gamma (\Pi_1^1, \Pi_1^2 \ldots \Pi_1^n; P_1^1, P_1^2 \ldots P_1^m; i_1; \Pi_2^1, \Pi_2^2 \ldots \Pi_2^n;$$
$$P_2^1, P_2^2 \ldots P_2^m; i_2; \ldots \Pi_v^1 \Pi_v^2 \ldots \Pi_v^n; P_v^1 P_v^2 \ldots P_v^m; i_v)$$

$$\text{for} \quad \begin{matrix} s = 1, 2 \ldots n \\ t = 1, 2 \ldots v \end{matrix} \quad . \quad (2)$$

The *technical coefficients*, relevant to the production of consumption goods in a given period, can be regarded as functions of the prices of the productive services available in this period. As has already been explained, part of these services can be conceived as "original" and part as "saved-up" from earlier periods. The prices of the latter are, under our assumptions, equal to the original costs of the previously invested services, plus the accrued interest during the whole time of investment. The technical coefficients, relevant to a given period, are therefore functions of the prices of all "original" services and of the rate of interest during this and the preceding periods. Since the assumption of perfect foresight does not necessarily preclude technical inventions (as has been explained in chap. II, sec. 1), it is possible that the functions alter for each new period. We thus get as many functions as we have unknowns of the type $Y_{rt}^{s\gamma}$, that is, $\frac{1}{2}mnv(1 + v)$. They are written:

$$\frac{Y^{sr}_{\tau t}}{X^r} = F^{sr}_{\tau t}(\Pi^1_1, \Pi^2_1 \ldots \Pi^n_1; \Pi^1_2, \Pi^2_2 \ldots \Pi^n_2; i_2; \ldots \Pi^1_t, \Pi^2_t \ldots \Pi^n_t; i_t)$$

$$\text{for} \quad \begin{matrix} r = 1, 2 \ldots m \\ s = 1, 2 \ldots n \\ \tau = 1, 2 \ldots t \\ t = 1, 2 \ldots \nu \end{matrix} \quad (3)$$

Since the principle that the prices of consumption goods must equal *costs of production* is valid here, according to the assumptions made, we obtain for every consumption good in every period an equation stating that the costs of the "original" services of different ages used up in the manufacture of the quantity demanded of the good, plus accrued interest charges,* corresponds to the value of the good, thus in all *mv* equations:

$$P^r_1 X^r_1 = \sum_{s=1}^{n} \Pi^s_1 Y^{sr}_{11}$$

$$P^r_2 X^r_2 = \sum_{s=1}^{n} [\Pi^s_2 Y^{sr}_{22} + \Pi^s_1 Y^{sr}_{12}(1+i_1)] \quad \text{for } r = 1, 2 \ldots m \quad . \quad (4)$$

. . . .

$$P^r_\nu X^r_\nu = \sum_{s=1}^{n} [\Pi^s_\nu Y^{sr}_{\nu\nu} + \Pi^s_{\nu-1} Y^{sr}_{\nu-1,\nu}(1+i_{\nu-1}) + \ldots$$
$$+ \Pi^s_1 Y^{sr}_{1\nu}(1+i_{\nu-1}) \ldots (1+i_1)]$$

Finally we can set up a system of equations for the *entire use of "original" factors*. The quantity of productive services, offered by the owners of these factors in each period, must, in a community of the type here assumed, be used up in the same period, either for immediate consumption or for investment. In estimating the amount of investment in a given period, we have first to sum the services saved-up from the said period but utilized in later periods. To this sum, however, a small addition has to

* It should be remembered that, as before, all prices both of productive services and of consumption goods are assumed to be paid at the *end* of each period. The interest charges for services invested in a certain period should therefore be reckoned from the end of this period to the end of the next period.

be made. If capital goods of *infinite* durability are produced, the process of maturing will not be finished with the νth period which is the last one covered by our analysis. A small remainder must exist, representing the utilization of the good after the νth period. Our assumption that stationary conditions prevail from the νth period onwards makes it possible to calculate this remainder.* The equations expressing the equality between the supply of and the demand for "original" productive services can therefore be written as follows,† $n\nu$ in number:

$$Y_1^s = \sum_{r=1}^{m}\left[Y_{11}^{sr} + Y_{12}^{sr} + Y_{13}^{sr} + \ldots + Y_{1\nu}^{sr} \cdot \frac{1+i_\nu}{i_\nu}\right]$$

$$Y_2^s = \sum_{r=1}^{m}\left[Y_{22}^{sr} + Y_{23}^{sr} + Y_{24}^{sr} + \ldots + Y_{2\nu}^{sr} \cdot \frac{1+i_\nu}{i_\nu}\right]$$

$$\cdot\quad\cdot\quad\cdot\quad\cdot\quad\cdot\quad\cdot\quad\cdot\quad\cdot$$

$$Y_\nu^s = \sum_{r=1}^{m}[Y_{\nu\nu}^{sr} + Y_{\nu-1,\nu}^{sr} + Y_{\nu-2,\nu}^{sr} + \ldots + Y_{1\nu}^{sr}]$$

$$\text{for } s = 1, 2 \ldots n \quad . \quad (5)$$

The total number of the equations is now $\nu(2m + 2n + \tfrac{1}{2}mn(1 + \nu))$, whereas the number of un-knowns (see the list above) is $\nu(2m + 2n + \tfrac{1}{2}mn(1 + \nu) + 1)$. Thus we want an equation for each period, in all ν equations. If we had expressed all prices in a certain consumption good, the number of unknowns would have been reduced by 1 for each period, and the problem would then have been fully determined. When the prices are assumed to be expressed in an arbitrary monetary unit, the problem is determined *except for a multiplicative factor*

* According to the explanations given in chap. II, sec. 4, the "maturing" of the services invested in a durable good can most appropriately be estimated by discounting the future values of its services at compound interest. We have thus only to sum up the infinite but convergent series whose first term is $Y_{\iota\nu}^{sr}$, second term $Y_{\iota\nu}^{sr}(1 + i_\nu)^{-1}$, etc.

† The last equation, for the νth period, assumes that stationary conditions have been achieved, and that the maximum length of the time of investment for the circulating capital is ν periods. Cf. above chap. II, sec. 5.

for each period. On the basis of the given data, we can therefore not determine the absolute height of the price level during the initial period, nor the movements of the price level during the following periods. As the height of the rate of interest, valid for loans from one period to another, must be dependent on changes in the value of the monetary unit, we can only determine its *relation* to the general price level.

From this we can draw the important conclusion that the assumption of perfect foresight does not necessarily contain any conditions with regard to the *movements of the general price level.* The price level may vary in an arbitrary way, that is, all prices may be proportionally increased or diminished from one period to another, without any consequences for the real import of economic transactions. (Disregarding possible changes in cash holdings and other complications connected with a monetary economy.) In particular when the changes in prices are foreseen by all, their effect can be fully neutralized through corresponding *changes in the rate of interest.*

[In the analysis given above we have not made use of such concepts as capital value, income, saving, etc In fact, these concepts are not indispensable for a theoretical treatment of the pricing problem, they are only of *secondary* importance. We may, however, add some observations respecting them since they can be determined on the basis of the terms employed above.

The total *capital value* (K_t) of all factors of production, including labour, at a given point of time, is obtained, if we discount and sum up the values of all productive services delivered during the succeeding periods. We can thus set up the following (ν) equations, referring to the value of all capital at the beginning of each period:*

$$K_0 = \sum_{s=1}^{n} \left[\frac{\Pi_1^s Y_1^s}{1 + i_1} + \frac{\Pi_2^s Y_2^s}{(1 + i_1)(1 + i_2)} + \cdots + \frac{\Pi_\nu^s Y_\nu^s}{(1 + i_1)(1 + i_2) \ldots (1 + i_\nu) i_\nu} \right] \quad (6)$$

* Since stationary conditions are assumed from the νth period, the discounted value of the services of that period has to be capitalized through division by i_ν.

328

$$K_{\scriptscriptstyle\mathrm{I}} = \sum_{s\ \text{and}\ r=\mathrm{I}}^{s=n;\ r=m} \left[\Pi_{\mathrm{I}}^s Y_{\mathrm{I}}^s - \Pi_{\mathrm{I}}^s Y_{\mathrm{II}}^{sr} + \frac{\Pi_2^s Y_2^s}{\mathrm{I} + i_2} + \frac{\Pi_3^s Y_3^s}{(\mathrm{I} + i_2)(\mathrm{I} + i_3)} + \right.$$
$$\left. \cdots + \frac{\Pi_\nu^s Y_\nu^s}{(\mathrm{I} + i_2)(\mathrm{I} + i_3)\cdots(\mathrm{I} + i_\nu)i_\nu} \right]$$

Since the negative term of the second equation, according to the equations of system (4) above, is equal to the value of consumption during the previous period, and since the other terms are equal to those of the first equation, multiplied by the interest factor valid for the first period $(\mathrm{I} + i_{\mathrm{I}})$, we can, in more general terms, state that

$$K_t = (\mathrm{I} + i_t) K_{t-\mathrm{I}} - \sum_{r=\mathrm{I}}^{m} P_t^r X_t^r \quad \text{or}$$

$$K_t - K_{t-\mathrm{I}} = i_t K_{-\mathrm{I}} - \sum_{r=\mathrm{I}}^{m} P_t^r X_t^r \quad . \quad . \ (6a)$$

If we further define total net *income* as the current interest on the total capital value of all factors (including labour) and total net *saving* as the difference between net income and consumption, we can write

$$S_t = i_t K_{t-\mathrm{I}} - \sum P_t^r X_t^r \quad . \quad . \quad . \quad . \ (7)$$

Since the right-hand side of equation (7) is the same as that of equation (6a), we get

$$S_t = K_t - K_{t-\mathrm{I}} \quad . \quad . \quad . \quad . \quad . \ (7a)$$

which states that, during a given period, the amount of net saving will be equal to the increase of the value of capital.

It is easy to show that this equation also holds true if we take the term capital in its more usual sense as including only external factors and not labour, and if we therefore define income as the sum of interest on capital (in this narrower sense) and wages.* But as we shall see later, if

---

* It is only in order to simplify the analysis and to evade the trouble of introducing a more complicated notation that we are here taking capital and income in the wider sense.

we drop the assumption of perfect foresight which has been maintained throughout, there will no longer be equality between saving and the increase in the value of capital.]

3. THE DEVELOPMENT OF PRICES AND INTEREST RATES

Under the assumption that the future is perfectly foreseen, all prices in all the periods included in the dynamic process thus become linked together in a uniform system. The equilibrium of this system is maintained by the same laws as under stationary conditions. Costs of production and prices coincide, and supply and demand are also equal, both for productive services and for consumption goods. The real difference from the stationary case lies in the circumstance that the primary factors, there regarded as given, are assumed to undergo change from one period to another. In this way a movement arises in the system. The task of theory is to elucidate more closely the general conditions on which this movement depends and to give exact expression to its course under all conceivable assumptions. We shall confine ourselves here to the following general reflections.

Other influences aside, the general connection not only between prices in a certain period but also between the different successive price situations has a marked tendency to smooth out and damp down all price movements in comparison with a community where the future is not completely foreseen. This relative stability in the formation of prices is increased by a certain regularity to be found in the changes of the functions for supply, demand and technical coefficients, which we have regarded as primary factors determining prices and as data in the problem. The situation can be characterized by saying that a continuous adjustment of the functions takes place with reference to current and expected future price developments.

If this tendency were alone operative, the community would in time reach stationary conditions. Population, capital and other factors affecting prices would gradually attain a relative size and nature such that at prevailing prices, conditions for a stationary state would come into existence. In the present case, however, the tendency cannot be fully realized, because the phenomena are also subject to changes of a more spontaneous character, not directly due to the economic situation. This is because the development of human nature is regulated not by mechanical but by organic laws, that give rise to new impulses and new acts breaking away from the stationary tendency. Furthermore, man does not control the external conditions of his existence. He cannot influence climatic conditions and so forth to any great extent, and changes of this kind therefore represent continually disturbing factors in economic life. But if all these changes, really primary in relation to price developments, were known beforehand (the angle from which we are discussing the problem), both the factors determining prices and the prices themselves would have the opportunity of adjusting themselves to the new conditions in good time. If for instance a certain commodity could be expected to be the object of a greatly increased demand in some future period owing to changed preferences among consumers (changes of fashion), the forces of production would be directed and adjusted to this branch of production a suitable time beforehand. The apparatus of production would thus be prepared to meet the increased demand and no substantial rise in price might be necessary. There would thus be no sudden transition. The development would have the character of a quiet and rounded wave movement.

What has now been said applies to price development as a whole. Concerning the *relative movements of prices and interest rates* under the assumption that the general price level remains constant a word may be added.

A change in the price of a *consumption good* from one period to another cannot be greater than the cost of such a shift in the process of production as will increase the supply in the period when the article is relatively scarce. As a rule such costs are not very large when production is to be delayed, in order to counteract a threatened rise in the price of an article. In any event they cannot exceed the costs associated with the storage of the commodity, including interest on the capital invested in the stocks laid up. In the other direction the difference may be greater, since it is more difficult to accelerate the maturing of goods in production. It is thus quite conceivable that there may be a considerable drop in the price of an article in a certain period, as the result of a technical invention then introduced. However, such cases are exceptions, in other cases the price movements in a downward direction will also be smoothed out.

Movements in the prices of original *productive services* arise only in so far as changes taking place on the demand and supply sides do not compensate one another. With regard to single categories of services, however, such compensation is probably the rule. The supply of a certain kind of labour, for instance, may vary through an increase or decrease in the number of new workers learning the trade. A change in the demand for this kind of labour can thus be supposed to keep pace with a corresponding change in supply. On the other hand, entrepreneurs will tend in good time to make use of every opportunity of substitution in order to adapt their demand to the situation on the supply side. The consequence of these adaptions is partly that the price movements themselves are weakened, and partly that they are spread over larger groups of services which form possible substitutes for one another, and thus their movement with regard to each category of services is still further reduced. On the whole then there remain only such slow and rather small adjustments of prices as are caused by population movements, the increase or decrease of capital equipment, the development of technique, etc. Since in real life it can be expected that these very changes counteract each others' influences on prices to a considerable degree, the influence of this cause of price movements will be much smaller than one might expect.

The fluctuations of the *rate of interest* under the assumptions made here must also be very small indeed, if we suppose that the general price level is kept fairly stable. This follows from what has just been said regarding the prices of consumers' goods and of original services. On account of the smooth and quiet character of general price movements it can be expected that the demand on the part of entrepreneurs for saving will also remain fairly constant (if exceptional cases are ignored, such as when a comparatively profound change in the process of production takes place as a result of technical inventions, etc.), and since the supply of saving under our assumptions will probably fluctuate relatively little, there is no apparent reason why the rate of interest should vary to any great extent. It should, however, be pointed out that even if such fluctuations should arise either on the demand or the supply side, entrepreneurs nevertheless have such extensive opportunities for substitution in the utilization of saving, that a smoothing out of the price curve can be expected to a *greater* degree here than elsewhere.

This thesis may most suitably be clarified by the examination of a concrete case. Suppose that under otherwise similar conditions there are reasons for expecting a considerable amount of saving in a certain future period, while the periods immediately before and after it remain

333

relatively normal in this respect. If this non-recurrent saving were not foreseen, the rate of interest (especially if we drop the atomistic premiss) would evidently then be greatly reduced and would later fluctuate on a level higher than in that period but lower than what was originally the case.* Again, if everyone correctly foresees what is going to take place and adjusts his actions accordingly, the process will differ greatly from that just characterized. For the apparatus of production will then be directed towards the absorption of the large non-recurrent saving. The result of this will be that the sudden dip in the interest curve will be smoothed out. The interest level will fall gradually from the old position to the new one over a stretch of time which includes periods both before and after the period when the saving takes place.

This may best be understood by imagining the way in which entrepreneurs would act if they foresaw a considerable drop in the rate of interest in the period of saving and subsequently a lower interest level. On the one hand they would obviously defer the normal new investments of the periods immediately preceding the saving until the period of saving itself and later periods, thus taking advantage of the lower interest costs. On account of this reduced demand for saving just before the period of saving, the rate of interest would start to fall even before the saving had taken place. Simultaneously, the increased demand in the period of saving and later would tend to raise the rate of interest at that time. On the other hand, entrepreneurs would prolong investments which would otherwise have matured during the period of saving and later. Such an extension of the time of investment would become remunerative on account of the lower rate of interest then in force. Thus, still more savings would be absorbed during this period and the interest level raised still further. The reorganization of the process of produc-

* We are supposing that after the non-recurrent saving has taken place entrepreneurs once more adjust themselves to more normal conditions. On account of the increase in the capital equipment resulting from the non-recurrent saving, the rate of interest in the future must be supposed to remain lower than before the saving occurred.

tion in these two respects would continue until a suitable smoothing out of the interest curve had taken place. This will therefore be the position at which the entrepreneurs aim from the very beginning, if they are fully cognizant of the situation.

In an analogous manner the smoothing-out process that takes place in other cases of expected fluctuation in interest rates can be explained, for instance, when savings are greatly reduced in a certain period or when a temporary increase or decrease in the supply of capital for some short future period can be foreseen.

Finally, under our assumptions there will be no change in the prices of *capital goods*, other than the addition in value due to services newly invested plus accrued interest on capital, and reductions in value due to the maturing of services. Capital values are accordingly altered only as a result of positive or negative saving. This does not apply solely to produced capital goods. The value of the original capital goods is also increased (diminished) through positive (negative) saving, in so far as the accrued interest on capital exceeds (or falls short of) the value of the services maturing during the period. In a study of the function of saving, this kind of saving which has reference to the original capital goods must clearly also be taken into account. As the problem has been stated here, this is all the more necessary, since all capital goods existing in the initial stage have been classified with original sources and only those produced later with the group of produced equipment. This point of view has probably the wider field of application, since it enables a pricing situation to be discussed without bringing up the question of the manner in which existing capital equipment came into being. But however the distinction is drawn, it must always be more or less conventional, and a limitation of the concept of saving to only one of the classes of capital equipment therefore appears to be unjustified.

In the above analysis we have ignored the fact that the general *price level* may fluctuate during the dynamic process on account of a change in the value of the monetary unit, involving a proportional rise or fall in all money prices. This does not, however, reduce the validity of the analysis of relative price movements just given. Nor is it of real importance for the problem in other respects—if we abstract from certain complications arising from the monetary system—since fluctuations in the general price level which are known beforehand can be neutralized by corresponding changes in the rate of interest, as has been shown particularly by Irving Fisher. Only in the analysis of the development of interest rates and of the factors intimately connected therewith—for example income and saving measured in monetary units* —is it necessary to take these circumstances into account. For our reasoning regarding the rate of interest to be applicable, it is evidently necessary that the general price level should remain fairly constant.

As pointed out above, no general rules can be laid down for the movements of the general price level in a community with perfect foresight. The determination of this factor calls for more specific assumptions with regard

* [The definitions given in the previous section of *income* as the current interest on all capital values and *saving* as the excess of income over consumption involve certain complications in this respect. It must be noted that increases in capital value due to a rise in the price level are included in income and saving thus defined. The terms thus acquire a purely monetary character. If we wish to study the function of saving, we must of course take account of possible changes in the value of the monetary unit. For a calculation of income and saving when the unit is constant, it is, however, not sufficient to carry through a division by a price index. It is also necessary to calculate what the rate of interest would have been, if no changes in the value of the monetary unit had taken place, and to employ this rate in the estimate of the value of capital and the estimate of income and saving based upon it.]

336

to the monetary system and the ruling principles of monetary policy.*

In a closer study of the dynamic problem under the assumption that the future is completely foreseen, the most important point to investigate is the manner in which a given process is altered by the introduction of primary changes of different kinds. Here the *ceteris paribus* premiss must be used with special care, for a foreseen change in one factor affecting prices must be connected with more or less widespread changes in other factors. The analysis therefore presents considerable difficulty, but it may nevertheless be expected to give results of immediate interest. Above all it should be possible to clarify to what extent the actual disturbances in economic life can be avoided or mitigated by increased foresight on the part of those responsible.

Instead of continuing our investigation of these problems, which have as yet been only very slightly studied,† we shall proceed to the complications which follow if we drop the assumption that the future has been completely foreseen.

* [We have treated this problem in the second part of this work, chap. I, sec. 5.]

† In the work already cited (pp. 213 ff.) Myrdal has an interesting study of how the "most advantageous method of construction" of enterprises is affected by certain foreseen changes relating to prices of products, materials, etc.

CHAPTER IV

IMPERFECT FORESIGHT

1. PERFECT FORESIGHT FOR SHORT PERIODS ONLY

In our next approximation to reality we assume once again that people have the same ideas regarding the future and everyone is certain that these ideas will be realized. We also assume that these views regarding the future have such a character that they would be completely fulfilled if it were not—and there lies the difference from the previous case—that unforeseen events occurred from time to time. As a result of these the actual course of events will differ from those anticipated by the members of the community in a greater or less degree. The simplifying assumptions made in chap. I, sec. 3, are still retained.

The discussion of this case can set out along the same lines as those used in the previous chapter. Starting from a certain period, we can set up a system of equations which will determine the development as anticipated. The data are the factors influencing prices entering into people's anticipations, i.e. the functions for supply, demand and the technical coefficients that everyone believes will apply during the various periods of the dynamic process. What is sought is the price developments that would occur if all anticipations were fulfilled. Since by our assumption unforeseen events go on occurring, causing people to modify their ideas regarding the future, we obtain for each new period of price determination a new price system, corresponding to anticipations during this period.

This mode of stating the problem will be found to be reasonably useful. For by studying the price development

338

anticipated in each period, a good basis is secured for the analysis of the actual course of events.

To start with, it may be assumed that the unforeseen events take place at the point of transition from one period of time to another. This appears not unreasonable when dealing with short periods. The price series anticipated in a certain period will then agree with the actual development of prices at least as far as this period is concerned. This first price situation will therefore be common to both series, and if the unforeseen events afterwards occurring do not cause too profound changes, the series will show many points of contact in the immediately subsequent periods also. The analysis of a *given* pricing situation can thus be directly linked with a study of anticipations during the same period. In such an analysis, the part of the anticipated series that will not be realized on account of later unforeseen events is also of interest. For it affects people's actions and thus constitutes a determining factor in the price situation of the initial period. In studying the pricing problem under the assumptions made here,* we can accordingly apply the analysis of the preceding chapter directly.

* The assumption, that in a given period of time people perfectly foresee the price level that will prevail in this period as a result of their actions during the period, is, strictly speaking, a necessary condition for an explanation of a price situation as a state of equilibrium, in the sense that there exists a *mutual* connection between supply and demand on the one hand and actual prices on the other, and that, therefore, at existing prices exchange can continue until full satisfaction has been attained. The assumption thus underlies most theories of price determination. If this abstraction is dropped, another method of analysis must be used. It must be imagined that people anticipate a certain price situation and therefore decide upon a certain volume of supply and demand, and that these decisions give rise to a price situation *different* from that anticipated. (Even if there should be agreement with regard to prices, the two situations differ with regard to the relation between supply and demand.) The new situation causes people to alter their decisions, and this in

339

Further, it is possible, setting out from the price series anticipated in a certain period, to investigate the manner in which the unforeseen changes taking place in the transition to the next period will modify the series of prices anticipated in this later period. This brings out the way in which one pricing situation is *transformed* into another, and also the importance of unforeseen changes for the actual development of prices.

On this latter problem, which is of both great theoretical and practical importance, we may here make a few observations of a general character. As has been mentioned, unforeseen changes result in modifications of people's previous ideas regarding the future. Herein lies the greatest deviation from the case treated earlier. On account of this circumstance we need two systems of equations—referring respectively to the situation before and after the changes have taken place—in order to elucidate the transition from one position to the other.

The other side of the problem is concerned with the fact that people *gain* or *lose*, in so far as they own capital assets, the values of which are disturbed by the change in anticipations. These *gains* and *losses*, as Myrdal has rightly shown,* "belong to quite a different category from incomes and costs." Whereas the latter may be regarded as prices (of productive services or products), the former "are not prices but changes in prices." The distinction may also be explained by saying that the income in the

turn gives rise to still another situation, again with new decisions, etc. In this case there is no mutual dependence between prices and the factors affecting prices at a given moment, but instead a *one-sided* causal connection in one direction or the other. A "zigzag" movement of this kind in the determination of prices exists in reality, above all in transactions unusually sensitive to price change, especially on the stock and produce exchanges. Here, however, we cannot discuss these highly dynamic price movements. [This problem has been taken up in Part I.]   * Op. cit., p. 44.

shape of interest obtained by a person from a certain capital refers to a certain *space of time*. But a gain or loss has reference to the *moment of time* when the owners of capital assets change their appraisal of its value, because of the unforeseen event.

Owing to these gains and losses—the size and character of which have been closely analysed by Myrdal under different assumptions* and which therefore need not be discussed here—another thesis ceases to apply when the future is no longer accurately foreseen. This is the view that the capital values in the community can be increased or decreased only through positive or negative *saving* of the same amount. For the concept of saving is distorted if an attempt is made to press into it the whole amount of the gains and losses just discussed. By the term saving we can only mean refraining from consuming *income*—for refraining from consuming *capital* we have the term "waiting"—although it is true that this can be interpreted in various ways, depending upon just what is meant by consumption and by income.† But, as has just

* Op. cit., chap. v.—If we drop the atomistic premiss, both gains and losses will be increased under the assumption made in the text regarding people's anticipations, but losses will rise more than gains, owing to a variety of circumstances, concerning which the reader may be referred to the work cited, pp. 75 and 89.

† If the concept of capital is made so extensive that human beings are also classed as capital, consistency requires that consumption for productive purposes shall also be regarded as saving. From certain points of view there are good reasons for this mode of defining the concept. From the standpoint of wealth, the development of productive capacities in labour is quite as important as that of material capital goods. And since a changed distribution of income often brings with it a shift in the proportion between these two types of the formation of "capital," an incorrect picture of the situation is obtained if one includes only that saving which is of a material nature. From other points of view, however, it may be desirable to confine both concepts to external material objects.—Another distinction used by us,—that between "gross" and "net saving,"—does not require any special explanation.

been said, it is in principle incorrect to regard the gains and losses as positive and negative income. From this it follows that they cannot be the objects of saving.* Saving, like consumption, takes place in time, it has a time dimension. The losses and gains, on the other hand, are strictly speaking timeless, so that in this respect again they evidently belong to quite different eonomic categories. This difference also appears in the manner in which capital values are changed, through saving on the one hand and through losses and gains on the other. Whether saving means that interest is added to capital or that there is new investment, the result will be a successive and continuous alteration in the value of capital. This is also true when saving is negative and consumption of capital therefore occurs. Gains and losses on the other hand bring with them *discontinuous* changes in capital values.

All this is of some importance when it is desired to determine the economic results of certain unforeseen events in a given case. For here the first task is to examine to what extent these events have given rise to gains and losses and have in this way increased or decreased capital values. From the above it appears that such changes in values are the most immediate results of unforeseen changes. It is another question whether the function expressing saving rises or falls as a result of the changes, whether for instance a loss of capital will be compensated in time through *increased* saving. It is true that such a tendency does not seem improbable, but this must naturally be *specifically* investigated in every case. In any event a warning should be given against the not uncommon fallacy of letting the criterion of *unchanged*

* [This applies to saving viewed *ex ante*. As we have shown above (p. 108), *ex post* estimates of savings for a certain period will include a part of the gains and losses, depending on the activities of that period.]

decisions concerning saving in such cases be unchanged capital values. On the contrary, an unchanged quantity of saving must evidently be associated with changed capital values. If saving both before and after the unforeseen event is supposed to be equal to zero, capital values in the succeeding periods must differ from the original values by the amount of the gains and losses.

2. Application to the Case of Unforeseen Saving

An interesting application of this reasoning is provided by the case of *unforeseen saving*. Owing to the fact that the saving is not foreseen, it gives rise to gains and losses in the same way as other unforeseen events. The increase in the value of the capital equipment directly caused by the savings and which on the material plane finds expression in the production of new capital assets or in the accumulation of interest on old ones, is accordingly modified in one direction or the other by these gains and losses, which to a greater or smaller degree affect the capital assets already in existence.

In order to shed still more light on the general nature of the problem we shall examine this last case somewhat more closely. Suppose, then, that we want to investigate (under certain given assumptions) the effects of saving that occurs unexpectedly in a certain period but is not continued in succeeding periods. It is assumed that no other unexpected primary changes take place. The analysis will be as follows.

In the transition to the period when the saving occurs people are assumed to acquire a knowledge of the consequences of the saving.* They consequently modify their

* As has already been pointed out above, without an assumption of this kind, it is impossible to explain a certain given price situation as a state of equilibrium with regard to the supply and demand then operative.

previous anticipations regarding the development of prices. The result will be altered capital values, i.e. gains and losses, even before the saving has taken place. If we add to the sum of these new capital values the total saving, we obtain the size of the capital of the community at the end of the period of saving. If one could then suppose that everyone, from the period of saving onwards, foresaw future developments completely, the capital of the community would evidently remain of this magnitude in succeeding periods, since by hypothesis there is no new saving, positive or negative, nor can any gains or losses arise. Again, if people's ideas as to the future during the period of saving are of such a nature that they are not realized, new gains and losses will arise in the transition to the next period. For no saving to take place in this period, all investment plans must evidently be directed towards keeping these new capital values unchanged. But if the anticipations in this period are also corrected in the transition to the next period, the result will be new gains and losses, and in this way the process may continue *ad infinitum*.

The assumptions made as to the anticipations of individuals in every particular case are evidently of decisive importance for the character of the process. In a theoretical case these assumptions should not be arbitrary in any way. The most natural assumption from the theoretical point of view is *either* that anticipations are such that they will be realized (as assumed above), *or* that in each period people are certain that the price situation then existing will be maintained in the future.

The reason for our choice of just this case as an example illustrating our previous reasoning is that it has already been treated in detail in a quite different manner by Gustaf Åkerman in the second volume of his important treatise on capital.* The most essential difference between the method outlined above and that applied by Åkerman† is that he consistently lets the capital of society measured as a "wage fund," that is as a sum of invested wages without regard to the accrued interest,‡ first increase by the same amount as the saving and then, when no more saving takes place, remain unchanged. This procedure is of course much simpler than that indicated by us. The question is whether it is logically unassailable.

Åkerman's method evidently builds on two premises. The first is that all savings are used for new investment of wages, and the second, that the wage total, represented by the old capital goods, is always equal to the wages originally invested.

It is true that the *first* premise is valid in Åkerman's special case, in which it is assumed that the production of capital goods does not require time, in other words, that interest on capital does not enter into the cost of production. But if this unreal assumption is dropped, it is evident that saving can also be used to prolong the time that elapses before a certain invested sum of wages matures. Therefore, not only the invested wages may be saved but also the interest that accrues on these wages from the moment of investment onward. In certain instances saving can be employed solely for a prolongation of the time in which services already invested mature. We refer to Wicksell's example of the store of wine,§ where the function of saving is to make possible a prolongation of the age of the wine already stored. Again, in connection with our earlier criticisms of

* *Realkapital und Kapitalzins*, vol. ii, chaps. xvii–xxi.—Åkerman is evidently speaking of unforeseen saving, although he does not state this expressly. Nor does he make it plain that the effects of perfectly foreseen saving are, as we have shown above, quite different.

† Another difference, also one of principle, is found in Åkerman's somewhat arbitrary assumption as to the anticipations of entrepreneurs. See on this and other questions touched on here, my review in *Statsvetenskaplig Tidskrift*, 1925, pp. 80 ff.

‡ See above, p. 313. The concept of wages in this connection is assumed to include also the payment of other original services than labour. § *Lectures*, vol. i, p. 176.

the wage fund theory, we must point out that in such cases the wage fund may not only be increased by a smaller amount than savings or remain unchanged in spite of savings, but it may even be *reduced* as a result of saving. The example which we have already used, of a community engaged both in agriculture and forestry can easily be constructed in such a way that this result will follow.* Thus it appears that Åkerman's method, even if it were otherwise correct, cannot be applied under assumptions corresponding to reality.

The *second* premise lying at the foundation of Åkerman's exposition is that the total of wages invested in one period in order to replace the services then maturing, and not available as new saving, is equal to the sum of wages representing the original cost of these services. This statement is true if the future is completely foreseen, and if, be it noted, at the same time the first premise, that interest does not enter into the cost of production of the capital goods, is also maintained. For if the value of a capital asset for instance is altered because of a change in the rate of wages anticipated with certainty from the very beginning, then this alteration will have been included in the original profit calculation. Thus it enters as a positive or negative item in the interest obtained from the investment. The reinvestment should therefore be determined by the initial costs of production.

But in the present case this scheme is disturbed by the *unforeseen* saving. This gives rise to a dynamic process, bringing with it *gains* and *losses* to the owners of the old capital goods. These gains and losses cannot, for reasons already given, be regarded as positive and negative items in the interest on the initial investment. They should instead be included in the value of the capital that is to bear interest in each period and be kept unchanged through the investment of new services replacing those that mature. Reinvestment in each period should therefore correspond to the reduction in value that the capital in

* Cf. above, p. 315, note. The example needs only to be varied by making the motive for the transfer from agriculture to forestry a small fall in the rate of interest, caused by a moderate amount of saving.

question undergoes because of the maturing services, without reference to whether it is greater or smaller than the initial value of the services in question. This means that the reinvestment does not correspond to the original costs of production of the capital asset but to its costs of *reproduction* in each period. And the latter differ from the former just on account of the changes that have taken place. A reinvestment on the basis of the original wage costs, which will therefore be greater or smaller than what is required (according to this view), will in the same degree include positive or negative saving, if this term is taken in the sense indicated above. The premise in question can therefore not be upheld from the point of view adopted here. In a dynamic community, where the future is not completely foreseen, capital does not maintain a constant size as a wage fund, if no saving (positive or negative) takes place in the different periods.* Thus Åkerman's method does not reach its goal even with the high degree of abstraction on which it is built, namely the assumption that the process of production does not require time. In an investigation of a dynamic process of the character in question one cannot side-step the trouble of calculating with gains and losses. The method previously indicated is therefore the only one that can be used.†

* Åkerman's assumption should therefore be formulated by saying that savings take place in the different periods to the extents necessary for the maintenance of a constant wage fund. As a motive for the use of *this* premise it might be said that, in reality, entrepreneurs are sometimes content to write off their capital goods according to their original value as shown in the books without taking later changes into account.

† The criticism brought forward here concerning Åkerman's treatment of the present question can by analogy be applied to other treatments of similar problems based on the assumption that the size of the capital of a community as a wage fund remains the same in spite of changes that have taken place. This assumption underlies for instance Wicksell's analysis of the consequences of a general tax on production (*Finaztheoretische Untersuchungen*, Jena, 1896, pp. 36 ff.), an exposition which I have already criticized (*Die Gerechtigkeit der Besteuerung*, Lund, 1919, p. 117, note) for analogous reasons.

3. FURTHER APPROXIMATION TO REALISTIC ASSUMPTIONS

We have now brought our investigation to a point at which a further approximation to reality is associated with such considerable difficulties that we shall restrict ourselves to a few comments on a special setting of the problem.

In the next stage of analysis the assumption previously made, that a particular future development appears quite certain to everyone, must evidently be replaced by the assumption that people's ideas regarding the future have the character of probability judgments. The future would therefore appear to them as series of more or less probable alternatives. The character of these *ideas regarding the future* depends upon two factors: people's power of making judgments regarding future developments, and their tendency to let their ideas be influenced by emotional considerations. How they *act* under the influence of these ideas depends in turn on a third factor, their evaluation of the risk believed by them to be associated with alternative courses of action. "These three intermingling factors: the *objective risk* actually run by the entrepreneur with his presumptions, his *views* with regard to this objective risk, and his *valuation* of the risk he imagines, are the main terms of the problem of the dynamic balance of costs, the problem of the profits of entrepreneurs."* By "objective risk" is meant a perfectly unemotional estimate of the

* Myrdal, op. cit., p. 103. What has been said applies not only to "enterprise" in the narrower sense but has a general application. See op. cit., p. 115: "From the viewpoint of the general determination of prices all human beings are entrepreneurs. Enterprise means making decisions of economic importance. Whether these decisions aim at action or inaction, the entire complex of risks enters into the underlying motives, as soon as different alternatives are open and the decision can be expected to be of importance for the size of future income and costs, or for the time when these latter will begin to be operative."

risks involved on the basis of the knowledge and experience actually possessed by the entrepreneur.

How a certain price situation is determined under these more complicated assumptions could be clarified by a system of simultaneous equations only in the special "hybrid" case discussed by Myrdal, where dynamic elements are included in a static system. We have already pointed out† that stationary conditions do not necessarily exclude all elements of risk. And a study of the complications due to the risk factor is of course much simplified, if it is based on the assumption that conditions remain stationary in spite of the fact that people do not fully foresee the future and therefore must reckon with risks.

But the introduction of the risk factor would mean that we could not as before work with functions referring to *total* quantities. We should be obliged to descend to *individual* functions, since the special mark of the fully dynamic problem is the difference between different individuals. The fact that people's anticipations take the form of scales of probability would also make the equations more complicated. Every particular form of enterprise is based on a calculation regarding investment—more or less approximate—with reference to more or less remote incomes and costs that are expected with differing degrees of probability to result. These expectations, reduced through the risk valuations of the entrepreneur, are discounted down to the present in the form of a capital value. Trying to maximise this value, the private entrepreneur operates in a market among other entrepreneurs, and the resulting price situation is *marginally* determined, both as far as concerns individual differences of estimates and valuations of risk and as regards the particular complications arising out of credit relations, the factors of inertia, etc.

† See above chap. ii, sec. 1, last paragraph.

The problem of equilibrium becomes of course more complicated than those treated above. In its general contours it has been elucidated to some extent in Myrdal's work.

In conclusion we only wish to remind the reader of the abstract nature of the assumptions under which we have proceeded in the whole of this investigation (see chap. I, sec. 3). These assumptions—of which the atomistic premiss is the most important—have been chosen in order to make a simple exposition possible. As long as the future is assumed to be fully foreseen, they do not, however, modify our conclusions to any great extent.

APPENDIX

THE PROBLEM OF BALANCING THE BUDGET

In 1927 a Commission was appointed to investigate the unemployment situation in Sweden. Its findings are important not only as a contribution to the solution of some of the problems of current economic policy, but also for pure science. Economic experts played such a large part in the investigation that the report may not unreasonably be considered the principal achievement of Swedish research into the problems of the trade cycle in recent years. In saying this we have in mind not only the monographs published as supplements, for which, besides the chairman of the committee, six professors and assistant professors of economics were responsible. The two reports of the commission itself also contain new theoretical and statistical material of high scientific value. This is no doubt largely due to Dr. Dag Hammarskjöld who held the post of secretary to the commission for some time. Nor does the scientific character of these reports detract from their interest for the layman. The first part forms a comprehensive handbook to the economic development of Sweden since the war, the second contains a survey of current problems in economic policy, taking account of their theoretical implications.*

It is very natural that the Commission should have devoted its attention principally to cyclical unemployment, since its work was necessarily influenced by the depression which came on during the time of its investigation. The progress of recovery since that time, however, does not in any sense diminish the importance of its achievement. What was proposed was

* *Arbetslöshetsutredningens betänkande (Unemployment Commission Report)* vols. i–ii (Statens offentliga utredningar, 1931, No. 20, and 1935, No. 6); *Bilagor* (Supplements): (1) Bagge (S.o.u., 1931, No. 21), (2) Huss (S.o.u., 1931, No. 21), (3) G. Åkerman (S.o.u., 1931, No. 42), (4) Hammarskjöld (S.o.u., 1933, No. 29), (5) Myrdal (S.o.u., 1934, No. 1), (6) A. Johansson (S.o.u., 1934, No. 2), (7) Ohlin (S.o.u., 1934, No. 12).

351

nothing less than an extensive programme aiming at smoothing out trade fluctuations by political action in various fields. The principal tool for this purpose is the rational direction of monetary policy. For this a method was outlined; but it was proposed to supplement it by measures concerned with financial, commercial and wage policy, in order to make monetary policy fully effective.

In the following pages, I shall confine myself to the following points concerned with the economic effects of financial policy: (1) The problem of balancing the budget in the long period. (2) Modification of the long period programme to counteract industrial fluctuations (when external relations allow of the pursuit of an active policy). (3) The effect of international complications. (4) Budgetary technique. The most convenient method appears to be to proceed by way of comment on the extensive investigation of these problems carried out by Professor Gunnar Myrdal at the instance of the Commission.*

1. The Long Term Solution

Every budget is of course formally balanced, since the sum of the items on the expenditure side must always be covered exactly by revenue. A demand for a balanced budget must therefore mean that the sum of *certain* kinds of revenue must be equal to the sum of *certain* kinds of expenditure. The most natural procedure is to start either from total *current revenue*, i.e. revenue other than that arising from the sale of capital assets or from borrowing; or from total *current expenditure*, i.e. expenditure that does not lead to an increase in the aggregate net assets of the community. If these two are exactly equal,

* Myrdal, *Finanspolitikens ekonomiska verkningar* (*The Economic Effects of Public Finance*), Statens offentliga utredningar, 1934, No. 1.

[Reference to Swedish conditions in sections 1–4 (written in 1934) thus refer to the state of affairs prior to 1935. An account of the important budgetary reforms of 1935–38 is given in section 5.]

[For a good treatment of these and connected problems from the English point of view, reference can now be made to Ursula K. Hicks, *The Finance of British Government* 1920–1936.]

the budget is obviously balanced in the sense that the net value of total public assets remains unchanged,— supposing that this is assessed on the same principles as those on which the budget is drawn up. If current revenue exceeds current expenditure, a corresponding rise in the net value of public assets occurs. Myrdal introduces the term "financial soundness" in order to characterize "the long term trend of development of the net assets of the body public." His intention is to make it clear that the problem of balancing the budget is concerned primarily with whether, and to what degree, the State (and local authorities) should increase or reduce their total net assets.

Myrdal points out that there are a number of advantages in a relatively high degree of "financial soundness" as far as long term policy is concerned. He also shows that it is particularly desirable to increase "soundness" when the net property of the state is small or negative, and current taxes are therefore so high that their incidence is necessarily unsatisfactory. "The dilemma, however, is that under our assumption with regard to the volume of direct expenditure, such a transition to a higher degree of financial "soundness," which would apparently be justified by the high level of taxation, demands an immediate and protracted increase of current tax rates, in order ultimately to obtain tax rates that are correspondingly lower, as a result of the reduction of loans, the paying off of debt or the creation of special funds."* It is a pity that he does not include a more complete treatment of the particular taxes through which the increase in the public assets might be financed. For it is not easy to base the argument for an increase in certain taxes on the ground that these very taxes are already too high and must therefore be reduced. The solution would seem to lie in higher taxes on *capital*

* Op. cit., p. 112.

353

(especially inheritance taxes, but also other true property taxes) in order by this means to secure lower taxes on current *income*.

When the problem is stated in this way, greater light is also shed on the real conflict of interest that exists in the political treatment of the problem. In general, a rising net value of public assets must be advantageous to the working classes, so long as the relief from taxation thus made possible is not offset by a flight or other loss of capital. On the other hand, the programme must tend to encounter opposition from the rich, who are forced to finance tax relief in the future by a reduction of their property now, but will have to share the benefits of the tax reduction with the whole community. A real divergence of political interest thus arises from the fact that an increase in the net assets of the state implies some mitigation of the inequality of the present distribution of wealth.

This is indeed the crux of the matter. The long term solution of the problem of public investment is of primary importance for the distribution of wealth. Its direct relevance for the problems of the labour market, especially the unemployment problem, is, comparatively speaking, less. Of course it may be argued that the scheme suggested would affect the internal supply of capital and that thus a change in the demand for labour might occur. It is also conceivable that a reduction of taxes on income made possible by a rise in net public assets, might make workers less unwilling to accept a certain reduction of their nominal income, and that the average level of employment might be somewhat increased. But these consequences of a particular solution of the problem of public property which might well be neutralized by each other or by other circumstances, can hardly be of decisive importance. From the point of view of the labour market there do not seem to be any arguments for departing from a comparatively high standard of "financial soundness," if this appears to be called for on other considerations.

The accepted standard of "financial soundness" in terms of Swedish financial traditions may be summed up by saying that the net assets (in the wider sense) of the State should in the long run be increased by the amount by which the value of new capital assets, not yielding a money income, exceeds the depreciation of old assets (of the same type), plus a certain amortization of public debt. Capital investment must therefore be financed to this extent by current revenue and not by loan. The standard set for the increase of the net assets of the Local Authorities is not the same, since on the one hand they have a limited right of borrowing for the acquisition of durable capital equipment (whether or not income yielding), which calls for exceptionally heavy outlay in relation to the normal yearly level; but on the other they are required to finance even self-liquidating capital expenditure of a more ordinary character out of current revenue. These principles have, it is true, no special significance,* but they appear to be as acceptable as any others. It would, perhaps, have been desirable to have a more exact statement of the rate at which public debt should be paid off. Amortization should if possible stand in some relation to total receipts from inheritance taxes and other genuine property taxes. But the chief limitation to the principle is its reference to long periods of time; it is essential to modify it for the solution of the annual budget problem.

* The principle adopted by the Swedish state is explained by the accounting system in force prior to 1935: no money values were in general set on capital assets not yielding money income, and a decrease of the net assets accounted for would therefore occur if such investment were financed by loans.

2. The Short Term Solution

The mitigation of economic fluctuations means, so far as the labour market is concerned, that unemployment is reduced in depression but in the boom may perhaps be somewhat greater than it would otherwise have been. The advantage of such a policy is that the reduction of unemployment is presumed to be much larger than its increase, so that there is a reduction in the average degree of unemployment in the long run.

This problem must necessarily be stated in terms of certain political assumptions which require specific justification on one point at least. Myrdal appears to assume that the direction of financial policy to ironing out trade fluctuations will leave the scope and extent of private activities unchanged in the long run. The Unemployment Commission is still more positive on this point. Its report is profoundly influenced by the view that government activities should not be expanded at the expense of private enterprise. Such an expansion may, however, be permissible when it does not cause a contraction of private activities, but takes place through the employment of productive resources that would otherwise have been (wholly or partly) idle. Whether or not one is wholly in sympathy with this view,* it may usefully serve as a starting-point for an analysis of the question of the degree to which the mitigation of trade fluctuations through financial policy is desirable.

In view of the intimate dependence of the internal

* The measures of financial policy that seem justified from this point of view may be characterized as the *minimum* concerning which the various political parties in Sweden agree. If the programme is shifted in a direction more favourable to state enterprise, it might include other measures more powerful in mitigating trade fluctuations, but which may gradually diminish private economic enterprise. The soundness of such measures, always a political question, is not discussed in this paper.

economic situation on the regulation of interest and loan rates by the Central Bank, and on the relation of the national currency to that of other countries, there can in my opinion be no doubt that any smoothing out of trade fluctuations regarded as desirable should be attained primarily through monetary measures. The primary responsibility for trade cycle policy must accordingly lie with the Central Bank, since it is intimately concerned with the responsibility for the care of the monetary system. Public Finance can therefore only be a supplementary instrument, and should if possible be co-ordinated with the policy pursued by the Central Bank. Myrdal and the Unemployment Commission seem to be of the same opinion on this point.

If such a financial policy is to be successful, it is important that it should not come up against difficulties arising from the relation of the country to other countries. There must accordingly be what Myrdal terms an "international margin" for an independent policy. Also, the technical budgetary apparatus and the character of public administration must be such as to make the policy feasible. Finally, there must be grounds for believing that fairly reliable short-term economic forecasts can be made.

It is necessary to make these assumptions more exact when the import of the financial policy is discussed in detail. It will be helpful to start first with relatively *favourable conditions*, and to investigate later how far the conclusions must be modified under more complicated circumstances.

The background against which a cyclical budgetary programme must be seen, is that public action has on the whole a "natural" tendency to intensify such fluctuations rather than the contrary. This means that after a slump has set in, a reduction of current revenue is anticipated

357

at the time when the budget is tabled, and also an increase in current expenditure due to emergencies arising out of the depression itself. For this reason the greatest possible economy is aimed at, both in current expenditure and in capital investment. The latter will thus be curtailed in the same way as in private enterprise. During the boom the situation is reversed: not only is current expenditure more generous, but there is also a more pronounced tendency to carry out constructional work, requiring loan funds, and thus the prevailing scarcity of capital is intensified.*

The least that can be demanded of public policy (assuming that there is scope for an active internal cyclical policy), is that it should not aggravate fluctuations, but should remain *neutral*. The majority of the Unemployment Commission have taken this cautious position, which agrees with the view expressed earlier by one of its members, Professor Bagge. This implies that the total volume of public works and purchases should be adjusted to a normal trend of development. They should accordingly not be made to depend on annual fluctuations in the business situation. The unavoidable surpluses and deficits on the revenue side in different years would then be evened out through

---

* The above shows, however, that the reaction of public policy to trade fluctuations is not *solely* additive. Fur during the depression there are usually "budget deficits" and during the boom "budget surpluses." This means that in the former case current expenditure tends to exceed current income, and in the latter case to fall short of it. This compensating tendency is strengthened by the efforts commonly made to utilize hidden reserves, in order to avoid sharp increases in taxation during depression, and by action in the contrary direction during a boom. These circumstances, also mentioned in Myrdal's work, are nevertheless not sufficient in themselves to counterbalance the intensifying influence already mentioned, which is above all due to the practice of synchronizing the volume of public investment with the general economic trend.

transfers from and to a fund created specially for this purpose, or by short term borrowing.

The realization of this programme would undoubtedly mean a real advance in comparison with traditional budgetary policy. And from the standpoint of economic policy the result should in many instances be fairly satisfactory, provided that the management of monetary policy, on which the responsibility for mitigating economic fluctuations primarily rests, is sufficiently active and efficient. But in my opinion it would be both inconsistent and unfortunate to commit oneself to this "neutral" financial policy so completely as to preclude the possibility of a more active policy when it is clear that it would give favourable results. Nor has this been the intention of the Unemployment Commission, since it speaks of "feeling one's way." The arguments supporting a "neutral" budgetary policy amount merely to saying that although certain deviations are reasonable in themselves they are not worth the risk, since they are difficult to carry out, and may often be ill-timed. In so far as it is believed that these difficulties can be overcome, the arguments for such a neutral policy lose their force.

I believe it is possible to find another solution of the problem, practically as safe as that proposed by the Unemployment Commission, and with more favourable effects on unemployment and industrial fluctuations. This solution presupposes, first that relatively elastic methods of balancing the budget (to be explained later), are sanctioned and generally practised, and secondly, that the commencement of all public works and orders capable of postponement, should rest on decisions of *two* types. First there would be a decision to *grant* the appropriation out of means available in the current annual budget, and, later, other decisions concerning the payment of the appropriated sum and the *carrying out* of the actual work itself. The effect of our solution would be that, after the reforms have taken effect, the authorities granting appropriations would be at liberty to react to industrial fluctuations in the way that seems to them most rational. Under our assumption it may be hoped that this reaction will have a tendency opposite to that which is common now. There is at present very little scope for postponement of work when appropriations have once been granted. The greater number of such grants are naturally made during a boom, when income flows more abundantly and the authorities take a comparatively optimistic view of the taxpayers' ability to pay. But it is quite natural and advantageous to postpone the utilization of appropriations, when circumstances permit, until a reversal of the economic trend has taken place, and costs have fallen to a more advantageous level.

The timing-of public works brought about by applying these principles is manifestly not affected by criticisms of the attempts made to accelerate public constructional work of various kinds during the recent depression. Such difficulties were due partly to insufficient preparation, whereby the work was begun too late, and partly to the fact that when they were decided upon it was necessary to estimate, consciously or unconsciously, not only their direct remunerativeness but also their advantages from the point of view of unemployment. Our programme presents no such difficulties. Moreover, it tallies well with the long term planning programme for public activity. The only difference is that planning is accompanied by a vote of appropriation, falling under the budget of the current year, but freedom in choosing the time for using the appropriation is allowed.*

* [A similar scheme is the approval of an alternative "emergency budget," to be applied if the economic situation deteriorates.—Cf. Section 5 below.]

I do not mean to deny that this type of solution has difficulties of its own, partly of a technical administrative nature, and partly depending on the correct interpretation of the economic situation. The former cannot be dealt with here. Only one point need be noticed—the solution would be facilitated if the financial policy of local authorities were placed partly under State supervision.*

Mistakes are naturally almost inevitable in interpretation of the economic trend. But such mistakes should by no means prevent the fulfilment of the crucial part of the programme, namely the postponement of constructional work, etc., during every boom until the following slump. The principal source of error lies in failure to realize when the slump is over, as a result of which the works may not be as evenly timed during the depression as would have been desirable. But even then the situation will always be better than if constructional work had been distributed indiscriminately over good and bad years.

If this programme were to be carried out at all fully, important advantages would be realized. (1) Financial gains would accrue to the State and to the local authorities through the reduction in the average level of costs for constructional work, etc. (2) There would be less unemployment and better utilization of productive capacity during depression years, and (3) more stable prices and less violent economic fluctuations, owing to the monetary

---

* In this connection it should be made clear that the solution of the problem for local authorities is especially urgent, since in their case the alternative principle of an unvarying volume of expenditure cannot as a rule be upheld. For a local unit the building of a new schoolhouse or poorhouse, is a relatively large undertaking of a non-recurrent nature. This constructional work cannot be evenly distributed over a period of years. The choice lies between timing it in a good year, when labour is scarce and the prices of materials are high, or waiting for a depression year, when the unemployed can be utilized and advantage taken of lower costs in other respects. The latter alternative is of course preferable from every point of view.

effect of the recurrent "under-" and "over-balancing" of the budget, through the adjustment of public expenditure between boom and depression years.

The programme is based on the principle that public authorities moved by the desire of securing financial gains, will act in such a way as also to secure the other two advantages which are of importance from the general point of view. In this respect the programme appears to be more effective than the "passive" financial policy advocated by the Unemployment Commission. Since it is politically quite neutral, its adoption seems justified, whenever conditions permit of an independent internal policy of economic stabilization.

To what extent this programme might subsequently be expanded by more drastic measures in order still further to stabilize industrial fluctuations is a question that must be dealt with in relation to a particular set of circumstances. We shall confine ourselves here to two points.

The most difficult problem in this field is the organization in the depression of *additional public works*, which are not directly remunerative but which lead to increased employment of labour and other factors of production, and thus appear advantageous from the angle of an unemployment or expansionist policy. Conflicts of economic interest often arise in judging the value of such works. Some of their effects have certainly no drawbacks from the point of view of private interests, for instance the reduced expenditure on unemployment relief and the improvement in the prospects of private industry due to the stimulus given to demand for goods of all kinds arising from the works. Other effects, however, bring advantages to certain groups only and are harmful to others. In so far as the public works mean higher prices for the services of labour, for raw materials, etc., there is a stimulating effect on the persons and enterprises selling these services and goods. But those who demand them in competition with the State, and whose own products have not been affected by a corresponding rise in prices, find themselves worse off than before. This is one of the most important causes of the frequent opposition to such public works, when they are not organized as unemployment relief of the usual type. Even if the Unemployment Commission is right in saying, that these works appear in a more favourable light when a considerable part of the productive capacity of a country is idle, the theoretical solution of the problem must build to a certain extent on premisses and valuations of a political character and the practical solution must build on the actual distribution of political power. Because of the intricate and delicate nature of this problem energy should in the first place be concentrated on the politically neutral programme characterized above.

In still another respect it appears that the measures justified from the strictly financial viewpoint should be supplemented by direct action aiming at economic stabilization. When the budget is "over-" or "under-balanced," the supply of net saving available for private investment is affected. The supply is reduced by "under-balancing" or current "deficits," when the public demands weigh heavily on the capital market, and increased in the opposite case. Since private demand for investment varies similarly, a better correspondence between these two factors is attained by the proposed policy. In this way, budgetary policy becomes a valuable aid to monetary policy in its task of *preserving equilibrium on the capital market.* Nevertheless, it is improbable that the stabilizing influence of budgetary policy will be of exactly the extent which is desired in every given case. For public activity is the result of the decisions of numerous different central and local authorities actuated by their individual considerations. The total result may therefore require adjustment in order to secure better correspondence with monetary policy. Such an adjustment would perhaps be brought about by providing that the directors of the Central Bank should each year advise the Government of the degree of "underbalancing" or "overbalancing" of the budget during the near future which would be desirable from the monetary standpoint. The budget should then be adjusted accordingly whenever possible. In this case budgetary measures would deliberately be resorted to in order to attain an end called for by monetary policy, namely, the maintenance of equilibrium on the capital market.

The views laid down here as to budgetary policy under certain simplifying assumptions are explained in more detail in Myrdal's work, in the Commission's report (chap. VII) and in Ohlin's supplement to the report (chap. V) where the implications of a public works policy are investigated. Although the authors of these works would probably not agree to all that has been said above, we seem on the whole to be of the same opinion with regard to the following main points:

(1) The trade cycle should not be allowed to affect *normal public activities*. This means that the tendency to reduce expenditure in bad years and increase it in good should be resisted in respect of normal activities. Any modification of financial policy in this direction which may be required for a special reason should be effected through adjustments in the earnings of the factors of production rather than through variations in the volume of their employment.

(2) Public *constructional work*, whether self-liquidating or not, should be distributed between depression and boom years in such a way that the best budgetary result is attained, i.e. the lowest costs with given advantages.

Such works should consequently be concentrated in depression years with their comparatively low level of costs, in so far as such a policy does not hinder the public bodies from carrying out their duties. Public action will then automatically give rise to a "counter-trend" with a stabilizing influence on the general trend.

(3) The *tax burden* should on the whole be lighter during the depression and heavier during the boom. This presupposes that the budget is "underbalanced" in the former case and "overbalanced" in the latter. The degree of government "over- or underbalancing" should be determined in consultation with the Central Bank, to ensure that budgetary policy is in conformity with the programme of monetary policy. Budgetary policy will then influence the supply of savings available for private investment, and ensure a better correspondence with the variations in demand during the different phases of the trade cycle.

3. MODIFICATIONS CAUSED BY INTERNATIONAL RELATIONS

So far the problem has been discussed without taking into account *international relations*. The complications arising when they are taken into consideration may conveniently be demonstrated by typical examples. For my part, I should be inclined to stress the importance of different currency systems in this connection. A few reflections on this point may therefore be added.

It appears to be a general rule that the gold standard increases the need for a cyclical budgetary policy, but diminishes the feasibility of carrying it out. The opposite is true in respect of independent currencies.

If it is on the *gold standard*, a small country like Sweden must for the most part adjust itself to international trade fluctuations. The opportunities for an independent policy are very limited, unless commercial policy is vigorously directed to this end. In any case, the risks attending a highly developed budgetary policy of the kind suggested above are considerable, particularly because of the unreliability of economic forecasting. For example, in a depression it may be asserted with a high degree of probability that a reversal of the trend is to be expected after a time. But it is difficult to foretell in what way this will affect the future level of prices. This difficulty is of fundamental importance, for an attempt to create an expansion by raising prices may have unfortunate consequences, if the right policy would have been the opposite one of accelerating the price fall, so as to reach equilibrium at a low price level as soon as possible. Our conclusion is that the mitigation of economic fluctuations by budgetary measures, though especially desirable in view of the limited possibilities of monetary policy in these circumstances, is only practicable to a comparatively limited extent. The rules of budgetary policy laid down above must therefore be applied with caution.

In a country with a *free currency*, on the other hand, I believe that the rules can be of greater importance. It is true that international trends are equally difficult to foresee in this case. External influences on national trends and the possibility of parallel internal and international developments must also be taken into account. But the crucial difference is that it remains possible to exercise a decisive influence on the future internal price level. The possibility of carrying out a financial programme of rational trade cycle policy is thereby substantially increased. During depression public works financed by loans which will tend to reverse the trend, may for instance be justified. The effect of these measures may perhaps be insignificant, owing to external depressing influences, but the danger that arises under a gold standard, that the government may be forced to repay its loans in a currency with a far higher value, is absent. Even if the general policy is that of maintaining more or less stable exchange rates, internal prices may be brought to any desired level by adjusting exchange rates at a single stroke. But when monetary policy is skilfully managed and the great possibilities of a free currency in the stabilization of general economic trends are judiciously utilized, the importance of certain portions of the budgetary programme outlined above is at the same time reduced.

4. THE ARRANGEMENT OF THE BUDGET

This brings us to the problem of budgetary technique. A financial policy of mitigating periodic fluctuations implies, as we have seen, that the budget is "underbalanced" during the depression and "overbalanced" during the boom. The problem is, then, how flexibility can be attained in the annual technical budgetary procedure without endangering the long term planned increase of public net assets in the wider sense. The main problem is to ensure that a budget "deficit" in one year will really be counterbalanced by a corresponding "surplus" in another, so that the long term net rise in assets will not fall below the desired figure.

Myrdal has linked his proposed solution of the budget problem with a demand for a recasting of the Swedish system of budgetary accounting so as to make it more comprehensive. Such a reform would in the first place imply that besides the direct monetary expenditures of the various departments the annual value of the services obtained through the utilization of real capital assets owned by the Government should be included in the accounts. The principle would be the same as that in force in the Swedish government-owned business enterprises, where interest and depreciation on invested capital are included in the books as outlays or costs.* This more comprehensive accounting system has the advantage that the principle now adopted in Sweden for balancing the budget (see p. 355) can be formulated more flexibly. Even non-remunerative capital investment can to some extent be financed out of loan, since future budgets will bear the charge for depreciation. Renewal funds will thus be expanded *pari passu* with the fall in the value of equipment, and net public assets will accordingly not be diminished.

However, as we shall see, even without departing from the traditional system of budget accounting, fairly good guarantees can be secured for the realization in the long run of such an increase in public assets as is regarded as desirable, if flexible methods of annual balancing are practised. For such a purpose it is of fundamental importance that the budget should be drawn up in such a manner that the degree of "over-" or "under-balancing" can be clearly realized in every case. This result can be attained quite as well under traditional methods of budget accounting as with a more complete system.† That an intentional abuse of the technique of balancing can go to greater lengths under the former system than under the new system is in comparison of subordinate

* [In 1935, since this paragraph was written, Sweden introduced this accounting system for all public real estate, cf. p. 378.]

† The following quotation from Myrdal (op. cit., p. 138) may accordingly be regarded as equally valid under the present system of budget accounting, if the budget were drawn up more clearly in the manner recommended here: "At least in this way every possibility of weakening the public finances in ways hidden from the public view and from public control is excluded. They may of course be weakened all the same, but then the weakening is conscious. The attainment of such increased clarity is in the last resort all that can be gained through methods of pure budget technique aiming at better guarantees for financial soundness."

importance. It is therefore by no means necessary to make the adoption of new principles of balancing the budget dependent on a recasting of the system of public accounts.

In order to elucidate my idea of the rational employment of the new budget technique, I have worked out below two alternative schemes for arranging the budget, of which the first includes only monetary receipts and expenditure but the second shows in addition also the calculated reserves and costs of the capital equipment owned by the State.

The *first* alternative keeps fairly closely to the system in use in Sweden before 1935. It is based on the principle that expenditure normally covered by taxes or by other true revenue is always included in the ordinary budget, whereas all other monetary expenditure is invariably accounted for in the extraordinary budget. All so-called current expenditure, i.e. that for current administration and other consumption purposes, interest on the public debt, etc., is accordingly referred to the ordinary budget. Capital expenditure, i.e. investment in capital assets, debt repayment and money appropriated to capital funds (this last item is not included in the table), are on the other hand divided between the ordinary budget and the extraordinary budget in accordance with the principle adopted for the long term increase of net assets. If it is desired that the Swedish tradition in this respect should be retained, the ordinary budget should thus be debited both with non-remunerative public investment and with certain regular repayments of the State debt. Other capital expenditure should be included in the extraordinary budget. This division of expenditure between the two budgets is conceived as institutionally established, through legislation or otherwise.

Such a method of drawing up the budget has the advantage that the extent of balancing can be directly

369

PROPOSED METHOD OF DRAWING UP THE BUDGET:

ALTERNATIVE I

ORDINARY BUDGET

Current revenue:		*Current Expenditure:*	
Taxes, customs, excise, fees, net income from State enterprises, interest on capital lent out, and other monetary revenue .. : : :: ::	$a+b+c-e$	Expenditure for consumption purposes, interest on public debt, etc.	a
Received from extraordinary budget	e	*Expenditure for maintenance and increase of capital:*	
		Expenditure for non-remunerative capital investments	b
		Regular amortization of public debt ..	c
Total	$a+b+c$	Total	$a+b+c$

EXTRAORDINARY BUDGET

Loans, and realization of capital assets:		*Expenditure for increase of capital:*	
From cash reserves .. .. : :	f	Expenditure for self-liquidating capital investments	d
Loans .. .. : :	$a+b+c+d-e-f$	*Transferred to ordinary budget*	$a+b+c-e$
Total	$a+b+c+d-e$	Total	$a+b+c+d-e$

ascertained from the current budget. If current income is exactly equal to the expenditure included in this budget, it will be balanced according to the established norm for the long term increase of public net assets. If current income (e) is larger or smaller than the expenditure in question ($a + b + c$), the budget is correspondingly "over- or under-balanced." In the table given above a case of "underbalancing" is assumed. The deficit in current income can then be made up by an amount specially assigned from the extraordinary budget. The size of this amount ($a + b + c - e$) shows the degree of "underbalancing." If it had been a case of "over-balancing," its size would have been evident from the surplus arising in the ordinary budget and appearing as a special item on the expenditure side ("transferred to extraordinary budget"). These transfers from or to the extraordinary budget will thus recur as additions to the expenditure or to the income side of the latter. The total of both budgets will accordingly be affected by them.

The application of new and more flexible principles of balancing implies that the budget need not be balanced in every single year, but that negative and positive deviations are allowable provided that they counter-balance each other in the long run. Therefore, if the budget has been "underbalanced" in certain years, a corresponding "overbalancing" must take place in the succeeding years. A definite tradition in this respect may perhaps develop, which would entirely eliminate the danger of a long series of "underbalanced" budgets. However, it would hardly be desirable at first to lay down general rules for the solution of the central problem in this connection, that is, the period within which a defined degree of "underbalancing" should be compen-sated by a corresponding "overbalancing." In general it may be taken to be a desirable objective, that the

371

surpluses and deficits of the ordinary budget should counterbalance each other fairly well over the course of the trade cycle. But since cycles may in the future be more irregular than hitherto, this principle cannot be laid down in terms of exact periods. Besides, it should be noted that economic fluctuations are not confined to trade cycles in the narrower sense. We have also to take into account other periods of advance and retrogression, shorter or longer, and it may be wise to modify the balancing of the budget accordingly. Further it should be remembered that the capital investment that is to be covered in the long run by tax revenue may show considerable variation. It may be desirable to even these out by corresponding formal "under- or overbalancing" of the budget. If these variations are spread over periods as long as decades, it would no doubt be best to attain the requisite adjustment in some other way, for instance by modifying the norm for the regular amortization of the public debt.*

The *second* alternative for arranging the budget differs

* This last case may well become acute in the near future, if it is decided to employ the permanently unemployed during the next decade on extra public works which result in a considerable increase of non-remunerative capital assets (e.g. roads). If the expenditure for this purpose is included in the ordinary budget, in accordance with the principles laid down above, and if the latter is nevertheless balanced and if the rate of repayment of the national debt is maintained, the result will be that the net assets of the State (in the wider sense, including these new capital resources) will receive unusually large increments during this decade. If it is desired to distribute this increase over a longer period than a decade, then either the balancing of the budget may be allowed to end in a deficit for this decade (to be covered by a corresponding "overbalancing" during the succeeding period), or else the regular repayments on the national debt for the decade in question may be reduced. Both of these methods have the same real import, but the latter would seem to be preferable, since for psychological reasons it is perhaps undesirable to operate with "underbalanced" budgets over such long periods of time.

from the first mainly by the inclusion of certain calculated items : on the income side the interest on buildings
and other real capital owned and used by the State, on
the expenditure side the value of the services rendered by
these assets (which can be dissolved into interest and
depreciation). As the interest item (g) appears on both
sides of the budget, its only effect will be an increase of
the total. The inclusion of the depreciation item (h) on
the cost side has a more important consequence, since it
enables us to calculate the total amount $(a + h)$ which
it is necessary to cover by the revenue (e) of the ordinary
budget, in order to maintain public wealth in the wider
sense. If, however, in accordance with the Swedish
tradition, a "balancing" of the budget implies not only
that the public wealth is maintained but that it is annually
increased by an amount corresponding to the regular
amortization of the national debt (c) plus the normal
increase of non-remunerative capital assets $(b - h)$,
then these two items must also be included with ordinary
expenditure, as normal appropriations to capital funds.
In consequence all investment, both non-remunerative
and self-liquidating, can be transferred to the extraordinary budget, to be covered either by the realization
of capital assets or by new loans. It will thus mainly
register the transfer of public wealth from one fund to
another. The amount of this will be varied by a change
in the sum transferred to or from the ordinary budget.

This budget arrangement [which is adapted to the·new
Swedish accounting system] has, of course, certain definite
advantages in comparison with the first alternative. It
exhibits more clearly the annual variation in public
wealth which the budgets imply. It also enables us to
compare them with an established standard of "normal"
annual increase of public wealth. Further it is not necessary to maintain the present distinction in the method of

373

PROPOSED METHOD OF DRAWING UP THE BUDGET:

ALTERNATIVE II

ORDINARY BUDGET

Current revenue:		*Current expenditure:*	
Taxes, customs, excise, fees, net income from State enterprises, interest on capital lent out, and other monetary revenues	e	Expenditure for consumption purposes, interest on public debt, etc.	a
		Calculated rent on real capital owned and used by the State—	
Calculated interest on real capital owned and used by the State	g	1. Interest	g
Received from extraordinary budget ..	$a + b + c - e$	2. Depreciation (Appropriation to sinking fund)	h
		Expenditure for increase of capital:	
		Increase of capital funds	$b - h$
		Amortization of public debt	c
Total	$a + b + c + g$	Total	$a + b + c + g$

EXTRAORDINARY BUDGET

Loans, and realization of capital assets:		*Expenditure for maintenance and increase of capital:*	
From sinking funds }	$b + f$	Expenditure on non-remunerative capital investment	b
From capital funds }		Expenditure on self-liquidating capital investment	d
Loans	$a + b + c + d - e - f$	*Transferred to ordinary budget* ..	$a + b + c - e$
Total	$a + 2b + c + d - e$	Total	$a + 2b + c + d - e$

financing non-remunerative and self-liquidating investments. All investments can be financed by loans or capital
assets without danger to the net public wealth, as long as
sufficient amounts are transferred to the capital funds in
the ordinary budget. It will thus be possible to evade
annual fluctuations of the tax burden arising from
the fluctuating needs of non-remunerative investment,
e.g. for social purposes or for armaments. We have
already mentioned the difficulties in this respect inherent
in the first method. It must be admitted however that
these difficulties are not insuperable.

In the above I have only attempted to explain the
main principles of the new budget technique. These
principles may of course be realized even if the details
of the budget are arranged in a different way from that
proposed here. It is accordingly of no real importance if
the deficits or surpluses occurring in the ordinary budget
are transferred to the extraordinary budget, as has been
suggested above, or are debited or credited instead to a
special fund, "the budget equalization fund" (cf. below).

The most important divergence between the method
for drawing up the budget recommended here and that
recently practised in Sweden lies in the fact that this
method shows more plainly the degree of "over- or
underbalancing." In 1931-4 when the budget was
"underbalanced" two different methods were employed.
First, certain items of expenditure were transferred from
the ordinary budget to the loan budget, and at the same
time certain future revenues were reserved for the rapid
repayment of the new loans. Secondly, certain capital
assets and funded reserves were drawn upon for the ordinary budget (among them non-recurring revenue obtained by changes in the manner of accounting, etc.). This
"underbalancing" was expected to be neutralized during

375

the next few years by a corresponding "overbalancing," arrived at by burdening the ordinary budget with the extra amortization of the public debt just mentioned, and with appropriations to special funds (in addition to the expenditures re-transferred from the loan budget).

What does not seem quite rational in this arrangement is that two different methods have been combined in order to effect the "under- and overbalancing." It is true that this combination may easily be explained on historical grounds; since it was formerly regarded as permissible to cover small deficits in the ordinary budget by making use of cash reserves. The departure from tradition would be minimized by retaining this method unchanged, and accounting for the financing of such loans as are needed to make up the balance, in the form felt to be least risky in the eyes of the general public. But as soon as new principles of balancing have been intentionally adopted, logic demands that one should go the whole way and do away with the old distinction between "underbalancing" as permissible when cash reserves are utilized, and as contrary to financial tradition when financed by loans (though in the case in question perhaps justified as an extraordinary measure for combating the depression). There is no difference in fact between these two kinds of "underbalancing'" and it is foolish to nourish the misconception just criticized by retaining the distinction.

It would be better to solve the problem on new and rational lines, so that the result will be fully satisfactory for the long period problem as well. In the first place, all cash reserves called upon should be entered in the extraordinary instead of in the ordinary budget. The deficit exhibited in the ordinary budget would then at the same time be fully accounted for. Whether it should be evened out by a transfer from the extraordinary to the ordinary

376

budget (the method advocated above) or by transferring certain specified items of expenditure from the ordinary to the extraordinary budget, is a question of relatively subordinate importance. As the latter method lacks the necessary flexibility, and it becomes more difficult to judge the degree of the balancing if items of expenditure are continually transferred from one budget to the other, the former alternative seems preferable.

The argument so far has been confined to the finances of the National Government. For Local Authorities the question requires different treatment, since the financing of non-remunerative capital investment by loan is allowed under certain circumstances. As a safeguard against continuous financial deterioration, Swedish law requires both large (75 per cent) majorities for decisions to raise new loans, and a certain amount of supervision by the Central Government. In spite of this, however, the finances of Local Authorities are markedly inflexible. All expenditure for administrative purposes and also for the normal increase of capital equipment has to be covered each year by current income, and assessments for local taxation are accordingly as a rule higher in depression years than otherwise. The introduction of more flexible principles of budget balancing appears to be a highly desirable reform in this sphere also. The creation of local equalization funds (with a certain amount of Government supervision) seems to be the simplest method of mitigating the unfavourable influence of industrial fluctuations on the finances of local units.

5. A Note on Swedish Budgetary Reform (1939)

The principle of counteracting the business cycle by underbalancing the budget in depression and overbalancing during the boom, has been put into practice in recent years in Sweden by Mr. Ernst Wigforss, the Finance Minister. As mentioned above (p. 375), an intentional underbalancing of the budget

377

was allowed in the last depression, mainly by issuing new loans for financing unemployment expenditure. These loans were of short currency only, since according to the plan they were to be repaid during the coming upward phase of the trade cycle, when the budget was to be overbalanced. This plan was, in fact, successfully realized: already by the middle of 1938 all the loans were fully covered.*

Since the new era of financial policy had its beginning in the midst of the depression, it was more difficult to realize the other part of the programme—the concentration of public investment in the downward phase of the business cycle. Such a timing of public works presupposes intensive preparation which had not been undertaken. Since then, however, considerable progress has been made in the direction of long-period planning of public investment, which will assist in mitigating business cycles in the future. This planning includes not only the investments of the Central Government and of State-owned enterprises, but also the investments of Local Authorities.

In order to secure a better approximation between the basic principle and existing budgetary technique, Mr. Wigforss has also successively introduced new methods of drawing up the budget of the Central Government.

The first step was taken in 1935, when real estate of a non-remunerative character was included both in the capital and in the income accounts of the State. A special capital fund, corresponding to the value of these assets, was established; at the same time the calculated value of the services rendered by them was included in the budget as expenditure, and the same amount *minus* sums transferred to special sinking funds appeared as the net income from the real estate fund (see the table on p. 380 and cf. p. 373). It was thus possible to finance capital expenses of this nature by borrowing without diminishing the accounted net assets of the State, and since the yearly depreciation of the assets was covered by current revenues in the budget of each year (as just explained), the maintenance of the value of Government-owned assets was also provided for.

* See E. Wigforss, "The Financial Policy during Depression and Boom, *The Annals of the American Academy*, May 1938, pp. 25 ff. Cf. also *ibidem*, p. 63, and Brinley Thomas, *Monetary Policy and Crises*, pp. 205 ff.

Meanwhile a more thoroughgoing budgetary reform was prepared by a committee of experts whom the Finance Minister had called upon to draw up a complete scheme for the rearrangement of the budget according to the new principles. This scheme was incorporated in the budget for the financial year 1938–39 and has been also applied, with small modification, to the budget for the following year. The main lines of the scheme are shown in the table below.* A few comments may be in order here.

The essential point is that the ordinary or current budget should include only such expenditure as should normally be covered by current revenue (and not by loan or capital assets). A positive or negative difference between current revenue and the corresponding expenditure should be expressly recorded as a surplus or deficit (as suggested above). But these surpluses and deficits are in this plan kept apart from the capital budget and transferred to a special fund, the so-called Budget Equalization Fund. In order that this fund, which should also register the difference between the budget estimate and the actual receipts and expenditure, should be kept at a certain level in the long run, it is intended that the budget for each year should contain a programme for the solution of the balancing problem for the succeeding ten years

As in the second table given above (p. 374), all capital expenditure which leads to an increase in the capital funds included in the public accounts, is carried to the capital budget. This budget will thus register total public investment, both self-liquidating and non-remunerative. But the methods by which the investment has been financed cannot be directly ascertained from the budget, since only one undifferentiated item appears on the income side. The necessary funds must, however, either be taken from sinking or other capital funds, or be created by new loans. (Cf. the table on p. 374.)

So far the scheme is in substantial accord with the second table above. But we now come to a point of difference: the item "Expenditure for increase of capital" entered on the expenditure side of the current budget in the table above does

* The real budgetary situation is assumed to be the same as in the tables given above, and the algebraic signs have the same meaning in both plans, so that a direct comparison between the proposals can be made.

METHOD OF DRAWING UP THE BUDGET APPLIED FOR THE BUDGET-YEAR 1938–39, IN SWEDEN

CURRENT BUDGET

A. *Proper State Revenues:*		
Taxes, Customs, Excise Fees, etc.		
B. *Income from Capital Funds:*		
I. State Enterprises		
II. Central Bank	$\Big\}$ $e + g$	
III. Real Estates		
IV. Loan Funds		
V. Shares, etc.		
Deficit to be transferred to the Budget Equalization Fund	$a + h + i$	
Total	$a + g + h + i$	

A. *Proper State Expenditure:*		
Services of the Various Departments		
B. *Expenditure for Capital Funds:*		
I. Public Debt (Interest)	$\Big\}$ $a + g + h$	
II. Sums written off New Capital Investment		
Total	$a + g + h + i$	

CAPITAL BUDGET

Funds Available	
Loans and Realisation of Capital Assets	$b + d$
Total	$b + d$

Capital Investment:	
I. State Enterprises	
II. Real Estate	
III. Loan Funds	$\Big\}$ $b + d$
IV. Shares	
V. Other Funds	
Total	$b + d$

not appear here. The underlying argument is that the budget is "balanced," if public net assets, as they appear in the accounting system, are kept unaltered. The expenditure side of the current budget, therefore, besides expenditure for consumption purposes and interest on the public debt, should only contain amortization items, corresponding to decreases in these assets.* An increase in the accounted net value of public property corresponding for example to the regular amortization of the national debt, is thus not necessary for "balancing" the budget.

This seems to be in full accordance with the original meaning

* In accordance with this view, another item "amortization of *capital losses*" was also entered in the current budget, in the original budgetary scheme proposed by the experts. It was argued that the maintenance of public assets presupposed that a decrease in them, occasioned by capital losses, should be compensated by corresponding appropriations in the current budget. Against this reasoning objections might be raised both from the point of view of principle and of practice. In point of principle it is hardly consistent to cover capital losses out of current revenues. A strict adherence to such a programme would lead to quite disastrous results in a depression period, when public, as all other values, are falling. Only such losses as refer to the activities of the current year should be covered by current revenue. In practice, the Financial Authority will probably not ascertain more capital losses than it finds convenient having regard to the budgetary situation. This more flexible application of the principle appears, thus, to involve the danger, that the balancing problem may be so manipulated that the public cannot discover how far it has really been solved. The amounts written off in the current budget may for example be diminished during the depression and increased during the boom. Thus the aim of the whole reform—that the public should be made aware of the real budgetary situation,— could very simply be sidestepped. It was therefore on good grounds that capital losses were omitted in the final scheme put into practice by the Finance Minister.

In the budget for the financial year 1939–40 an item called "Losses on Capital Funds" is included on the expenditure side of the current budget. This item, however, refers not to capital losses in the true sense, but to such more normal losses, connected with the capital funds of the State, as are expected to be realized during the current year. The reasoning above does not apply to losses of this type which of course, like other regular yearly expenses, should be covered by current revenue.

of a "balanced" budget. But it corresponds less well to the standard of "financial soundness" accepted in Sweden (see above p. 355), which not only implies that the net property of the State should be maintained, but that it should be *increased* in a certain degree. From this point of view, the budget is "balanced," if it provides *both* for a certain accounted increase in the net public assets, caused by the regular amortization of the national debt, *and* for a certain other increase, appearing in the accounting system or not, corresponding to the excess of new non-remunerative investments over the depreciation of the old ones.

The first kind of increase in public wealth has, as just mentioned, clearly been omitted in the present budgetary scheme. The practical importance of this deviation from the traditional standard of "soundness" is, however, not very great, since only a fairly moderate amount is in question. But an odd consequence of the arrangement may be pointed out.

If a reduction of the national debt or some other form of increase in public net assets (other than non-remunerative investments) is desired, it can, on this arrangement of the budget, only be realized by an increase in the Budget Equalization Fund and a corresponding "overbalancing" of the budget. Should the programme for increasing public wealth be extended over a period of several years, the Equalization Fund will thus lose its original meaning, and its part in achieving the solution of the short-term balancing problem will be somewhat obscured. If such a plan were to be realized, this complication should therefore be met by the appropriation of the required amount from the Equalization Fund to the Capital Budget.

Of greater importance is the second kind of increase in public wealth, namely that of non-remunerative investment, yielding no money income. A strict application of the new scheme outlined above would certainly have implied that this increase would also have disappeared. If such investment is entirely financed by borrowing, and if the yearly appropriation in the current budget only corresponds to their actual depreciation, there will neither be any accounted nor any hidden increase in net public assets.

In the scheme outlined above on p. 374 this difficulty was met by the introduction of a special appropriation in the current budget for "increase in capital funds," corresponding to the excess of new non-remunerative investments over the depreciation of the old ones (b–h). In the Swedish budget for the financial year 1938–39, another arrangement was made by which the same result was at least partially obtained. With regard to new non-remunerative investment it was decided that a substantial amount (25–50 per cent) of their costs should immediately be written off and the corresponding appropriation made in the current budget (indicated in the table by the letter i). This important modification of the reform of 1935 (see above) represents in fact an approximation to the old treatment of such investment, the real import of which was that they were written off 100 per cent immediately. Since i is probably less than (b–h), the real increase in public wealth will be smaller than with the old method of balancing the budget, assuming that the amount of investment does not change. It should be observed that this increase in wealth, just as under the old system, does not appear in the book values, since it only corresponds to the excess of the sums written off over the actual depreciation of non-remunerative investment.

We may therefore conclude that the traditional standard of "financial soundness" in Sweden has been somewhat modified by the recent budgetary reform: the accounted increase in wealth has been omitted and the hidden increase *ceteris paribus* diminished. But it seems probable that sufficient compensation will be given by an increase in the total amount of non-remunerative investment.

Finally we may briefly refer to the methods adopted in Sweden for the adjustment of the budget, if changed economic conditions should make a subsequent correction desirable. The traditional method was the presentation of a supplementary budget, when an increase in the appropriations proved unavoidable. This method was, however, not sufficient for a flexible adaptation of expenditure to business fluctuations, for after the adjournment of the Riksdag in the end of May, the Government has no constitutional power to take the financial measures which might be necessary in case of a recession in trade. Therefore, in the first half of 1938, when it was difficult to foresee whether a downward phase of the business cycle would begin during the financial year 1938–39, a special "emergency budget," adapted to a state of depression, was

383

passed as a complement to the regular budget which was based on the assumption that no material change in the conditions of trade would take place. The emergency budget includes conditional appropriations which may be used only in case of a substantial deterioration of business conditions. Whereas the regular budget thus has the character of a minimum budget adapted to the needs of the boom, the emergency budget represents together with the regular budget a maximum budget adapted to the needs of depression. Since the question of how to finance the conditional appropriations is not solved in the emergency budget, it follows that it may lead to a deficit. The new system with a supplementary emergency budget has not yet been tried out, since so far it has not been necessary to put it into force. But the method seems to go a long way towards overcoming one of the greatest difficulties connected with a financial policy directed to mitigate business cycles, that of correctly judging the coming development of trade.

The budgetary scheme now applied in Sweden is thus on the whole clear and simple and in conformity with the new principles for balancing the budget.

INDEX

Consumers' goods, basic price equation for, 141–3; causes of changes in quantity of, 156–7.
— — industries, changes in productivity of, 218–22, 227–30.
Co-ordinated ("*gestaffelte*") production, 299 n.
Costs, of maintenance and repairs, 83; of production, equations for, 282, 306, 326.
Cumulative processes, defined, 153; described, 171; Wicksellian, 168, 169 n.; in *ex ante—ex post* terminology, 175–6; caused by a lowered rate of interest, 161 ff.; by a raised rate of interest, 183 ff.; independent of the rate of interest, 167.
Current revenue and current expenditure in the budget, 352–3.

Dahlgren, E., 121 n.
Davidson, D., 226 n.
Depreciation, 83, 100 n., 299 n., 347.
Development, theory of, 51–60, 136.
Disequilibrium method, in price theory, 60, 175, 260 ff.
Distribution of incomes, changes in, making saving equal to investment, 174.
Divisibility of factors and products, assumption of defined, 274.
Durable capital goods, treatment of in price theory, 291 ff.
Dynamic theory, general and special, definitions of, 31–2; structure of, 35–40; based on disequilibrium, 60–3; based on equilibrium in two senses, 64–9; the disequilibrium method explained, 51–60; the equilibrium method applied, 158–60, 318–21, 338 ff.

Elasticity, of consumers' demand, 221, 224–5; of the credit system, 237; of expectations, 49 n.
Entrepreneur, defined, 78; as subject of estimates, 97.
Equilibrium, stationary, 32; temporary, 64–9, 158–60.
— rate of interest, 249–51, 262–4.
Estimates, *see* Prospective and retrospective estimates.
Ex ante—ex post terminology, 63, 68; applied to the cumulative process, 175–6; *see also* Prospective and retrospective.
Expectations, single-valued and many-valued, 41; influenced by past events, 49; forming the basis of plans, 49–50, 62, 65; importance of for the cumulative process, 171 n., 180–3, 186; *see also* Foresight.
Export surplus, 123–4.

Financial soundness, of the budget, 353–5.
Financial transactions, defined, 76; *see also* Capital; Investment.
Firms, as economic subjects, 74; income of, 82–7, wealth of, 89; undistributed profits of, 87 n.

*

Interest, differentiation of rates of, for loans and deposits, 194–6; for different types of investment, 197–8. *See also* under specific heads.

—, level of rates of, in the absence of capitalistic production, 288–91; determined in static theory as a function of the size of the real capital, 301 ff.; movements of under perfect foresight, 149–50, 333–5; determining the amount of real investment, 133; effects of its lowering, 161 ff.; of its raising, 183 ff.

International margin, for financial policy, 357, 365–7.

— relations, importance for price theory, 243–4.

Intertemporal relations, between expectations and planned actions, 45; between prices, 142.

Investment, financial, net value of, defined, 77; relation of to income and to financial transactions, 85.

— gain, 104.

—, real, net value of, defined, 77; relation of to income from factors, 80; *see also* Period, Saving and investment.

— —, cost of, 67 n.

Johansson, A., 351 n.

Keynes, J. M., 66, 95, 261, 265.

Kock, Karin, 121 n., 188 n.

Labour disputes, effect of on the price level, 218, 222, 226.

Large and small scale production, significance of the assumption that they are equally remunerative, 275–6, 281 n.

Laws, economic, 24.

Long and short term loans, *see* Interest.

Losses, capital, amortization of in the budget, 380 n.; *see also* Gains and losses.

Lundberg, E., 59 n., 128 n., 167 n.

Mackenroth, G., 24 n.

Marginal efficiency of capital, 261.

Marschak, J., 63, 106 n.

Marshall, A., 68, 286 n.

Micro-economic and macro-enconomic terms, 74; developments, 51–2; relations between micro-economic values, 78–111; relations between macro-economic values, 111–35.

Mobility of factors and products, assumption of defined, 274–5; importance for the theory of price movements, 164–8, 177–9, 183–5, 191–2.

Monetary policy, aims of, 199 n.; programme of, 200; the two standard objectives of compared, 230–2; methods of, summary of their application, 232–4.

Money, as cash, 77; as wealth, 90; *see also* Cash holdings.
Multiplicative factor, in price theory, 283, 309, 327.
Myrdal, G., 27 n., 63, 150 n., 261 n., 262 n., 274 n., 286 n., 295 n.,
    337 n., 340–1, 348–50, 351 ff.

National income, methods of calculation of, 120–5.
Natural rate of interest, 247–8, 261–2.
Neutral financial policy, 358.
— rate of interest, 252–7, 264–8.
Normal rate of interest, 245 ff.
Notation, algebraic, methods of, 74–5.

Ohlin, B., 64, 256 n., 351 n., 364.
Original factors of production, 293, 297.
Output, *see* Input and output.

Perfect foresight, *see* Foresight.
Period of income, 102, 105, 108–9, 144.
— of investment, influenced by the rate of interest, 170, 296, 302–3,
    310 n.; weighted average of, 308 ; unweighted average of,
    314.
— of registration, of planners, 42, 49; shorter than the "period with
    fixed relevant plans," 50, 52.
— —, of the economist, 53–4; application to static theory, 302; to
    dynamic theory, 125, 158, 318, 339.
Pigou, A. C., 23 n.
Plan, economic, defined, 37, 40; content of, 42 ff.; characterized
    with regard to its definiteness, 45–6; the planning process,
    40–2; four types of changes in planning, 47–8.
Points of estimate, 74.
Policy, economic, based on economic theory, 22–3.
Price movements, methods of dealing with, 60–9; determined by
    anticipations under perfect foresight, 149, 332–7; primary
    causes of under imperfect foresight, 151 ff.
Pricing process, elements of, 60.
Productivity, function of, 281 n.; changes in, distinguished from
    changes in quantity of factors, 210–11; increase in, causing
    a rise in retrospective income, 103.
Profit and loss account, 82–5, 110–11.
Prospective and retrospective estimates, 63–4; relation between, 90–6,
    125–35; expectations influenced by retrospective estimates
    and by their deviations from prospective estimates, 91–2;
    prospective profit rate, 261.
Public investment, non-remunerative and self-liquidating, 369 ff.
— works, during the depression, 362–3; of constructional type, 364.

Quantity theory, 141, 235 ff.

Receipts and expenditure, equation of, 79.
Risk, 348; *see also* Uncertainty.
Robbins, L., 24 n.
Robertson, D. H., 167 n., 199 n., 236 n.
Rosenstein-Rodan, P. N., 261 n.

Saving, defined, 77, 341; causes of changes in, 154–6; changes in cash holdings, also of relevance for, 236; effects of changes in, 205–10; method applied in the investigation of, 343–7.
— and net value of real investment, relation between for a single economic subject, 88; relation between for a community *ex post*, 119–20; effects of a difference *ex ante*, 126 ff.; in a closed community, 127, 130–1; the adjustment of, to investment through "unintentional" changes in, 131, 132 ff., 175–6; through "intentional" or "voluntary" changes in, made possible by a redistribution of incomes, 174–5.
— and changes in wealth, relation between under perfect foresight, 329; in prospective and retrospective estimates, 99–100; in estimates referring to actual values of wealth, 108.
Securities, *see* Capital, financial.
Simplifying assumptions, use of, 28–31; applied in the traditional theory of price, 274–6, 339 n.
Short and long term loans, *see* Interest.
Socialistic community, pricing problem in, 69–73.
Static theory, its relation to dynamic theory, 31–2; the static premise, characterization of, 286; does not exclude uncertainty, 287; not appropriate as a starting-point, 33–4; but of a certain use, 34–5; consequences of for the theory of price, 302; difficulties of, 309–13.
Stocks, changes in, caused by altered interest rates, 169–70; by expectations, 228.
Streller, R., 31 n.
Supply of services of factors, functions of, 279, 305, 324–5.
Svennilson, I., 41 n., 42 n., 53 n., 58 n.

Taxation, for financing an increase in gold reserves, 242; higher taxes on capital for securing lower taxes on income, 353–4.
Technical coefficients, 279–81, 306, 325.
Theory, economic, aim of, 23, 25; based on general terms, 27–8; structure of, 35–40.
Thomas, B., 378 n.

Time factor, disregarded in price theory, 271–4; complications of for price theory, 284; in the absence of capitalistic production, 288–91; with instantaneous production of durable goods, 291–6; with roundabout processes of production, 296–301; *see also* Uncertainty.

Timing, of public expenditure, 360 ff.

Trade cycles, 133, 198, 356 ff.

Uncertainty factor, elimination of in price theory, 273; of relevance also under stationary conditions, 287; importance of for dynamic theory, 348–50.

Under- and overbalancing of the budget, during the trade cycle, 363–5; consequences for budgetary technique, 367 ff.

Undistributed profits, *see* Firms.

Unemployed resources, importance of for the cumulative process, 176–9.

Unemployment, caused by a too high rate of interest, 185; mitigated by financial policy, 356 ff.

Unemployment Commission in Sweden, 351–2, 356 ff.

Unforeseen events, treatment of in price theory, 339.

Uniformly progressing or retrogressing communities, 286 n., 318 n.

Unintentional savings, 95, 103, 131.

Use of factors, equations of, 282, 307, 326.

Valuation attitude, 39, 42.

Voluntary saving, *see* Saving and investment.

Wage fund, concept of capital as, 313–16, 345.

Wages, effects on the price level of a rise in, 209.

Waiting, defined, 341.

Wealth, value of, 78, 89, 120; changes in, 98–9; changes in subjective value of, 108.

Wicksell, K., 26, 166–8, 182 n., 245 ff., 277 n., 280 n., 281 n., 295 n., 303, 308, 310 n., 314, 345, 347 n.

Wigforss, E., 377 ff.

Windfalls, *see* Gains and losses.